THE PORT OF MISSING MEN

The PORT of MISSING MEN

BILLY GOHL, LABOR, AND BRUTAL
TIMES IN THE PACIFIC NORTHWEST

AARON GOINGS

UNIVERSITY OF WASHINGTON PRESS
Seattle

Design by Jordan Wannemacher
Composed in Sentinel, typeface designed by Jonathan Hoefler

26   25   24   23   22   5   4   3   2   1

Printed and bound in the United States of America

UNIVERSITY OF WASHINGTON PRESS
uwapress.uw.edu

LIBRARY OF CONGRESS CATALOGING-IN-PUBLICATION DATA
Names: Goings, Aaron, author
The port of missing men : Billy Gohl, labor, and brutal times in the Pacific Northwest / Aaron Goings.
Description: Seattle : University of Washington Press, [2020] | Includes bibliographical references and index.
Identifiers: LCCN 2019045335 (print) | LCCN 2019045336 (ebook) | ISBN 9780295747415 (hardcover ; alk. paper) | ISBN 9780295747422 (ebook)
Subjects: LCSH : Gohl, Billy, 1873–1927. | Labor leaders—Washington (State)—Grays Harbor—Biography. | Labor unions—Washington (State)—Grays Harbor—History—20th century. | Serial murders—Washington (State)—Grays Harbor—Case studies. | Murderers—Washington (State)—Grays Harbor—Case studies.
Classification: LCC HD6509.G55 G65 2020 (print) | LCC HD6509.G55 (ebook) | DDC 364.152/32092 [B]—DC23
LC record available at https://lccn.loc.gov/2019045335
LC ebook record available at https://lccn.loc.gov/2019045336

ISBN 9780295751207 (paperback)

♾ This paper meets the requirements of ANSI/NISO Z39.48-1992 (Permanence of Paper).

TO JESS

CONTENTS

PREFACE

My entry point into the world of Billy Gohl came in 2001 when I sat down at the microfilm readers at the Timberland Regional Library in Aberdeen, Washington, to explore issues of the *Aberdeen Daily World* from 1911 and 1912. Aberdeen and the wider Grays Harbor region was rife with labor conflict during those years, marked by struggles between local employers and members of the Industrial Workers of the World (IWW or Wobblies). In August 1911, the Aberdeen City Council passed an ordinance forbidding street speaking in the city's downtown, an effort to prevent the IWW from organizing in public. That day I found out a great deal about the Wobblies, the Aberdeen City Council, and the overtly antilabor news coverage provided by the *Aberdeen Daily World.*

But I also found something else. Early on in my research, a front-page headline from the August 10, 1911, *Daily World* caught my eye: "Business Men Helped Convict Gohl." The article below it discussed a debate in the Aberdeen City Council over the use of municipal funds to pay private detectives for their 1909–10 investigation into the criminal activities of William "Billy" Gohl. The article provided a detailed history, stating that much of the investigation into Gohl had been carried out by employees of the Thiel Detective Service, a leading spy firm that, like the Pinkerton Agency, had a notorious reputation for breaking unions and radical organizations using whatever means necessary. In addition, the article showed that it had been private individuals—local businessmen, united into a shadowy citizens' committee—that had paid most of the Thiel detectives' bills.

So much about the *Daily World* article piqued my curiosity. While I had work to do on my senior thesis, I couldn't shake the feeling that I had stumbled on something important. Billy Gohl—long known as the Ghoul of Grays Harbor—was one of the most famous residents in the history of Washington's coast, a convicted murderer and alleged serial killer whose reported crimes have continued to interest Northwesterners for over a century. As a native Aberdonian and Grays Harborite, I grew up hearing stories about Gohl. Teachers mentioned him in school, and some residents strongly hinted that Gohl and his victims haunted old buildings in downtown Aberdeen. Having read some of the pulp nonfiction tales about Gohl's dastardly deeds, I also knew that he was a local Sailors' Union agent, although his biographers have taken pains to downplay his life as a worker and union activist. But my early research suggested that the Gohl story was every bit as much labor history as it was true crime.

Digging deeper into Gohl's life and times, I had several questions. First, why did the city government outsource the investigation of Gohl to a notorious company like the Thiel Detective Service, one with a reputation for bending the truth—and the law—to assist employers with their "union problems"? Next, why did it fall to employers, united into a citizens' committee, to lead the investigation? What did these men have to gain from Gohl's downfall? Were they just civic-minded and good-hearted men who put community and safety before all other concerns? Or was there more to that story? After all, these business-men who formed the citizens' committee routinely coordinated to bust unions. Furthermore, why did these employers choose the name "citizens' committee" for their group? Grays Harbor employers knew full well that citizens' committees were widely known throughout the country for using a range of legal and extralegal tactics to bust unions. These men surely knew about citizens' committees: in late 1911 and again in 1912 they formed such committees in Aberdeen and nearby Hoquiam to violently expel the Wobblies from Grays Harbor.

After a few more days exploring newspaper articles related to Gohl, I put that on the back burner and returned to my senior thesis. But I couldn't shake my suspicions that there was a bigger story needing to be told, and this book is the eventual result of that hunch. I have spent much of my career studying and teaching the history of labor, the Left, and reactionary groups and individuals who battled working-class activists. My research has investigated dark subjects: vigilantism, immigrant exclusion, the Ku Klux Klan, and the tragic incident known as the Italian Hall Tragedy, when more than seventy striking mine workers and family members died in Calumet, Michigan, on Christmas Eve in 1913. Still, none of that research and subsequent writing has been met with the surprise and resentment stirred up by my investigation of Billy Gohl, a man who, by all accounts, belongs in the spot he has long occupied: on the list of America's most prolific serial killers.

Many Pacific Northwesterners have heard of Billy Gohl, and nearly as many think they know a great deal about him. During the more than a decade I've spent researching this book, I've encountered dozens of engaged antiquarians with an interest in Gohl. More than a few have questioned my intellect, sanity, and even morality for having the gall to ask whether the "Ghoul of Grays Harbor" story is a myth or more complex than previously conceived. Despite the blowback, my research was guided by several questions. Was Gohl actually guilty of the one murder for which he was convicted? More important: did he really kill so many of the class of young men for which he spent his life advocating (according to abundant historical evidence)? Much as convicted criminals (guilty or innocent) today often represent the race, class, and gender prejudices of American society, Gohl represented the social fault lines of his own time.

ACKNOWLEDGMENTS

Many people helped me write this book. I owe a tremendous debt to the Institute of Advanced Social Research at the University of Tampere in Finland, where I worked as I shaped the book into its final form. My fellow fellows at the institute: I have much appreciated your insights and support. I also enjoyed one year as a Fulbright Scholar at the University of Jyväskylä in Finland. It is no stretch to say that this book would never have been completed without the generous intellectual guidance and financial assistance provided by these fine institutions.

I also wish to thank the University of Washington's Labor Archives, the Washington State Archives in Olympia and its Southwest Regional Branch, the Polson Museum in Hoquiam, and the Washington State Library. These institutions hold tremendous collections of materials, and the staffs at all of them are first-rate.

A special thank you to the Saint Martin's University Faculty Development Committee and College of Arts and Sciences, which awarded funds to support some of the research that went into this book.

I would also like to thank the University of Washington Press, especially Andrew Berzanskis, Chris Dodge, and Margaret Sullivan, who did so much to encourage me in all the developmental stages of this book. Thanks as well to the manuscript's peer reviewers who provided great ideas that helped shape the book.

Thanks are due to everyone who helped make this book possible. I've been fortunate to get to know so many activists and scholars who have generously contributed their time and ideas. Thanks especially to Roger Snider, Brian Barnes, Matti Roitto, Helena Hirvonen, Keri Graham, Heather Mayer, Pertti Ahonen, Rex Casillas, David H. Price, Peter Cole, Jeremy Milloy, Gary Kaunonen, Bill Messenger, Jeremy Hedlund, Brandon Anderson, Jess Bever, Laurie Mercier, Chris Henry, Vince O'Halloran, and Shanna Stevenson. I owe a special debt to my mentors Mark Leier, Betsy Jameson, and Karen Blair for their years of generosity, kindness, and intellectual guidance.

I am indebted to the many archivists and librarians who helped along the way. Thank you to Roy Vataja, John Larson, Tracy Rebstock, Amber Raney, and Lanny Weaver. To John Hughes, my friend and historian extraordinaire: thank you for your advice as I have navigated the sometimes bumpy world of Pacific Northwest history. Thank you to the members of AWPPW Local 211 for teaching me so much about the importance of solidarity.

My greatest debts are owed to my family. To my wonderful aunts and uncles, brothers and cousins, in-laws and nephews: thank you for your sweetness, generosity, and good humor. I dedicate this book to my parents—Chris and Mike—and to my partner, Jess. This book would have been impossible were it not for your love and support.

THE PORT OF MISSING MEN

INTRODUCTION

AS THE NONUNION crew of the lumber schooner *Fearless* sailed out to sea on June 2, 1906, a small boat carrying a group of heavily armed unionists approached in the dark. Within a few moments, the night sky became alight with scores of rounds fired from revolvers and shotguns on both boats. After the gunfire subsided, the small vessel retreated to shore under the cover of darkness, and the crew of the *Fearless*, happy to have been spared their lives, abandoned their voyage and returned to shore. The *Fearless* crew had made the mistake of trying to ship lumber despite the pending threat of a strike by members of the Sailors' Union of the Pacific (SUP). Their voyage began in Aberdeen, Washington, one of the West Coast maritime workers' strongholds and home of SUP agent William Gohl, whose ferocious militancy would gain him fame and notoriety throughout the West.

Gohl settled in the Grays Harbor area in 1903. He became the agent for the Aberdeen local of the SUP in July 1903 amid the rapid expansion of both the regional labor movement and the rich lumber trade that by the first decade of the twentieth century had become the most prolific on the globe. Gohl brought with him years of experience as an itinerant wage laborer, just like millions of other men and women during the early twentieth-century North American West. And, like many other workers, he used this experience to fashion strategies and tactics to battle against saloon owners and boardinghouse keepers, all widely considered by workers to be parasites. Within a few years of his arrival on the harbor, Gohl established himself as one of the most prominent regional trade unionists. Along with his fellow maritime workers he created a fiercely militant labor movement, one capable of shutting down the region's lumber trade.

Gohl has been the subject of dozens of short articles.[1] His attraction, however, has nothing to do with Gohl's labor or community activism. Instead it is morbid curiosity about the "Madman of Aberdeen," the "Ghoul of Grays Harbor," and the "[Man Who] Launched 100 Murders," as he is labeled in titles of some of those works about him. The popular travel book *Weird Washington* devotes two pages to Gohl and uses his life to "explain" why Grays Harbor has such a violent past.[2] One of the only eateries in Aberdeen that has survived the decline of the lumber industry is named Billy's, after Gohl, and in 1969 local historian Anne Cotton wrote that Gohl "is Aberdeen's only first-rate tourist attraction."[3] During Gohl's seven years in Aberdeen, scores of workingmen were found dead, floating in the Chehalis and Wishkah Rivers. This "Floater Fleet," as the bodies became known, worried local workers unaware of the cause or causes of this spate of deaths and elites facing the public relations nightmare of having their town known for this. Studies have estimated that between forty and two hundred men were found dead in this manner between 1903 and 1910 and during the first three months of 1907 no fewer than ten men found their watery graves in the area.[4]

In February 1910, two men discovered a body, allegedly belonging to sailor Charles Hadberg, floating in Indian Creek, a small stream on the south bank of the Chehalis River, west of Aberdeen.[5] Three months later, a Chehalis County (soon to be Grays Harbor County) Superior Court convicted Gohl for Hadberg's murder and sentenced him to life in prison at the Washington State Penitentiary at Walla Walla. He would die seventeen years later at the Eastern State Hospital at Medical Lake, where authorities transferred him in September 1923 after declaring Gohl insane.[6] Following his February 1910 arrest,

Gohl became the subject of a massive campaign by local employers and their allies in the mainstream press to pin the region's crimes on him and "his gang." On the day of his arrest the *Aberdeen Daily World* blamed Gohl "for many of the members of the 'floater fleet,' comprising more than 40 bodies."[7]

Rumors of Gohl's crimes made headlines in local newspapers, and spread throughout the Pacific Coast as the regional press fixed its gaze on Grays Harbor. A *San Francisco Call* headline declared: "Gunness Farm Mysteries May Have Parallel. Believed that Grays Harbor Holds Evidence of Many Brutal Murders."[8] Years later, rumors of Gohl's crimes made their way into US federal investigations. For the 1914 Congressional Report on Industrial Relations, a witness provided false allegations of Gohl's criminal acts to demonstrate the perils faced by Pacific Coast shippers. He alleged that William Gohl killed "two sailors not members of the Sailors' Union of the Pacific on one of our coasting vessels, the schooner *Fearless* ... who boarded the vessel at night while she was lying in Grays Harbor."[9] Gohl has retained an important place in the history of American violence. More than fifty years after Congress issued its "Report on Industrial Relations," Hugh Davis Graham and Ted Robert Gurr issued their "Report to the National Commission on the Causes and Prevention of Violence," titled *Violence in America: Historical and Comparative Perspectives*. Formed in 1968 in response to the murders of Martin Luther King Jr. and Robert Kennedy, the National Commission on the Causes and Prevention of Violence was a massive project involving scholars from several academic disciplines, brought together to analyze and interpret the many facets of violence in America. The final report included a story about Gohl. In the chapter on American labor violence, Graham and Gurr concluded falsely that "two men working on the vessel *Fearless* were killed in Grays Harbor, Wash., by strikers led by the union agent, William Gohl, who was subsequently convicted and sentenced to prison."[10] Clearly, the myth of the Ghoul of Grays Harbor extended beyond his home region.

Gohl was not the only convicted murderer in early Grays Harbor history, and the jury had difficulty coming to a unanimous decision about his guilt. Yet, by the time the jury convicted him of a single murder, Gohl had been tried and convicted in the public mind of being a monster, a cold-blooded killer who had spent seven years ravaging the Grays Harbor area. The case against him, said Gohl, appeared to be "the dream of some dime store novel writer," as the union agent joined his attorneys and fellow unionists in alleging that employers had conspired to remove Gohl from his place in the labor movement.[11] But with the combined efforts of capital and state determined to silence Gohl, a pulp novel plot was more than enough. Gohl's public notoriety as a mass murderer, what could be called "the myth of the Ghoul of Grays Harbor," has turned rumor to truth in the minds of many Washingtonians. Still, this widespread view ignores the fact that of all the convicted murderers in the region's early history, Gohl was the only one capable of shutting down the highly profitable Grays Harbor lumber trade. It ignores the important historical context, which shows how frequently—around Grays Harbor and throughout the United States—employers acted collectively to eliminate labor and left-wing activists.

But why should we care about this sailor turned militant labor activist once we have stripped him of the sensational notoriety drawn from his alleged crimes? Some may argue that without his complicity in the Floater Fleet, Gohl loses his importance as a historical agent and ought to take his place on the scrap heap of history. This book instead proposes that Gohl's life story retains its coherence without making the man into a monster, and that it can be greatly improved with a sharpened analysis based on Gohl's and other workers' relationship with capitalism. Gohl's life, from his union and family relations to the efforts by employers to put him in prison, can best be understood through class analysis.

Gohl's biography can teach us a good deal about the US West in the early twentieth century. Prior to settling permanently in Aberdeen, Gohl lived the life of a migratory laborer, sharing experiences with tens of thousands of merchant seamen and millions of itinerant workers in the West.[12] This was a hard and even brutal life, one filled with violence and exploitation. Historian Mark Leier concluded,

"Often disparaged as hoboes, tramps, bindlestiffs, vagrants, and bums, their labour was essential to the industrial economy."[13] Second, William Gohl settled into a rather important position in the social fabric of the Grays Harbor working-class community. He belonged to several clubs, and his work as a union agent took him throughout the area's working-class districts, where he was responsible for making sure that only unionists in good standing got jobs aboard lumber schooners. Because of Gohl's prominence in the community, he is a useful lens into class and community relations in a lumber town during the first decade of the twentieth century, a time when eventual residents carved the towns of Aberdeen and Hoquiam out of the forests and established the harbor as one of the world's great lumber centers. Third, since Gohl was a prominent unionist and strong proponent of militant direct action at the point of production, following his actions can illuminate a broader view. In this scene, brutality was common as Pacific Coast sailors confronted their employers and sought to escape the poverty and hazardous conditions ubiquitous in their trade. Fourth, because of Gohl's tremendous community activism and because of the extensive archival collections that exist because of his trials and imprisonment, there is a far greater record of his life than for most American workers and union officials of the time. Thus, while most of the early twentieth-century working class lived relatively anonymous lives, Gohl's life—his involvement in labor and community activism, his social and political views, and his criminal activity (both real and mythical)—is available for historical scrutiny. For all these reasons, we can learn a great deal about American labor history by studying William Gohl.

Grays Harbor occupies the southwest corner of Washington's Olympic Peninsula. Workers built the harbor towns of Aberdeen, Hoquiam, and Cosmopolis between the 1880s and 1910s. The abundant evergreen forests also provided the region with its main industries. Logging, lumbering, shingle production, and the shipping of wood products employed tens of thousands of workers during the early twentieth century. Local laborers cut and shipped wood on an epic scale. Harbor mills regularly cut the most lumber of any in the

United States, while the region's teamsters, longshoremen, and sailors were responsible for shipping record-breaking amounts of lumber annually, earning the harbor's annual title as world's largest lumber-shipping port. In 1924 Grays Harbor became the first port to ship out over a billion board feet of lumber by water, a feat that earned heavy praise of local boosters: "Grays Harbor would be the only lumber port in the world able to talk in billions while others were talking millions in the lumber game."[14]

Grays Harbor's "lumber game" produced on a vast scale. But the game was dangerous for those who produced and transported the lumber, marked by not infrequent violence. Sometimes overlooked in studies of violence is the significance of social class. In the past, as in the present, class determined much about individuals' lives. Although one's relationship to the means of production did not dictate that he or she would join a radical political group or the chamber of commerce, it did influence where people lived, how they vacationed (if they vacationed at all), what they ate, what schooling they received, and how they died. It was thus class that determined who died in the forests, mills, and docks around Grays Harbor. The so-called "industrial accidents" that caused so much death and pain in working-class families' lives were not "acts of God," such as lightning striking some hapless victim. Instead, the types of workplace violence that occurred around Grays Harbor were the result of class relations, caused by relations of production and the property—machines, natural resources, and work spaces—of capitalists.

Billy Gohl was no saint, but his greatest sin may have been that he partially subverted this relationship between class and violence, stoking fear in bosses, who, like generals, most often died at ripe old ages in their beds.[15] Gohl threatened employers with bodily harm, thereby threatening to reverse or at least equalize the violent relationship that rewarded bosses for speeding up production to unsafe levels and allowed sea captains to commit acts of violence against sailors with little fear of punishment.

During the first three decades of the twentieth century, loggers died at a much higher rate than did workers in any other job on the Pacific

Coast. Lumber manufacturing was the second-most-dangerous occupation in the region, and workers regularly lost fingers, hands, and
arms to swirling saws. Dozens of SUP members perished each year by
drowning: in shipwrecks, after being knocked into the water by shifting cargo, or after slipping on a wet deck. Pacific Coast sailors knew
lumber ports like Grays Harbor well. Most coastal vessels carried
lumber from the forests of the Northwest to California, Mexico, and
beyond. Merchant seamen lived extremely harsh lives. They faced
countless dangers aboard ship, and discipline by bosses—masters and
mates—bordered on sadism. Those mythologized for courage ("going
down with the ship," if it came to that) frequently whipped and beat
workers and sometimes shot them.[16] For all the rowdiness of sailor
towns, the key unifying element in the lives of the sailors descend-
ing on saloon and whorehouse was not debauchery but their raw
exploitation under capitalism. Wages, work hours, and working conditions were notoriously bad, even for unionized sailors.[17] During
long trips from Grays Harbor to Hawaii or China, seamen slept in a
tiny, cramped forecastle.[18] Peter Gill, the Seattle Sailors' Union agent
and a friend of Gohl, wrote that the "life of a sailor was hell.... Brutal
treatment at the hands of ship's officers [was] common."[19]

Employers and much of ruling society viewed sailors as less than
human. Few subordinate groups have been so consistently dehuman-
ized as sailors. Many of those acquainted with seamen's lives—friends
and foes alike—compared the condition of their labor to chattel
slavery.[20] In his biography of Sailors' Union leader Andrew Furuseth,
historian Herman Weintraub compared the lives of sailors and
slaves: "Seamen were whipped, beaten, kicked, clubbed for minor
offenses, or no offenses at all. It is true that such treatment was the
exception, but so was the whipping of slaves. The fact remains that
both the slave and the sailor were subject to beatings at the will of the
master, who could administer them with almost complete immunity.
This unlimited authority presented those who possessed it with a
strong temptation to use it."[21]

As a sailor, Gohl had directly experienced some of the most stag-
gering cruelty of masters and mates, the likes of which had been

recorded in an 1895 pamphlet written by the International Seamen's Union, *The Red Record*. Designed to attract mass attention to the plight of sailors, the pamphlet documented many of the most violent attacks upon seamen, including the *Solitaire* case, in which the ship's second mate knocked a sailor down and jumped on his chest, ultimately killing him. When the body was finally inspected four days later it was so darkened that the captain informed authorities that the man had died from consumption.[22] This brutal treatment was known as "buckoism," and "bucko mates" and sadistic captains were rarely punished for it.[23] As Gohl moved to land, becoming what sailors referred to as a "white-shirt sailor," it did not take him long as union agent to recognize that the exploitation and violence of capitalism was not confined to floating workplaces. As a leading player in the early labor struggles of the lumber industry, known widely for dangerous working conditions and violent anti-unionism, Gohl knew that the whip of the ship captain was mirrored on land by the lumberman's axe handle and the night watchman's pistol.

Although Gohl has been treated unfairly by popular historians and "true crime" writers, he has been ignored by academics. The well-known caricature of Gohl would fit comfortably in studies of the frontier myth and historiography of the "Wild West," a region where independent, self-made men conquered nature with intellect, bravery, toughness, and disdain for authority. Many of these studies emphasize violence, both its mythical and real components, and as historian Susan Armitage concludes, "Of all the qualities of the frontier myth, surely the most troublesome is the emphasis on violence."[24]

The mythical frontier holds an important place in the American imagination and history. But *The Port of Missing Men* fits better in the field of social history. As historians Elizabeth Fox-Genovese and Eugene Genovese argued, the central question in social history is "who rides whom and how."[25] This books seeks to contribute to the vibrant social history of the North American West, which in the words of historian William G. Robbins studies the region by asking "questions that revolve around the influences of capitalism, corporate leverage in manipulating natural resources, and the changing place of the region in the global economy."[26] Using this methodology, the story of a serial killer who took advantage of a supposedly "wide-open town" loses much of its resonance. More important is what the study of power structures can tell us about the processes that create a sick society.

The history of Billy Gohl and Grays Harbor is one of class war, epitomizing such struggles around the globe. In the early twentieth century, Gohl held numerous union offices in the Pacific Northwest, influenced local politics, crafted organizations to institutionalize working-class solidarity, and led strikes that threatened the booming Grays Harbor lumber trade. Across the United States, activists like Gohl organized to build and strengthen a labor movement as unions fought for better wages and conditions and control over the workplace. In their important book *Against Labor: How U.S. Employers Organized to Defeat Union Activism*, historians Rosemary Feurer and Chad Pearson argue, "At the end of the nineteenth century, employers and others referred to these activities as 'the labor problem.' In many cases, they responded forcefully, creating frameworks that remain important today."[27] Studies such as *Against Labor* provide valuable insights into the diverse tactics used by employers and their allies to fight labor. Bosses built organizations ranging from chambers of commerce to vigilante clubs, lobbied politicians to pass antilabor laws, and influenced elections and political appointments to guarantee that those in public office, from president to city council, favored capital's interests. *The Port of Missing Men* shows that local employers in the Grays Harbor area followed national trends in union-busting, making frequent use of common antilabor tools such as injunctions, arresting picketers, and hiring strikebreakers prepared to bust skulls. But when these tactics failed to end labor's threat, management turned to more creative forms of strikebreaking. Indeed, US history abounds with examples of bosses eliminating union activists and working-class radicals by whatever means necessary.

Even a cursory reading of US labor history would make someone suspicious of the "Ghoul of Grays Harbor" myth. During the early twentieth century, employers and workers routinely committed acts

of class violence on picket lines, shop floors, and in the wider community. Another site of violence was the legal system, as police, prosecutors, and judges aided antiunion employers by jailing union organizers
and radicals. Labor spies often provided much of the evidence necessary to convict American working-class activists, and the annals are
full of martyrs, working-class activists sentenced to death or long
prison sentences. The names of Haymarket, Haywood, Joe Hill, and
Sacco and Vanzetti still resonate as potent reminders, but many more
class war prisoners and martyrs are forgotten.

Labor historians have done much to unearth evidence of the diverse
methods used by employers and their allies to combat unions and
working-class radicals. In his book *Union-Free America*, historian
Lawrence Richards identifies a persistently antiunion culture among
the American middle and employing classes, writing that "the image
of the unruly, dangerous, even revolutionary nature of the proletariat
remained a constant throughout [the late nineteenth and early twentieth centuries]." This anti-unionism was partially rooted in a view
that members of the working class were inferior to their employers.
"The proletariat . . . was un-American in every sense of that word: it
was composed largely of immigrants and their children; and it was
wedded to radical and foreign ideologies," Richards concludes.[28] Fundamental to this contempt for working people was a belief in social
Darwinism: employers were entitled to rule society because they
had worked hard to gain their position. Bosses did not shy away from
spouting this perspective. During the 1914 U.S. Commission on Industrial Relations, Grays Harbor area lumberman Neil Cooney spoke to
his beliefs in individualism and the self-made man: "I came to this
country from Canada right off the farm 34 years ago a common laborer,
built myself up to the position I have, and had no education."[29]

In the Grays Harbor area in the early twentieth century, attacks on
labor involved capital's traditional weapons: cooperative police, a
captive legal system that arrested and jailed labor activists, and vigilante citizens' committees. But local employers also enrolled the
assistance of outside labor spies, men whose skills supplemented less

experienced locals in dealing with Gohl and the powerful labor movement he helped organize.

Few aspects of American life are as sacred as employers' right to control the workplace. Bosses have nearly unchecked power, protected by the state and endorsed by the corporate media, to hire and fire who they want, determine wages and hours of work, and shape work processes to maximize productivity. Twentieth-century US history has a handful of examples of the state stepping in to enforce labor regulations such as safety and hours laws, minimum wages, and collective bargaining rights, all notable exceptions to bosses' hegemony over the workplace.

With limited influence in national and state politics, late nineteenth and early twentieth-century workers relied on direct action at the point of production to bring about workplace change. In every instance employers saw these challenges for what they were: assaults on their managerial prerogatives to run their property and manage their employees as they saw fit. To protect their class interests, employers adhered to a standard antiunion playbook relying on collective action of their own at all levels of American society, including legislative lobbying, physical violence, and antilabor propaganda campaigns.

A biography of Billy Gohl will most likely interest those drawn to the story of a serial killer. But Gohl was also a white working-class man living in a time and place of dynamic change. The pages that follow discuss the big questions: "Did Gohl do it?" "Did he kill them?" But they also shed light on the lives and struggles of Gohl and others like him on behalf of workers who were ground down by industrial capitalism and sometimes died in its jaws.

Unionization efforts by Pacific seamen focused on combating the abuses of employers and their auxiliaries. By the time Gohl became agent for the Aberdeen SUP, the union was a strong force in the Pacific Coast and among the oldest and most powerful labor organizations locally. As union agent, Gohl represented seamen who had suffered the worst abuses and routinely served as attorney for union sailors in court. An articulate spokesman for his trade and the labor movement, Gohl sometimes penned op-eds for local newspapers and gave interviews to local journalists. The most common subject of his writings was the exploitation of sailors, both at sea and on land, and the need to protect these men through legislation and a strong union movement. Gohl described the International Seamen's Union, a federation of sailors' unions including the SUP, as "desiring to work for the improvement in the material, mental, and moral condition of men employed on vessels in any capacity. It desires the friendship and help of all Trade unions or other organizations of labor, and further desires to the best of its ability, to render the same in return."[30] The union agent's work continued even after members' lives ended, which, during the early twentieth century, they did with shocking frequency. Each time a seaman died, Gohl, like other union agents, was responsible for finding and informing his next of kin; passing along what few possessions belonged to him; arranging, paying for, and often speaking at the unionist's funeral; and speaking with authorities and journalists about the sailor and his death.

Gohl was part of the political, social, and economic fabric of the Grays Harbor region, but he also thrived amid street-level skirmishes in the class war. His role in the region's labor conflict took a drastic turn in June 1906 as the SUP declared a coastwise strike. Among employers and newspaper editors Gohl gained a reputation for violence, as the union agent led a force of approximately one hundred sailors and longshoremen in armed attacks against employers, scabs, and deputized "special" police. Their success at shutting down all coastwise shipping horrified local employers who had just begun enjoying enormous profits from reconstruction following the April 1906 San Francisco earthquake and fire. Following the strike's resolution in October 1906, harbor bosses—abetted by state officials and spies—combined to defeat the region's militant maritime unions.

The coordinated antiunion campaign silenced Gohl and sent him off to prison where he lived the rest of his short life. In prison he was cut off from society as he knew it, including his friends and family, worked at hard labor, and was subjected to the harsh depredations of the institution not yet known as the correctional center. Within a year of his conviction his old union was in tatters, and the thoroughly organized waterfront he had helped create was subjected to an "open shop" regime.[31]

Besides being a labor history, this book is also a biography of William Gohl, whose efforts on behalf of his union have been so distorted that "common knowledge" of his life bears no relation to reality. Eccentric and hardheaded though he may have been, Gohl shaped his class experiences into a wide variety of offensive and defensive tactics against the employers who exploited his and his fellow workers' labor, the state that remained so closely beholden to the interests of capital, and the dominant society that despised him and his kind.

Beginning in early February 1910, an ambitious group of editors and journalists stocked with rumors and sketchy testimonials provided by labor spies and Gohl's political enemies joined a well-heeled group of employers and started pounding the "Ghoul of Grays Harbor" myth into the collective consciousness of the region's residents. On April 7, 1910, the *Aberdeen Herald* headline "Gohl, Leader of Gang of Murderers" represented the popular opinion of the man, just as it does now.[32] Dozens of popular historians and true crime writers have done little more than repeat the same tales spun by those reporters in 1910. By uncritically repeating the story, these historians exceeded expectations of the original mythmakers, since by focusing so much attention on a single man—serial killer or not—they have masked much of the region's wider violent past. We should not be surprised, then, that famed Northwest journalist and popular historian Murray Morgan devoted the greatest part of a book chapter titled "Grays Harbor: The Era of Violence" to Gohl's alleged crimes.[33]

Ed Van Syckle's popular 1980 history of Grays Harbor, *They Tried to Cut It All: Grays Harbor—Turbulent Years of Greed and Greatness,* is characteristic for its treatment of Gohl. Van Syckle, a longtime journalist in the region, titled his pertinent chapter "That No-Good Billy Gohl," and his handling of the story resembles the newspaper articles written seventy years earlier: "Billy Gohl was the scourge of the waterfront, the torment of lumbermen, and an affliction of shipmasters and shipowners. Because he could do so much mischief with but little more than a wave of his hand—and a few threatening axe handles—Gohl tied up ship loading, delayed sailings, fouled up provisioning, caused lawsuits over late lumber deliveries, roused the saloons, intimidated pimps and gamblers, 'cut' the whores and generally did pretty well for his finances and his egomania. And already he was on his way to becoming a terrifying criminal, the murderer of many men."[34] Few writers on Gohl have matched the dramatic punch of Murray Morgan, who declared: "These anonymous dead men, culled from the hordes of migrant laborers who had flocked to Grays Harbor to cut trees, came to be known as the Floater Fleet." Not mincing words, Morgan concluded: "Billy Gohl was credited with launching most of them. If he was responsible for even half of the floaters found in the harbor during his day, Gohl was America's most prolific murderer. Over a ten-year period the fleet numbered 124."[35]

Writers on Gohl have openly expressed elitist views about working people, making condescending and offensive comments on their appearance, language, and manners—specifically applying them to Gohl, his family, and his fellow unionists. Although these writers might claim to be producing factual accounts free from prejudice, the reality is often a work of intense class bigotry that transforms unionists into criminals, strikers into rioters. Elitist views toward workers do not merely entail terminology but also infect the argument and choice of evidence to examine and hold up. Indeed, as historian Mark Leier wrote, "If one believes the working class smells, one writes differently than if one believes it is heroic."[36] Given this, it should surprise no one that "ghoulists" avoid quoting or even examining Gohl's own extensive body of writings. When Gohl's purported words are used, they take the form of thirdhand rumor allegedly uttered by the Ghoul of Grays Harbor after a night of drunken carousing. To some overtly antilabor writers on Gohl, it is clear, unions mean gangsters and corruption. Popular historian Stewart Holbrook's *Holy Old Mackinaw: The Natural History of the American Lumberjack* lists "Gohl, Billy, gangster" in its index.[37]

The stories presented in writings about Gohl do not hold up to scrutiny. Over and over, misrepresentations are presented as fact, fiction as truth. To be clear: the overarching tale of the "Ghoul of Grays Harbor" is fiction. It is sheer myth that holds that he murdered anywhere from forty to two hundred men, thus making him one of the most prolific serial killers in US history. He did not. The state convicted Gohl of first-degree murder for the death of Charles Hadberg and for this crime alone. The jury reached this verdict even after the man who pulled the trigger on the firearm killing Hadberg, sailor John Klingenberg, admitted to the crime after being drugged, kidnapped, and otherwise mistreated before, and during, the interrogation that produced his confession. As to the claim that Gohl murdered scores of other men, this is based on pure conjecture and contradicted by many facts. Gohl was at the vanguard of efforts to remove "falltraps" from saloons, which he accused saloon keepers of using to drop drunk or drugged men into the Wishkah and Chehalis Rivers after stealing their money.[38] This was the method that writers on Gohl have supposed he used to killed his victims.[39] Gohl also fought to have streetlights installed along the river banks, a measure he correctly assumed would make the cities safer. Furthermore, public records state that most of the "floaters" found during Gohl's life on the harbor resulted from unsafe living and working conditions. Most importantly, Sailors' Union members comprised a high percentage of the "floater fleet," and Gohl was dedicated to these men, whom he called "comrades."[40] He treasured their camaraderie, and they idolized his courage and militancy, as demonstrated in the many elected positions he held in their union.

The pages that follow bear little resemblance to earlier writings about Billy Gohl. While acknowledging Gohl's hand in a handful of violent acts, I avoid portraying him as a caricature. I place Gohl in historical context, viewing his work and struggles as parts of wider societal processes. Unfortunately, like Billy the Kid and Jesse James, Gohl "the Ghoul" has become ensconced in the mythology of the Wild West, and the person is rare who knows of Gohl but doesn't call him a "serial killer." Gohl was a prominent labor leader, and local elites saw him as an enemy who needed to be silenced. To accept as history the stories peddled by his enemies and uncritically repeated in self-published books is wrongheaded. For the myth to succeed it needed to destroy the life and reputation of an activist labor leader and turn Gohl into a monster. For the truth to be known, one needs to make Gohl human again.

1

BILLY GOHL'S WORLD

DECADES BEFORE BILLY Gohl became "The Ghoul of Grays Harbor," he was born in 1873 in Germany and named Wilhelm Johann Hermann Gohl. Gohl's home country and name are two of the few details of the man's life that appear in multiple sources. Indeed, Gohl is a case study in the difficulties of researching the lives of itinerant workers, those who spent most of their lives toiling in anonymity. More than a century after Gohl's name appeared in headlines across the Pacific Northwest and beyond, it remains difficult to speak with confidence about the first thirty years of his life.

Details about Gohl's early life have been embellished or fabricated, both by Gohl and others. A basic sketch of his early years was published in September 1904 in the *Grays Harbor Post*, a labor newspaper, and given Gohl's friendly relationship with the *Post*, it is likely that he was the source for the article. The bones of Gohl's life story can be cobbled together from censuses, court records, penitentiary reports, and articles in the labor and mainstream press. One thing that needs to be noted is that although articles about Gohl refer to him as "Billy," he exclusively went by the more formal "William Gohl." One of the first instances of his name appearing as "Billy Gohl" came in an attack on Gohl in a 1906 letter to the editor of the *Aberdeen Daily Bulletin* written by E. B. Benn, with whom Gohl had a political

disagreement.[1] Although Gohl referred to himself with the more
formal "William," he's been dubbed "Billy" for more than a century.
For clarity, I adopt the nickname "Billy" throughout the book.

Despite discrepancies in details about Gohl's life, some facts are
clear. Several sources record his birthdate as February 6, 1873, for
one. In the late nineteenth and early twentieth century Gohl would
enjoy the relative freedom of life as a member of the industrial working class in Germany and the United States. During the late nineteenth century, these countries emerged as the world's two greatest
industrial superpowers. Nearly all sources agree that Gohl spent his
early years in Germany. As a child growing up in rapidly industrializing Germany, he witnessed the growth of a new world. Prior to 1867,
Germany was an association of central European states—the German
Confederation—including Bavaria and Prussia. Born out of wars of
unification and conquest, a new German state centralized power
into the German Empire in the 1870s and 1880s, becoming one of the
world's great powers. The new state harnessed natural resources
throughout the country and the work of millions of industrial laborers, along with manufacturing prowess, to give Germany by 1890 the
world's second-largest industrial output after the United States. This
was the industrializing Germany that produced Karl Marx and the
powerful German socialist movement. To borrow from Marx, the history of capitalism is one of "blood and fire," and as an adult William
Gohl came to understand this line from Marx's *Capital*.[2]

Gohl never publicly commented on the shocking rise in poverty
and inequality that took place during his and his parents' generations
in Germany. But by the early twentieth century he had developed a
critique of industrial capitalism, especially of the inequality and
uneven legal playing field that many of his era saw as an inevitable
result of western Europe's and North America's dominant socioeconomic system. Gohl, like so many unionists, was especially galled by
the horrid conditions experienced by laborers. In a 1906 letter to the
editor of an antilabor Grays Harbor newspaper, Gohl explained that
his fellow unionists struck because, as human beings, they deserved at
least a certain minimum quality of life: "So I do not wonder when the

sailors kick, because they are human and at least should receive fair wages and clean, roomy decent quarters to live in."[3]

As a prolific reader and keen observer of power relations, Gohl criticized the power of capital over the Gilded Age state. He took note of the ways employers used their influence in the judicial, executive, and legislative branches of government to bust unions. In 1906 he joined two other officials in the Sailors' Union to draft a resolution for the Washington State Federation of Labor (WSFL) condemning the use of court injunctions to break strikes. During the late nineteenth and early twentieth centuries, employers regularly sought injunctions against strikers to prevent them from picketing factories, mines, docks, and other workplaces. Heavily aligned with capital, US courts issued more than four thousand such injunctions between 1880 and 1930.[4] Gohl and his fellow unionists wrote: "We hereby protest against any use of the writ of injunction that will in any way interfere with the right to quit work, the right to peacefully induce others to refrain from going to work or to in any way, individually or collectively, buy or refuse to buy any article the maker or vendor of which is using his industrial power to destroy personal liberty."[5]

William claimed to have attended school in Berlin until age twelve, when he entered the Leibnitz Gymnasium.[6] His schooling paid off in later years as his eloquence and studiousness made him a tremendous asset as a union agent. Equally important, his ability to speak both German and English allowed him to translate for fellow unionists, and he had considerable writing talent. Approximately twenty of Gohl's writings exist, mostly letters to the editor in local and union newspapers during his six-plus years as an SUP official. In 1910 the *Vidette*, published in the Chehalis County seat of Montesano, noted: "Gohl is a German, has a slight accent, but uses good English and talks fluently."[7] Despite the intended praise, the *Vidette* understated Gohl's talents in speaking and writing. In an op-ed written to the *Aberdeen Daily Bulletin*, a Republican organ read by elites on Washington's coast, Gohl wrote regarding dishonest bargaining methods used by shipping bosses: "We believed that [our] demands were reasonable and expected to have entered into a new agreement without parley. To our surprise, the owners refused at first to consider any change in the agreement. We had asked for bread and received stones."[8]

According to the short *Grays Harbor Post* biography, Gohl worked as a seaman for fourteen years. Like most sailors, Gohl experienced a cosmopolitan life: the very nature of the occupation meant visiting far-flung port cities and mixing with different peoples and cultures. The SUP, which Gohl belonged to for more than a decade, serviced ports as far away as Africa, Asia, and Australia. William talked of having friends as far away as Hawaii and England, and he visited Australia during his years at sea.[9] He spent his last several years of freedom in Aberdeen, but he continued to travel throughout the American West and retained friendships with persons near and far. Not surprisingly, his closest friends were officials in the Sailors' Union: Peter B. Gill of Seattle; Harry Ohlsen of San Pedro, California; Charles Sorensen of Honolulu; and E. Ellison, secretary pro tem of the SUP, based in San Francisco, with whom Billy carried out correspondence. William also considered a "Mrs. William Bailey" of Norfolk, England, to be a friend, meaning that he had friends living on islands in both the Pacific and Atlantic—also perhaps unsurprising given his years at sea.[10]

Late nineteenth-century shipping was Gohl's world, as he spent most of the free years of his adult life directly involved with shipping on the US Pacific Coast. As historian Bruce Nelson showed in his seminal work on Pacific Coast maritime unions, the life and work of seamen revolved around the "foc'sle and sailortown," locations of masculine labor, culture, and bonding.[11] Many Pacific Coast port towns were home to famous waterfront districts—sometimes called red-light or "restricted" districts—where workingmen roamed between ships and docks, saloons and cigar stores, boardinghouses and brothels.

Gohl worked aboard deep-sea vessels, traveling to ports around the world, as well as coastwise ships, usually schooners bringing lumber from the Pacific Northwest to markets in California, Mexico, and beyond. The lumber trade occupied most of the Pacific Northwest maritime transport industry in the late nineteenth and early

twentieth centuries. Made up of captain, mate, carpenter, cook, able
seamen, and donkeyman (the marine worker responsible for the
steam-powered donkey engine), schooner crews varied in size
between eight and twenty men.[12] Pacific sailors, particularly those
who, like Gohl, worked on lumber schooners, were skilled both at sea
and on land, and were capable of loading and unloading lumber in
isolated ports in the absence of a permanent body of longshoremen.[13] This was difficult and critical work. A crew of seamen skilled
in loading lumber could ensure a fully, properly, and promptly loaded
vessel.[14] Indeed, as scholars have long noted, maritime workers
occupy key "choke points" in the global economy and are thus in
unique positions to disrupt the flow of goods.[15]

Ships served as workplace, home, kitchen, dining room, and site of
all recreation for the seamen when they were at sea. Although punc-
tuated by excitement—times of stormy weather, rough seas, or inter-
personal violence—most of a sailor's life at sea was mundane, day
after day performing routine tasks before retreating to one's bunk to
rest or read. Gohl wrote, "The crews are compelled to eat their meals
on the deckload [open deck]. The forecastles, where the sailors live,
are generally three-cornered holes and all hands can not always get
out of their bunks and dress at the same time."[16] The forecastles on
ships built in the late nineteenth century were roomier than those
built before the Civil War, but conditions in these living quarters
remained cramped. A surgeon with the Marine Hospital Service
described the forecastle: "No prison, certainly none of modern days,
so wretched but life within its walls is preferable, on the score of
physical comfort, to the quarters and the life of the sailor on the vast
majority of merchant vessels."[17]

Especially in the rough waters of storms, vessels sometimes
became delayed or even were lost at sea. Newspapers in ports like
Seattle, San Francisco, or Grays Harbor ran worrisome reports of
delayed ships feared lost. In 1909 it took the *Minnie E. Caine* ninety-
seven days to reach Grays Harbor from China. Shortly after departing
the Chinese coast, the schooner had encountered a typhoon that "carried away her sails and everything loose on deck, and destroyed a

large part of the ship's provisions." Forced to traverse the Pacific with no sails and few provisions, the crew grew ill and nearly starved. The *Aberdeen Herald* wrote of "the captain dangerously ill and the crew so weak as to be almost helpless from hunger."[18] In an editorial in the *Aberdeen World,* Gohl expressed the importance of hiring skilled seamen: "Their hazardous calling demands the highest intelligence, and a clearly defined knowledge and understanding of every particular branch of his occupation are absolutely necessary if the seaman is to protect ship, passengers, and cargo when emergencies arise."[19]

Prior to labor reforms of the early twentieth century, seamen were prisoners of the captain. Unlike most onshore workers, who could, at least in theory, quit work if they found it intolerable, sailors were legally bound to captains and were considered wards of the state. In response to the class system created under industrial capitalism, workers and intellectuals adopted the term "wage slavery" to compare wage work with chattel slavery. Maritime labor was wage slavery in its purest form, because, once at sea, ships were inescapable.[20] Strikes aboard ship would be considered a mutiny by captains, mates, and legal authorities. Captains had a great deal of latitude for dealing with mutineers aboard ship, and few of these masters were ever punished for meting out corporal punishment to rebel seamen. If a mutinous crew survived the journey, captains could, and often did, appeal to legal authorities to arrest and prosecute seamen for their crimes. Sentences for challenging a sea captain's will were harsh. Citing the case of a ship on which "beatings, kickings . . . and pistols were the order of the day," historian Bruce Nelson concluded: "It is at least highly probable that before 1900 the average seaman in the foreign trade witnessed this kind of sadism on occasion and continually lived in its shadow."[21]

Writer and onetime sailor Jack London based his title character in the novel *The Sea-Wolf* on the real-life cruelty of notorious sea captain Alexander MacLean. Although the novel contains many disturbing scenes, one practically jumps off the page—an episode when the captain's violent deeds are described by a sailor: "This Wolf Larsen is a regular devil, an' the *Ghost*'ll be a hell-ship like she's always ben since he had hold iv her. Don't I know? Don't I know? Don't I remember him in Hakodate two years gone, when he had a row an' shot four iv his men? Wasn't I a-layin' on the *Emma L.*, not three hundred yards away? An' there was a man the same year he killed with a blow iv his fist. Yes, sir, killed 'im dead-oh. His head must iv smashed like an eggshell."[22]

In attacking a 1902 bill "to make seamen serfs to the ship," proposed by Congressman Amos Allen of Maine, the *Coast Seamen's Journal* invoked the Declaration of Independence: "We have been assured that slavery is a thing of the past, that, no matter what the original limitations of life, liberty, and the pursuit of happiness, these blessings are now extended equally to all colors—white, black, yellow, and copper."[23] But "a state of slavery does exist," continued the *Journal*, even if "general opinion is sometimes oblivious of important details."[24]

For good reason, most of the histories of the Industrial Revolution focus on factories and mines, two central sites of industrial labor, brutal hours of work, and capitalist accumulation. But as historian Leon Fink's epic history of merchant seamen describes it, shipping was "the world's first globalized industry," one that carried industrial capitalism across the seven seas.[25] When at sea, sailors worked aboard floating factories. They performed long hours of hard labor under strict supervision by bosses with the ability to punish them physically—up to and including death—if a sailor objected too strenuously.

The difficulties of a sailors' life did not end when he came to shore. In the late nineteenth century, boardinghouse owners known as crimps were matched only by ship captains in the infamy of their trade and the hatred heaped upon it by seamen and the labor movement in general. Crimps controlled the supply of maritime labor to ships. To obtain employment, sailors needed to go through crimps, and crimps had relationships with shipowners and captains who paid them to provide workers. As itinerant workers, most sailors lived in boardinghouses when not at sea. Every Pacific Coast port city had crimps who exploited sailors by offering them room and board and then plying them with drink. A successful crimp would overcharge for these services, running the workers into debt, and then sell them their next job aboard ship.

After years of plying his trade as a seaman, Gohl explained some of the crimp's nefarious activities:

> The "divekeeper" therefore becomes one of the most obnoxious obstacles in the educational department of the seaman's union. This fellow is very vigilant. He knows whenever a vessel reaches port how many men are to be paid off, and about how much money is due the prospective "sucker." As soon as the vessel is about to make fast her lines, a booster, or at times, the "boss" himself, is at the dock to greet the crew and one by one the crew are asked forward to have a drink. Money is on many occasions advanced and when the seaman goes to the deputy collector to receive the balance of his pay, there you will find a few "friends" waiting to guide the sailor to some place where he may indulge in a sociable drink.[26]

Some crimps joined disreputable ship captains and merchants in procuring seamen via shanghaiing: abducting a sailor and forcing him to work on a ship. To help meet labor needs, captains (or more likely their associates on land) abducted potential seamen, typically drugging them or knocking them out, took them aboard ship, and kept them locked up until the vessel was at sea. At that point, the involuntary seaman would be made an offer: work or starve. In a 1985 study of the practice of shanghaiing in early San Francisco, Lance S. Davidson stated: "As early as 1852, twenty-three shanghaiing gangs operated on San Francisco's waterfront."[27] In 1906 the US Congress passed legislation that prohibited shanghaiing and provided for potential imprisonment for violations.[28]

Tragically, for decades after this practice gained exposure and condemnation, it persisted in American port cities. One of the better-known cases involved William O'Rourke Jr., a son of a prominent New York politician, who found himself abducted, gagged, placed aboard a sealing schooner known as the *Carmencita*, and imprisoned in San Francisco. When "set free" on the schooner, it was already three days out to sea, and he was forced to either work aboard ship or starve.[29] An equally notable case entails circumstances even more disturbing. In June 1912, the steam schooner *Corinthian* ran aground on the Humboldt Bar, with two men—a sailor and a University of California student—being shanghaied and forced to work until their deaths in the shipwreck.[30]

Like his comrades at sea, Gohl understood the dirty business of procuring seamen. In June 1906, amid a seamen's strike, he argued that employers had resorted to shanghaiing men and boys in San Francisco and forcing them to work as scabs aboard ship as they traveled north along the coast.[31] By the 1910s, due to pressure from unionists and their legislative allies, shanghaiing began to be prosecuted, although punishments for this ostensibly serious crime were remarkably minor. In 1915 John Curtin, a San Francisco crimp, was fined ten dollars for attempted shanghaiing.[32]

Sailors' dangerous, difficult jobs earned them neither a high standard of living nor the respect of the public. Large swaths of the population viewed seamen as incorrigible and in need of surveillance and assistance from the state and charitable organizations.[33] Paul Taylor, who in 1922 wrote an institutional history of the Sailors' Union, stated: "Thus the 'drunken sailor' became a familiar figure on the waterfront, and much justification was afforded for the judgment that 'Jack' was 'intemperate, rough, and turbulent in character.'"[34] Sailors' Union leader Andrew Furuseth denounced these condescending attitudes, noting that religious groups liked to state "in their official reports, that they had done excellent service during the year among 'the criminals, the prostitutes, and the sailors.'"[35]

Like those doing many other difficult manual labor jobs in the industrial world, sailors died with some regularity at work. In 1906, 113 Great Lakes seamen died, with at least 30 of that number due to drowning or being lost overboard.[36] The *Coast Seamen's Journal* took matters of worker safety seriously and ran pieces, ranging from short death notices to long articles, on at least 107 SUP members who died between September 1903 and September 1904.[37] Sailors' deaths were so common that even this, the union's newspaper, published only short notices about union member fatalities. For example, when Andrew Petersen Wiklund drowned at San Pedro in March 1905, the *Coast Seamen's Journal* published only a twenty-two-word death notice.[38]

Sailors perished in shipwrecks, drowned when they fell off docks or gangplanks, and died from a host of accidents aboard ship. Dangerous conditions, old and improperly maintained equipment, short crews, unsanitary food and water, and environmental dangers such as freezing nights at sea contributed to injuries and illness. This was "slow violence," to use the term coined by literary scholar Rob Nixon to describe "an attritional violence that is typically not viewed as violence at all" but that is common to working-class life over the long term. In the late nineteenth century seamen accused captains of running ships shorthanded, preferring to save money over making a safe workplace, while seamen fell victim to consumption and scurvy.[39]

During Gohl's time at sea he experienced nearly every conceivable disaster, with sailors struggling to survive in the face of storms, fires, shifting cargoes, and massive waves slamming into the ship. The March 8, 1900, issue of the *Aberdeen Herald* provided a window into the life and death struggles for the men at sea. It included a notice of the injury sailor John Albert sustained when he fell down the hatchway of the barkentine *Benicia*; two weeks after his fall, Albert's condition remained so serious that he was transferred to a marine hospital in Tacoma. The same issue notified readers that the body of sailor Charles Ecelsen had surfaced in a local waterway six weeks after his fall overboard from the schooner *Charles R. Wilson*. Albert's fall and Ecelsen's death occurred in 1900, when the harbor boasted a small population and only a handful of mills and saloons. Just as population, lumber production and shipments, and the number of saloons all increased, so did the number of deaths and crippling injuries.[40]

Gohl knew a great deal about one experience unique to seafarers, as the short *Grays Harbor Post* bio stated: "He has braved the perils of the sea in several shipwrecks."[41] Newspapers published in port towns stretching from Aberdeen to San Francisco regularly reported on shipwrecks. In March 1906, the schooner *Sadie* had to be towed into Grays Harbor by a tugboat after being "battered and bruised, and looking like the ghost of some old pirate ship after a losing fight with its enemies." Battered by a storm for more than ten hours, the ship's crew lost all their belongings as water deluged the ship.[42] From its earliest existence, the Sailors' Union provided a benefit to shipwrecked union members. Gohl likely benefited from these funds to survive during those years.[43] In 1900 Gohl worked aboard the *Lizzie Theresa*, a bay schooner operating out of San Francisco. The *Lizzie Theresa* didn't take its sailors to distant points such as China or Hawaii, common destinations for Pacific seamen, but operating any vessel brought the potential for danger. In March 1900, the schooner's captain, Albert Sims, drowned after the *Lizzie Theresa* capsized, dumping the crew overboard.[44] It is possible that Gohl was a crew member of the wrecked *Lizzie Theresa*. If so, he would have had firsthand experience with the importance of the union's shipwreck benefit fund. Three months after Sims's death, Gohl worked aboard ship with the dead captain's replacement, Jack Conrad.[45]

Gohl was one of those fortunate enough to survive his days at sea. Not only did he live, he emerged with his health intact and an eagerness to become an important member of his adopted community of Aberdeen. By all accounts, Gohl was a physically impressive specimen, although Gohl's size has been exaggerated both to satisfy readers' sense of awe about the "Madman of Aberdeen" and to impress twenty-first-century American readers, who are, in many cases, larger than their early twentieth-century counterparts. Several writers have contended that Gohl stood six foot two and weighed more than two hundred pounds. A 1908 medical report provided for Gohl's application to the Fraternal Order of Eagles says otherwise. Standing five foot seven and weighing 173 pounds, Gohl was barrel-chested and physically fit.[46]

As historians B. R. Burg and Ira Dye have shown, throughout US history, sailors have commonly sported tattoos.[47] According to one physical examination, Gohl had three tattoos: an anchor with letters "W.G." on the inside of his left forearm, a crowned serpent on the inside of his right forearm, and a compass and star on the center of his chest.[48]

If a sailor's life at sea was a mixture of unfree servitude and bore-dom, his life on land mixed equal parts excitement with exploita-tion and danger. Although a sailor's job title was "seaman," sailors spent much time on land while longshoremen loaded and unloaded cargo. At their most efficient, ships could be loaded in a matter of hours. But delays, with causes ranging from accidents to strikes or a glut in the market, kept vessels docked at ports, delaying their trips for weeks or even months. Few seamen had a permanent residence on land, and those who did lived in shacks hastily constructed along waterways. Boardinghouses provided housing for most seamen in cit-ies such as San Francisco, Seattle, and Aberdeen.

At the taking of the 1900 US Census, William Gohl lived in a San Francisco boardinghouse occupied by men, who, like him, worked aboard ships. Unlike in factory or mining towns, where workingmen lived with women (and sometimes worked among them), itinerant loggers, road construction workers, and seamen in the West chiefly lived and worked with other men. Although Gohl's residence appeared in the US Census, he doesn't show up in the San Francisco city direc-tories around the turn of the century. This isn't surprising, as city directories routinely missed itinerant laborers such as seamen. This evidence suggests that in the years before becoming a union agent Gohl did not settle into a permanent home. The 1900 Census records him as a "roomer/boarder," living with other crew members on the *Lizzie Theresa*, hardly an indication of a close relationship between him and the permanent community of San Francisco.

Like all US Census records, Gohl's entry in the 1900 tabulation provides only the sparest details of his life and community. Censuses miss a great deal. For example, in interviews, Gohl stated that he worked in mining and construction in Alaska in 1900–1901. From his jail cell in February 1910, he told a reporter of his work life and expe-riences similar to those of millions of migratory workers of the era: "I worked for the Pioneer Mining company at Cape Nome and Anvil Mountain in 1900 and 1901 as a contract laborer and also helped to build the lighthouses at Fort Wrangel and Juneau Pass."[49] Fur-thermore, numerous sources suggest that Gohl lived in—or at least visited—Aberdeen long before settling there in 1903 as union agent.[50] It is quite possible, even likely, that William spent considerable time in Aberdeen, San Francisco, and many other port towns prior to making the Grays Harbor area his permanent residence in 1903. From 1900 to 1903, William received correspondence at the Aberdeen and Seattle Sailors' Union halls.[51] Sailors were perhaps the most itinerant of all workers, and it seems that Gohl or anyone else would have been well served by spending time in a community prior to dispatch there as a union officer.

Gohl was living in Aberdeen by October 16, 1903, on "Black Friday," one of the most infamous dates in that city's history. That day, a fire broke out in downtown Aberdeen, tearing through the city's buildings. All told, the blaze took the lives of four people and destroyed 140 buildings.[52] Gohl apparently informed a reporter of his experiences on Black Friday and thanked his dog Boatswain for saving his life. In a series of pieces entitled "Remarkable Canine Stories," the *Seattle Times* reported that on the morning of the fire Gohl and a friend named Tom Swanson had been fast asleep in the cabin they occupied "when Boatswain's nostrils first scented the acrid smell of smoke." After Boatswain's whines failed to awaken the men, "the dog with almost human intelligence pulled the blankets and other coverings from the beds of both men, and in that manner, together with his barkings, brought them to consciousness and safety in the nick of time."[53]

Given the widespread sympathy with dogs and dog lovers, it is surprising that people writing about Gohl haven't picked up on this story. But it is a useful reminder that Gohl was a real person, a flesh-and-blood individual who should not be lumped into the category of "serial killer." In fact, the story of Gohl and his dog provides a useful window into Gohl's early days on the harbor. "In the dog's youngest days he was the sole companion of Gohl; inseparable from his master; at his heels in daytime and at his bedside at night," according to the *Times*. Unfortunately, according to Gohl, Aberdeen children persistently teased the dog, leading Boatswain to become "unmanageable." Gohl gave his companion to a ship captain, who apparently brought the dog on working vessels throughout the Pacific. Boatswain became a "sea dog" who made stops "at Peru and other Southern countries, returning eventually to the Sound and Grays Harbor." Like Gohl, Boatswain survived at least one shipwreck and became, in the words of the *Seattle Times*, "famous the length of the Pacific Coast and the talk of the Honolulu docks."[54]

Most of Gohl's rooming house mates were Scandinavian immigrant sailors, and at the turn of the century the terms "Scandinavian" and "sailor" were nearly synonymous. Twenty of his roommates were Scandinavians, while Gohl was one of five German immigrant seamen living at that one address.[55] More than one observer described the Sailors' Union as the "Scandinavian Navy," with Norwegians,

William Gohl, 1904, from a series of short biographies of local union officials that appeared in the *Grays Harbor Post*. After years as an itinerant seaman, in 1903 Gohl settled into life as the Aberdeen agent of the Sailors' Union of the Pacific. *Grays Harbor Post*, September 4, 1904.

Swedes, and Danes comprising most of the union's membership.[56] Norwegians occupied all levels of the sailors' workforce, from top union officials Andrew Furuseth and longtime Seattle agent Peter B. Gill to able seamen and deck boys.[57]

The virtual slavery experienced by sailors, the exploitation they experienced at the hands of crimps, their dangerous job, and the dehumanizing views held by much of the public toward them all motivated Pacific Coast sailors to band together into unions. The SUP, founded in 1891 through the amalgamation of the Coast Seamen's Union (CSU) and Steamship Sailors' Union, organized into seven locals, whose members sailed the Pacific Coast and beyond.[58] Unionists spread the organization up and down the coast, from San Pedro and San Francisco to Port Townsend and Seattle.

The Sailors' Union sprang in part from radical and militant influences of the country's wider labor movement during the late nineteenth century. The radical milieu included diverse ideologies and organizations, prominently including anarchists, socialists, communists, and members of the Knights of Labor, a federation that topped out at 700,000 members in 1886.[59] Six years before merging with the Steamship Sailors' Union to become the SUP, seamen formed the Coast Seamen's Union in San Francisco. Members of the International Workingmen's Association (IWA) led the unionization drive. Also known as the First International, the IWA was a radical political organization influenced by Karl Marx but also the anarchism of some of its other leading members. During the early 1880s, the IWA enrolled several thousand members in locals scattered throughout the American West.[60]

The IWA and the CSU are unknown to most Americans, but their ideologies and labor activism emerged from the same radical milieu that animated the wider Gilded Age labor movement. Two of that era's labor conflicts—the 1886–87 Haymarket tragedy and the 1905 assassination of former Idaho governor Frank Steunenberg—illuminated a great deal about the nature of late nineteenth-century and early twentieth-century class conflict. The fact that both culminated in nationally covered political trials indicated the influence wielded by capital. They also provide context for the labor struggles that broke out in the early twentieth century in the Grays Harbor region and the ways capital and the state responded to the labor movement's—and especially Gohl's—place in those conflicts.

Few years in labor history have been so influential as 1886. That year saw the Knights of Labor peak in membership and influence and the eight-hour-day strike called by the Knights and trade unionists for May 1. The strike and its tragic aftermath birthed May Day, International Workers' Day, an official holiday of the labor movement in many countries outside of the United States where it was born. The incidents surrounding May Day 1886 provide diverse lessons, but to workers they provided clear evidence of the state's potential—by means of police, politicians, and courts—to serve as assistants to capital in union-busting campaigns.

On May 1, 1886, hundreds of thousands of workers, including forty thousand in Chicago, went on strike, all demanding the eight-hour workday. On May 3, police attacked a strike demonstration at the McCormick Harvester factory in Chicago, killing at least two protesters and injuring others.[61] The next day, anarchists joined a host of diverse working-class radicals in a meeting to protest the police violence. After hours of speeches, police raided the gathering, looking to break it up with force. During the police attack, an unknown party threw a bomb into the crowd. When the bomb exploded, police fired wildly into the crowd. Between the bomb and shootings, several police and workers died. The bombing led to a red scare that swept across the nation. State and capital combined to persecute radicals and the wider labor movement. In Chicago, the state tried and convicted eight anarchists for the bombing, even though some of them weren't at the meeting. Following months of protests and condemnations of the frame-up of these men, widely seen in working-class circles as political prisoners, the State of Illinois executed four of the prisoners. Today known as the Haymarket Incident or the Haymarket Affair, the trial, executions, and protests of the unjust treatment of the "Haymarket martyrs" inspired generations of labor and Left activists.

In the late nineteenth and early twentieth centuries, the American West experienced numerous bitter, violent labor conflicts, which in the words of historian Melvyn Dubofsky comprised "class war on the industrial frontier."[62] One of the flash points in the western labor wars was in northern Idaho in the silver and lead mines of the Coeur d'Alene district. In 1899, miners affiliated with the Western Federation of Miners (WFM) struck, demanding compliance with the union's pay scale. On April 29, 1899, dynamiters blew up one of the region's mines, killing one person. In response to the dynamiting and to strikers' successes at shutting down the region's mines, Idaho governor Frank Steunenberg placed the area under martial law and requested federal troops from President William McKinley. The president complied, sending in soldiers to occupy the region. Troops arrested sixteen hundred strikers and supporters, tossing them into foul cells with little protection from the environment. During their internment, several strikers died. By the end of the strike, the mine owners and state government had crushed the local union. Defeated in northern Idaho, the WFM remained a powerhouse of western labor, one led by militant socialists such as the legendary "Big Bill" Haywood and Charles Moyer. Understandably, unionists harbored deep resentment toward the union-busting governor and mine owners.[63]

Six years after the miners' strike, a bomb went off at the home of Steunenberg, killing the former governor. Harry Orchard, a deranged drifter with a long and varied criminal past, had stalked Steunenberg for months before killing him. Authorities quickly arrested Orchard, discovered bomb-making materials in his room, and placed him into custody. Given the deceased governor's history of union-busting, influential mine owners and state officials suspected union involvement in the murder. The antilabor press, which had long viewed the WFM as little better than foreign terrorists, fanned the flames of suspicion, running articles that blamed union leaders for the bombing. With Orchard detained, antilabor spies went to work. James McParland, a Pinkerton detective made famous by his work in the Molly Maguire cases in Pennsylvania, led the investigation, and he obtained access to Orchard. Backed by influential businessmen, McParland was able to gain for Orchard a plea deal in exchange for his confession that he had been the "tool" of WFM officials who had paid him to murder the former governor. Given Orchard's confession, antilabor spies kidnapped WFM officials Bill Haywood, Charles Moyer, and George Pettibone in Colorado and transported them to Idaho against their will. In prison, McParland coached Orchard on what testimony to provide in court each day. In the words of historian Philip S. Foner, who uses an alternative spelling of the Pinkerton agent's name: "McParlan's reports on his conferences with Orchard are in the Hawley and Borah manuscripts . . . and they reveal not only that the Pinkerton agent coached Orchard as to what he should say on the stand and just whom he should implicate in the murder of Steunenberg, but he reminded Orchard that the witnesses in the Molly Maguires' case who followed his (McParlan's) advice and testified for the State 'went entirely free' and 'saved their own neck.'"[64] Fortunately, McParland's efforts to implicate Haywood, Moyer, and Pettibone in Steunenberg's murder failed, in part because the state lacked witnesses to corroborate Orchard's confession. The combined efforts of capital, state, and their sidekick private detectives to bring down the WFM's top leaders bear striking similarities to the campaign against Gohl that would take place a few years later.[65]

Clearly, much about American society—its police and courts and professional strikebreaking operations—made building a labor movement difficult. Not surprisingly, then, efforts to establish the Sailors' Union proceeded in fits and starts. Through the last two decades of the nineteenth century, most shipowners and captains preferred to hire nonunion sailors. The existence of union and nonunion ships led to tense exchanges between union and nonunion sailors in port, sometimes docked next to one another. The Sailors' Union hired staff to recruit unionists, but organizing efforts sometimes devolved into bloody flare-ups between seamen. In 1892, in one of many waterfront disturbances, a nonunion sailor stabbed Sailors' Union member Otto Anderson to death in San Francisco. Unionists sometimes committed acts of sabotage, such as cutting nonunion vessels' ropes to set them adrift.[66]

A common organizational tactic used by unionists was to approach and sometimes board ships to persuade nonunion sailors to abandon ship. This persuasion took many forms, including verbal coaxing, threats, and physical attacks. In December 1892, Grays Harbor unionists attempted to board the nonunion schooner *Eureka* to convince the sailors to join their organization but abandoned the effort when met by men "well armed, determined to fight if necessary."[67] Two months later, SUP officer Albert Rabe "enticed" nonunion sailors on the *Catherine Sudden* and "persuaded [them] to desert." Showing whose side the law was on, the ship's captain had Rabe arrested.[68]

Like other unions, the Sailors' Union benefited from the impressive economic upturn at the turn of the century. High demand for maritime labor provided workers with leverage to drive up wages, improve conditions, and strengthen their union. During an 1899 strike, union and nonunion seamen alike refused to work unless they received pay in line with the union wage scale. Shipowners quickly acceded to union demands, providing the sailors with an important victory to boost their ranks. From 1898 to 1901, the union expanded from under one thousand to a full three thousand dues-paying members.[69]

By 1904, the union's 4,222 members, organized into eight branches, had won contracts with the Shipowners' Association of the Pacific Coast, the Steam-Schooner Managers' Association, and the Oceanic Steamship Company. Union contracts mandated pay of at least $45 per month for able seamen working on steam schooners, and lower amounts for seamen working on sailing vessels. However, according to the 1903–4 California Bureau of Labor Statistics report, seamen working on steam schooners averaged eight months of work per year, making for average earnings of $350 per year. This was far lower than the annual wages of unionists in many crafts.[70] Sailors' Union contracts also mandated a nine-hour workday, fifty cents daily overtime pay and lunch and coffee breaks. Union benefits included $50 for shipwrecked unionists, $75 to pay for members' funerals, and $3 weekly strike pay.[71]

The Sailors' Union also wrested control over hiring, taking that away from crimps, captains, and owners. By 1902, SUP contracts included standard language reading: "None but union men shall be employed and the engagement of the crew shall be done through the Union's Offices."[72] Unionists considered this achievement—gaining control over hiring—to be their most significant achievement.

There is good chance that Gohl was on hand in San Francisco in the summer of 1901, when the Bay City erupted into the Pacific Coast's century's first knock-down, drag-out industrial fight. By the turn of the century, San Francisco was arguably the nation's strongest labor city. The majority of workers in several trades belonged to unions. To encourage closer cooperation among the city's transportation workers, unionists formed the City Front Federation, a coalition of fourteen unions, including its longshoremen, teamsters, and sailors. San Francisco employers responded to the growth of the city's labor movement by uniting along class lines into the antiunion Employers' Association.[73]

Whether Gohl was on hand in San Francisco during the strike, took part in one of the smaller struggles in other port cities impacted by the strike, or read about it in the country's newspapers, it provided some clear lessons. Originating as a lockout of San Francisco teamsters, the conflict ballooned as the fourteen-thousand-member City Front Federation went out in sympathy with their teamster comrades. The strike was a bloody affair. Unionists patrolled the waterfront and issued passes to other union members, allowing them to go unimpeded to the waterfront. Showing that the relative ethnic homogeneity of the sailors could become a potential liability through nativist appeals, an antilabor newspaper labeled Sailors' Union leader Andrew Furuseth as "this Scandinavian dictator of ours" who "wants his Scandinavian scum to be permitted . . . to beat American citizens into a bloody pulp with slung shots and bludgeons."[74]

To a unionist like Gohl, the Bay Area at the turn of the century proved to be fertile training ground. Employers coordinated their activities through the Employers' Association, showing a united front to break the labor movement and leading the city's labor council to dub the organization a "secret order of industrial assassins."[75] The association hired strikebreakers and labor spies from Curtin's Detective

Agency. Municipal police, nonunion workers, and college students joined in the attack on organized labor, while antilabor newspapers did all they could to depict the strikers as violent, foreign ruffians. Gohl applied the lessons he learned in the 1901 strike to the situation around Grays Harbor. Most notably, he built the Waterfront Federation there, one that, as in San Francisco, united the Aberdeen and Hoquiam waterfront and transport unions into a body that promised united labor power.[76]

Gohl's experiences as a Pacific sailor had taught him a great deal about the daily lives and troubles of itinerant workers. But if he required any lessons about the nature of class and conflict in industrial capitalist American society, the 1901 waterfront strike certainly taught him about its fundamental aspects. Less than two years after the strike, Gohl's comrades voted him agent for the Aberdeen branch of the Sailors' Union of the Pacific, a position he used to mitigate the dangers faced by working men like himself.

2

BILLY GOHL'S
GRAYS HARBOR

BILLY GOHL'S SETTLING in Aberdeen coincided with a massive population growth around Grays Harbor, particularly its industrial cities of Aberdeen and Hoquiam. Between 1900 and 1910, the region expanded from a series of small, isolated villages into major industrial cities. In 1900, the entirety of Grays Harbor County (called Chehalis County until 1915) had only a little over 15,000 residents, with Aberdeen counting only 3,747 population. At the turn of the century, Aberdeen was a small town. Most of its buildings lay in a section of town about four blocks long by four blocks wide, bordered by the Wishkah River to the east, the Chehalis River to the south, Market Street to the north, and I Street to the west. A scattering of homes lay beyond this section of town, but the dominant presence was that of industry, with mills, docks, and services marketed to workers all lining the Chehalis and Wishkah riversides. Made of wooden planks, Aberdeen's streets gave pedestrians the impression that it was a frontier town. In 1906 the *Aberdeen Daily Bulletin* trumpeted the buildings going up across the city: "Everywhere cottages and residences are going up and yet there is a big demand for new quarters."[1]

Although Gohl spent much of his life at sea and in port towns such as San Francisco, he likely would have experienced sensory overload when he first stepped ashore in Aberdeen. The sight of massive evergreen forests nearby, the smell of sawdust, and the sounds of carousing and fighting emerging from the saloons likely impressed Gohl. The ubiquitous dampness too—moisture in the air and covering all surfaces—would have been impossible to miss. Coastal cities are known for their humidity, but no other US city lay at the intersection of the North Pacific Ocean and the rainforests of the Olympic Peninsula, showering Aberdeen with more than one hundred inches of rain per year. Robert Weinstein, author of a pictorial history of the early Grays Harbor region, described it: "Mud seemed everywhere always, and whatever was damp glistened with a dull wet luster. Infrequent dry days at the harbor were eagerly used to dry sails that always seemed to be damp; wet sails were a nuisance. They dripped water endlessly, and sailors knew that unless they were dried at every opportunity, mildew would inevitably rot them at the seams."[2] By 1910, Aberdeen and Hoquiam ranked as two of the ten largest cities in Washington State. But the cities' population went only so far in explaining the region's significance. Aberdeen and Hoquiam, along with the small company town of Cosmopolis, formed the "Harbor Towns," a nearly contiguous zone of industrial production and transportation, connecting the region's vast forests to the markets that lay beyond the sea. By 1905 the harbor was already the world's largest lumber port, a position it retained for decades thereafter. Speaking of the region's industrial might, one booster claimed that the port shipped enough lumber to "load a train one-half mile in length, every day in the year." During Gohl's residency there, most of its lumber shipped by sea. In 1906 the region's mills shipped more than 360,000 board feet of lumber by water, almost double the 185,000 feet shipped by rail.[3] From June 1905 until June 1906, "over 600 ships loaded at Aberdeen during the year ending June 30."[4] Grays Harbor shipped more than four hundred million board feet of lumber on 422 steam and 136 sailing vessels in 1910. And production continued to climb for years thereafter.[5]

For men like Gohl who sought to build and maintain "the brotherhood of the sea," Grays Harbor proved to be a tough assignment. Even among cities of the so-called Wild West, Aberdeen had an exceptionally sordid history. A "wide open town," Aberdeen boasted dozens of saloons and brothels, and accounts of deadly brawls, shoot-outs, and knifings colored the town's early history. Popular historians Stewart Holbrook and Murray Morgan each devoted a great deal of ink to recounting the rough details of turn-of-the-century Aberdeen. Holbrook, America's most prominent popular writer on logging and lumber, described Aberdeen as a "den of skullduggery" that "fairly swarmed with cutthroats and harpies."[6]

Writers on Gohl have long emphasized the man's toughness, setting him firmly in the roughest spaces of Grays Harbor: the waterfront, the saloon, the brothel, and the picket line. There is plenty of good reason why Gohl has long been situated in these spaces: his job placed him at the intersection of the Chehalis and Wishkah Rivers, in an area of Aberdeen surrounded by mills, docks, saloons, boardinghouses, and brothels. Two of his primary tasks as union agent— ensuring that only unionists got jobs aboard ship and managing the affairs of the dozens of seamen who perished on the harbor—required Gohl and all Sailors' Union agents to interact with the grittiest parts of working-class life: disease, alcoholism, police, jails, fistfights, and death. In a characteristic treatment of Gohl's "life and crimes," one writer comments that Billy "was a good-sized fellow, and apparently this was put to good use in ending barroom fights."[7]

Historians of gender and labor have shown the importance of analyzing masculinity to better understand working-class life, insisting, in Ava Baron's words, on "the significance of gender regardless of women's presence or absence."[8] Often, notes historian Stephen Meyer, "notions and ideals of manhood varied with age," with young men conforming to patterns of rough manliness by fighting, drinking heavily, and aggressively pursuing sexual partners.[9] As working men grew older, they often sought working-class respectability through marriage, stability within a community, proficiency in a craft, and involvement with a trade union. Although this formula isn't determinative, it does provide a useful guide to better make sense of working-class men's life courses, which millions of twentieth-century American men, including Gohl, followed.

A group of men and at least two children pose outside of Emil Olson's saloon, one of the many waterfront saloons in Aberdeen during the early twentieth century. On the second floor is the Aberdeen Sailors' Union of the Pacific hall. *Courtesy of Polson Museum, Hoquiam, Washington.*

Four activities comprised much of the masculine life in the Grays Harbor waterfront district: working, drinking, fighting, and sex. In this it resembled the lives of young working-class men throughout industrial America. Nearly every working-class social activity in the Grays Harbor vicinity involved consuming alcohol and tobacco, and the pages of the local press and jail registers show ample evidence of the frequency of fighting, particularly in and around the saloon districts of Aberdeen and Hoquiam. As the *Aberdeen Herald* wrote in January 1903: "Five different rows in five different saloons, Saturday night together with a free for all lunch at J. Bowes' establishment meant a lively time for one policeman."[10]

Most of Aberdeen's saloons lay in a small section of town known as the restricted district. The number of saloons climbed from eight in 1895, to twelve in 1899, twenty-four in 1903–4, thirty in 1908, and thirty-seven in 1909.[11] Big Fred Hewett's Humboldt Saloon achieved notoriety as a watering hole for loggers and sailors, its proprietor described by Murray Morgan as "a black-mustached behemoth whose love for loggers was as deep as his scorn for all lesser breeds."[12] Loggers and seamen gained legendary status for their partying while in town for holidays, strikes, or shutdowns. Local saloons lay next to unlit and unguarded bodies of water. Pages of the local press carried accounts of intoxicated sailors and loggers falling into the waters of the Chehalis and Wishkah Rivers and drowning. Between 1907 and 1915, at least nineteen adult Finnish immigrants were killed by alcoholism or by accidentally drowning in Grays Harbor, a death commonly related to the victim's intoxication.[13] Drunken brawls too were frequent. Aberdeen longshoreman John Thorsen died as the result of a "drunken row between three Swedes and four Norwegians," after an assailant hit him over the head with a large piece of lumber.[14]

Gohl took great pleasure in the rich and festive working-class cultural activities in the region. Nearly all these activities occurred in men's spaces such as union halls, smoke-filled saloons, and fraternity clubhouses. Commenting on the significance of itinerant laborers to the industrial West, historian Carlos Schwantes wrote, "Undoubtedly the single most distinguishing feature of the wageworkers' frontier was the army of itinerant laborers who were constantly shifting from place to place and from job to job."[15] For many migratory workers, including Gohl, life brought few encounters with women. In 1890, Washington State had a population only 33 percent female, but over the next two decades that number climbed to 41 percent in 1900 and 42 percent in 1910. The region's gender ratio tilted slightly more toward males than did the entire state's population. At the turn of the century, Grays Harbor (Chehalis) County's population was 39 percent female, and a decade later women constituted only 36 percent of the county's population.[16] On the docks, where seamen and longshoremen labored, the population was almost entirely male. Few women worked in the Pacific Northwest lumber and maritime transport in the late nineteenth and early twentieth centuries, and Grays Harbor remained a single-industry region throughout Gohl's life.

The main exception to the seamen's homosocial lives came from prostitutes, the women whose "oldest profession in the world" was as important to American working-class life as any other. In her perceptive study of class and gender in the mining region of Cripple Creek, Colorado, Elizabeth Jameson noted: "Prostitution was inevitable, too, given mining-town demography. Single men found companionship in cribs and dance halls, where they bought dances, alcohol, and conversation as well as sex."[17] Likewise, historian Mary Murphy found that in early twentieth-century Butte, Montana, prostitution constituted one of the most common types of women's paid employment.[18] While describing western mining towns, Jameson's and Murphy's conclusions were equally true of lumber towns, particularly in the working-class spaces along a waterfront.

In Aberdeen and Hoquiam, as in other cities, legal authorities regulated sex work by arresting and fining prostitutes. In April 1908, after the Aberdeen police court collected $400 in fines from prostitutes, one newspaper provided a frank assessment of the reasons for policing the restricted district in this manner: "Two objects are accomplished by the present method of police court procedure. Much time is saved to the officers, and a complete record is kept of persons who are habitants of the restricted district, this record being corrected once a month."[19]

The City of Hoquiam police records are intact and along with the 1900 US Census suggest a lively sex work industry on the harbor, one with approximately dozens of prostitutes employed during the first decade of the twentieth century. The census for Hoquiam alone counted fourteen prostitutes, while the census-taker for Aberdeen refrained from listing any ladies of the night, despite Aberdeen's far more famous red-light district.[20] The City of Hoquiam got its cut of the proceeds, looking the other way for twenty-nine days a month before marching the brothel keepers and prostitutes into jail and charging them with working in a house of ill repute. Most months, the women escaped with a ten-dollar fine, while owners might be subjected to a fine double or triple that size. The city's cut of the sex trade could be considerable, as most months Hoquiam authorities fined thirty or more sex workers.[21] Researching his book *They Tried to Cut It All*, Grays Harbor area journalist Ed Van Syckle gained access to the Aberdeen "prisoner record" for the year 1907. On June 28 of that year, the record lists more than one hundred prostitutes who worked in Aberdeen's restricted district. According to Van Syckle, Aberdeen's prostitutes each paid a $10 fine, while "the keepers and procurers were assessed $25."[22]

Rumors of Gohl's indulgence in the bottle color much of the writing on his life, gaining Billy a historical reputation as a heavy drinker who took full advantage of Aberdeen's night life. Few work groups are so identified with liquor as are sailors. Although the phrase "drunk as a sailor" no doubt stems from class and ethnic prejudices, the reality is that the men of the sea could not avoid the sights and sounds of saloons along Pacific Coast waterfronts. It seems certain that Gohl did imbibe. Surrounded by saloons, saloon keepers, bartenders, and drunks, he would have been hard-pressed to stay sober. Dozens of saloons lay less than two blocks from his residence, and he would have passed a score or more of these places between his home and place of work. The union agent retained a semi-permanent residence in the Capital Rooming House alongside none other than Fred Hewett, proprietor of the Humboldt.[23]

The historical record clearly establishes that Gohl liked to drink and got into his fair share of scraps. But as his life of itinerancy and physical labor shifted to the life of an office-holding landlubber, he took steps toward the life of a respectable workman when he met and married Edith "Bessie" Hager.[24] Bessie was a working-class woman, one of nine children born to a farm family in Johnson County, Missouri. Born in 1879, Bessie experienced some hardships in early life. Her father, Samuel, was sixteen years her mother's senior and by the time of Bessie's birth was already sixty-one years old. He died when Bessie was only two, leaving a large family with few resources.[25]

Bessie Gohl's past is even more opaque than William's, and, given the fondness of those writing about Billy Gohl to exaggerate and condescend toward working people, it is difficult to separate truth from fiction. Among the few sources from Bessie's early years in Aberdeen is her marriage certificate, whose few details include her age, twenty-five in 1905, and residency in Aberdeen.[26] Many writers about Gohl have speculated that Bessie's actual occupation was "dance hall girl," or prostitute, and that she met her future husband at work. Although it is impossible to confirm the story, writers about Gohl sometimes quote *Grays Harbor Post* editor J. W. Clark as saying: "Billy got mean drunk one night and got fresh. She landed one on his chin that knocked him down, then kicked him in the ribs. Billy admired her courage. He liked that kind of rough and tumbled courtship and shortly thereafter they got married."[27] The sexist framing aside, this might hold a kernel of truth. Working-class Grays Harbor women like Bessie were constrained in their life choices. As adults, most would marry or work for wages in low-paying service industries or sex work. More than one hundred prostitutes lived in Aberdeen during the early twentieth century. Given the locations of William's home and workplace, it's likely that most of the women he met were sex workers. Many western prostitutes did marry, and some ended up owning their own brothels or dance halls.[28]

Bessie and William married on May 16, 1905, in the Chehalis County seat of Montesano.[29] As William gained prominence, the couple's relationship received attention in the press. The newspapers Gohl read all contained "society" or "happenings" columns, the former speaking to elite readers of the *Aberdeen Daily Bulletin*, the latter to the more working-class readership of the *Grays Harbor Post*. The *Post* described the Gohls' relationship as a loving and supportive one. In the summer of 1907, as William recovered from a nasty infection, the newspaper praised Bessie for helping to stave off an amputation as Gohl's "swelling extended from the hand to the shoulder and only the most careful nursing by Mrs. Gohl and excellent surgical care by Dr. Watkins prevented the loss of the finger, if not the hand."[30] The *Post* described a family visitor to the Gohls' home in February 1908: "J. T. Monroe, a brother-in-law of Mrs. Wm Gohl, arrived in the city Wednesday from Mena, Ark. for a visit. Mrs. Gohl was pleasantly surprised, not having seen Mr. Monroe for thirteen years."[31] While local reporters would call for Gohl's blood after his 1910 arrest, the *Tacoma*

Daily Ledger described him in this manner: "His relations in his own home were of the most pleasant character. He always appeared very fond of his wife, and the two were to be seen frequently taking a quiet stroll together."[32]

The Sailors' Union forbade its officers—including branch agents like Gohl—from drinking on the job, work that included officiating union meetings.[33] Still, union halls were situated in areas surrounded by saloons, and the SUP hall was on the second floor above a saloon. Tempted on all sides, unionists sometimes drank before and even during meetings. In addition to drinking, smoking, speech-making, and joking, the men at these meetings got into heated debates that sometimes ended in violence. At a 1906 Sailors' Union meeting in Aberdeen, sailor Manuel Mesba lashed out at union agent Gohl, who was likely heading the meeting and who had Mesba removed from the hall because of his objectionable behavior. The incident was only temporarily defused, however, because Mesba waited outside the hall with a knife to ambush the agent. Gohl was warned against confronting the man, but, ever defiant, he tried to speak with Mesba. When Gohl neared, the sailor pulled out his knife and inflicted a deep cut in Gohl's arm. Rather than urge his fellow workers to attack Mesba, Gohl had the man arrested.[34]

As with this assault on Gohl, many of violent acts reported in the local press took place between workers fighting over political or ethnic differences. On occasion, unionists fought scabs, Finns battled Greeks, and cops beat up inebriated workmen. Local newspapers delighted both in reporting on these assaults and inciting future violence. The *Grays Harbor Post* reported on one fight between police and seamen in January 1906. After a night in jail, the men "were put through a sweating process by the officer after which they were conducted out of town by Officer Birmingham." The men started out of town, then returned to Aberdeen and were confronted by Birmingham, gun in hand. The police officer claimed that one of the men grabbed his gun, but Birmingham "made a bound" for his assailant before the man fled from the cop.[35]

Gohl's comrades in the Sailors' Union took part in their fair share of the fights. In July 1904, an Aberdeen police officer arrested sailor William Ditman, but before they reached the police station, five other sailors attempted to rescue Ditman. In the resulting fray, police, joined by wealthy locals, did battle with the six seamen. The *Daily Bulletin* added some color commentary: "In the melee where belaying pins were opposed to billy clubs and bare fists, the brave leader of the bunch received a broadside in the nasal organs that shivered his timbers and swamped the decks in gore. The engagement was quickly over, and, when the smoke of battle had cleared away, four of the invaders were below hatches, and two had set sail and disappeared."[36]

Boardinghouses, hobo camps, and shantytowns provided common housing types for workers. Homeless encampments and riverside shacks housing unemployed and migrant laborers have always been a part of industrial American life. In the first decade of the twentieth century, Aberdeen and Hoquiam had a large transient population, who lived in ramshackle structures adjacent to the Harbor's waterways or in even less permanent tent colonies. Knowing that sailors frequently lacked for permanent housing options, Gohl helped his fellow unionists construct shacks: homes that they could call their own, even if they were crude.

Workers built shacks alongside the harbor's waterways. Municipal authorities did not see the shacks or hobo camps as legitimate homes or attempts by the less fortunate to shelter themselves. Instead, police, prosecutors, and judges punished them for their living arrangements. In March 1906, Aberdeen police rounded up and jailed five "tramps" who camped near the Wilson Brothers Mill. The *Aberdeen Daily Bulletin* applauded the move for ridding the city of what it saw as a nuisance, writing: "The police made a good capture this morning and broke up a gang of hoboes that have been infecting the town for some time past. . . . The officers rounded up the whole gang, five in all, and escorted them to the city jail."[37]

Industrial capitalism pushed large parts of the working class into poverty and homelessness. Grays Harbor area police regulated the

Wooden shack on the water at Indian Creek. Gohl helped itinerant sailors construct these homes to mitigate the brutality and exploitation the men faced at the hands of crimps and boardinghouse masters. *Courtesy of Southwest Regional Branch, Washington State Archives, Olympia.*

poor, arresting and interning workers for a variety of crimes specific to their class. In April 1906, the *Aberdeen Daily Bulletin* reported: "Nine Vags Deported—During the past two days nine men have been arrested by the police upon vagrancy charges. The men included several hoboes, who were not needed here, so far as Chief Christensen could determine."[38] During periods of intense unemployment and poverty, local jails became little more than warehouses for the poor and homeless shelters for those whose poverty had been criminalized. An illustrative case came in April 1906, when police arrested a "one-armed vagrant" living in Aberdeen.[39] The police record for the City of Hoquiam is especially telling on this matter. In 1913, as the economy faltered and unemployment soared throughout the Pacific Northwest, the Hoquiam jail housed scores of impoverished workers under the charges of "vagrancy," "bumming," and "sleeping [in public places]" or of just being a hobo. During 1913, the city jailed 365 persons on these charges, one for every day of the year.[40]

Saloons, brothels, and sports events provided diversions for the men whose labor took the trees out of the forests, cut them into lumber and shingles, and shipped these products to market. Such diversion was needed, because industrial life in lumber country resembled a horror story. Workers were maimed and perished at frightening levels throughout the late nineteenth and early twentieth centuries. Gohl's historical notoriety stems in part from the mistaken belief that he bore responsibility for making the harbor a dangerous place. In fact, the main danger to residents came on the workplace. As historian Eric Loomis writes, "Both camp and mill workers felt the pain and shock of severe injury in a dangerous and highly mechanized working environment."[41] Loggers were maimed and killed by falling trees and swinging cables; mill workers had their bodies cut into pieces by spinning saws and their arms crushed by machinery. Huge stacks of lumber sometimes fell on workers as they hurried between tasks, and other injuries and drownings frequently followed simply slipping on a ship's deck or a wet dock. Front pages of local newspapers were grim reminders of the toll taken by accidents in industrial Grays Harbor. Nearly every day, a worker died or was seriously injured in the area's lumber industry. On March 10, 1906, mill worker Ernest Skog had his leg caught between machinery "and crushed so as to cause hemorrhage of the arteries," while F. C. Vining, who worked at the Western Cooperage Company, had part of his little finger cut off by the same machine that had injured two other men shortly before.[42]

Workplace injuries and deaths were a grim reality in the lives of workers in the Pacific Northwest lumber country. Chances were good that a spinning saw or falling logs would eventually get them, while the rowdy nightlife and poverty pushed many workers to alcoholism and suicide. For more than a decade newspapers carried stories of logging and milling machinery hacking off workers' arms or falling and crushing men's skulls.

Numerous seamen took their own lives in Aberdeen and Hoquiam during the early twentieth century. In May 1907 Sailors' Union member Joseph Matuservitsch arrived in port and began "acting strangely."

Police responded to his behavior by locking him in jail for several nights. After his release, the sailor went to a lodging house and slit his own throat.[43]

During the first three decades of the twentieth century, loggers died at a much higher rate than workers at any other job on the Pacific Coast. Lumber manufacturing was the second-most-dangerous occupation, while shingle manufacturing likewise took its toll in human blood.[44] These dangers are evident in the case of logger Con Murray, who perished in a "frightful manner" after a "sudden increase of speed on cable" trapped him between a swinging log and tree trunk. Murray's death affected his fellow workers, who observed the logs "crushing the heart and intestines" as the logger cried out "My God! I'm killed!"[45] In February 1909, a flying cable hit logger Swan Johnson while he was at work in the woods; the cable "struck him in the back of the head, crushing his skull and causing death about an hour later."[46] Deaths such as Murray's and Johnson's were not inevitable, but they were the product of specific technological innovations and highball logging (speedups), run by foremen and massive firms motivated only by higher production. "As they are too fatigued by the hard and rigorous work of the woods to be alert," argued journalist Charlotte Todes, "and as they are being speeded up at a rate which makes it impossible for them to think of personal safety, accidents will continue to mount."[47]

Maritime workers too performed dangerous tasks that frequently led to injury and sometimes death. In 1900 the *Aberdeen Herald* went into detail to describe the death of a dockworker: "H. Hain, a longshoreman, fell overboard and was drowned at the Cosmopolis dock Monday morning. Although seen falling into the river and his comrades ran to his assistance, he did not rise after first sinking, and it is thought that he struck against the piling in his fall. . . . The body has not yet been recovered."[48] The many dangers of the docks stalked the longshoremen's every move. In July 1904 longshoreman Karl O. Lehte broke his ankle when he was hit by a swinging load of lumber.[49]

Much of the historical attention paid to seamen's deaths has focused on those deemed to be the results of criminal activities. But

Grays Harbor seamen were injured and perished on the job almost routinely. In May 1908 sailor Richard Wechter fell from the steamer *Wimbledon,* broke his neck, and died. Later that year, the *Aberdeen Herald* reported on the injury of a "sailor named Klinkenburg," quite possibly the Danish-born seaman John Klingenberg, who sustained a compound fracture of a leg when it was crushed by a falling pile of lumber on the steamer *Newburg.* In July 1904 a hawser slipped and crushed George Erlenson, a twenty-five-year-old Swedish immigrant and tugboat mate, killing him. As was the norm, the Sailors' Union coordinated the funeral.[50] In early 1905 Aberdeen sailor John Lind fell overboard from the schooner *Resolute* and drowned as the vessel carried lumber between Grays Harbor and Mexico.[51]

From his home and office beside the Wishkah, Gohl had a front-row seat to observe the everyday lives of the harbor's working people, which too often entailed scenes of shocking brutality and gross exploitation. Disturbed, the union agent worked to ameliorate the worst of these ills. But neither Gohl nor the labor movement operated in a vacuum. On the other side of picket lines and political debates were men with tremendous resources who viewed the region's wealth as their own and its towns and workplaces as theirs to command and defend. Throughout Gohl's years on the harbor, the competing interests and goals of labor and capital repeatedly came into conflict. These conflicts routinely flared into open class warfare, with William Gohl at its center.

3

UNION

SIGNS OF WEALTH and inequality appeared throughout the Grays Harbor region, as the families who owned or bossed the lumber trade lived in luxury, enjoying many of the same amenities as their counterparts in major American cities. This inequality did not go unnoticed by harbor workers such as Gohl, who demanded their own part of the tremendous wealth generated by their labor. Although divided by ethnicity, race, politics, and other factors, workers nearly all believed they deserved a larger piece of the pie. But unionists did not fight for fatter paychecks alone. Some, including Gohl, worked to expand the labor movement and aid workers in more precarious positions. Some, again including Gohl, drew motivation from racist and xenophobic ideologies and used their unions to limit the pool of labor, specifically to deny jobs to immigrants and nonwhite workers. During Gohl's first three years on the harbor, a growing number of workers organized unions and challenged employers to achieve these aims.

Gohl's life cannot be understood outside the context of both the local labor movement and the wider West Coast maritime labor movement, in which he was a central figure. Maritime workers, particularly those on the West Coast, have often been at the head of radical working-class movements, including the famed "march inland" in the 1930s of the Pacific Coast longshoremen's union and the International Longshore and Warehouse Union (ILWU) boycotts on all German, Japanese, and Italian goods in the late 1930s and early 1940s.[1]

Four decades before the founding of the ILWU, however, Grays Harbor maritime workers made an inland march of their own, albeit at the local level. In April 1898 John Gronow, an ex-sailor and agent for the Seattle SUP, moved to Aberdeen and immediately established an SUP local.[2] It was among the first unions in the region. The sailors' agent also proved vital in the organization of a longshoremen's union shortly after his arrival. By August 1898 the Aberdeen dock workers were said to be "thoroughly organized."[3] Between 1898 and Gohl's arrest in 1910 on murder charges, maritime unionists held every leadership position in the local labor movement, from vice president of the Washington State Federation of Labor and president of the Grays Harbor Trades and Labor Council (GHTLC) to head of the local Labor Day committee.

The significance of Gronow and other maritime workers in this growth cannot be overstated. Labor leaders praised his efforts on behalf of Grays Harbor's workers. Gronow was a "pioneer" of the labor movement who "with the authority of the Sailors' Union at his back, the true spirit of unionism within his soul," built "such a splendid foundation that those who came later had something to stand upon."[4] He served as the lone Grays Harbor delegate to the founding convention of the WSFL in January 1902, when he and Seattle SUP agent Pete Gill introduced the resolution to form the state labor federation, and he was elected to the first executive board of that body.[5] After the creation of the state federation, Gronow served as the main link between local labor and state labor bodies and national union leaders.[6] He held meetings with American Federation of Labor (AFL) cofounder and president Samuel Gompers, WSFL president William Blackman, and state and national organizers who visited Grays Harbor at his invitation.[7] Grays Harbor unionists' efforts yielded impressive results, as by mid-1902 the local union movement was thriving.[8] At the 1902 Labor Day parade in Aberdeen, five hundred of the eight hundred local unionists, representing thirteen unions, marched across

Aberdeen, a feat of strength that according to the *Aberdeen Herald* "was a revelation to many."[9] The local movement developed into a number of extraordinarily stable unions that by 1905 boasted a combined membership in the thousands.[10] Thus, Blackman was not exaggerating when he stated in 1906 that Grays Harbor had "more organized men in this section, according to the population, than any other place in the state."[11]

For union agents such as Gronow and Gohl, the closest contact with employers would have been with shipowners, the men whose wealth came from the work done by Gohl's comrades aboard ships. Shipowners consisted both of lumbermen who owned vessels to supplement profits and those who specialized in shipping. Lumber interests dominated the region's economics and politics. As historian Charles Pierce LeWarne concluded: "Grays Harbor had a sturdy lumber baronage centered around the elderly founders and their scions who still headed most of the lumber firms. Often the same individuals controlled real estate, finance, and utilities; they and their families provided cultural and fraternal leadership and were politically active, usually as Republicans."[12]

At the fore of Grays Harbor business activity were several men who dedicated themselves to welding a powerful, united front against labor. Like workers, Grays Harbor employers were enthusiastic joiners. Most lumbermen belonged to several trade and commercial associations, including the local chambers of commerce and commercial clubs, regional and national lumber associations, and exclusive fraternal organizations such as the Elks and the International Order of Hoo-Hoo. As early as 1891 they began to form "Business Men's Protective Associations" and chambers of commerce, which, in their own words, were replicas of trade unions, in that they sought to "work together for the accomplishment of any purpose."[13] The mill owners and boss loggers also coordinated their mill shutdowns. These annual and semi-annual suspensions of production tossed thousands of lumber workers out of work anywhere from a week to sixty days.[14]

Pacific shippers also practiced collective action to protect their class interests. To set rates and fight unionization, these men formed the Shipowners' Association of the Pacific Coast (SAPC) in 1886. Based in San Francisco, in its early years the association demanded that seamen abandon their union books, which carried proof that members were up-to-date on their dues, and replace them with employer books, which enabled bosses to evaluate sailors and use those evaluations for hiring decisions. SAPC rules dictated: "Each and every member of this association shall be required upon joining to agree to act with the other members in all matters that may be adopted by the members or directors of said association." Association members paid dues to a defense fund used during strikes. As a rule, the owners preferred to fight rather than concede to union demands, even during boom periods.[15] Shipping was the lifeblood of Pacific commerce, and the SAPC received backing from the largest employers' combinations on the West Coast. By 1892, according to economist Paul Taylor, the Shipowners' Association had grown tired of fighting the SUP and "was about ready to give up. But the Manufacturers' and Employers' Association of California, which was active in breaking up unions, took hold of the shipowners' struggle."[16] Troubles peaked in 1899 as union and nonunion sailors clashed on lumber docks. In February 1899, a Seattle union agent declared: "Unless the Shipowners' Association gives up trying to put scab seamen on coasting vessels, a general strike will be ordered, and every sailing vessel on the coast tied up as soon as she gets into port. The union men will not accept less than $40 per month."[17]

The Aberdeen SUP branch floundered before 1902, owing to the lack of industry-wide contracts. As at other ports, conflicts between union and nonunion seamen sometimes turned violent. The most explosive conflict between union and scab sailors came in late 1899 in a gunfight hailed as the "Battle of the Wishkah" by one local newspaper. In November nonunion workers loaded the barkentine *Benicia* with lumber from an Aberdeen mill. Docked next to the *Benicia* was the *A. J. West*, a lumber schooner worked by a union crew. After alleging that unionists had threatened the nonunion crews, the captain of the *Benicia* secured assistance from the Aberdeen city marshal, who deputized Charles Fenwick, a locally based ship captain and agent of the Shipowners' Association, to guard the nonunion ship. On the morning of November 26, union sailors approached the *Benicia* to persuade the crew to join the union or abandon the ship. To deter the unionists, the freshly deputized Fenwick and the nonunion crew exchanged gunfire with the unionists. Union member Charles Larsen received two wounds in the abdomen. According to Sailors' Union agent John Gronow, the bullets hit Larsen while he "was in the act of peaceably going on board of his own vessel, the *A. J. West*. This man had to pass the *Benicia* in order to reach his own vessel." Shortly after the gunfight, the *Benicia* put out to sea, with none of its crew or guards arrested for their involvement in the gunfight.[18] Fights of this type broke out throughout the 1890s in Pacific port towns.

Several harbor employers belonged to the Shipowners' Association, and these men maintained an agent in the area dating back before the turn of the century. Prior to 1902 when the association signed a coastwise agreement with the SUP, the Shipowners' Association served principally as herders of scabs, providing nonunion sailors for employment by their members. As seen in the November 1899 *Benicia* incident, association employees also functioned as armed guards for nonunion seamen. Seamen despised the association and rightly placed it in the same category as notorious union-busting institutions like the Citizens' Alliance and Pinkerton National Detective Agency. Gohl held fast to these views, declaring in June 1906 that the Shipowners' Association was "controlled by the Citizens' Alliance."[19]

The Pacific Coast maritime agreement did much to alleviate tensions between sailors and shipowners. In 1902 the *Aberdeen Herald* commented on an agreement between the Sailors' Union and the SAPC: "The new agreement is one satisfactory to both parties in all ways, and will prevent a reoccurrence of the troubles. Quite a number of ships plying to Grays Harbor are affected by the agreement."[20] By 1902, in addition, the Steam-Schooner Managers' Association, representing steam and freight vessel owners, came to terms with the maritime unionists.[21]

Seamen up and down the coast built the Sailors' Union into a powerful organization, and in Grays Harbor none stood as tall as John

Gronow. But organizing and maintaining unions in a place like Grays Harbor was a difficult and dangerous occupation. After many years at the head of the local labor movement, the prestige and benefits of his position no longer satisfied Gronow. He left the Sailors' Union behind in July 1902 to purchase the appropriately named Union Saloon, deep in the heart of Aberdeen's Sailortown. Not surprisingly, given Gronow's background and his saloon's location, his business was a prime meeting spot for union men.[22]

As the harbor's maritime trade expanded, so did the number of union sailors living and working in the region. The union's growth depended on the ability to stay apace with increased numbers of vessels and sailors coming into port. Branch agents held weekly meetings to induct new members and held court for all seamen new to the port. According to the SUP's *Constitution and By-Laws*, the branch agent was to "ascertain what kinds of crews are in the vessels . . . and see that the crews of all outgoing vessels are in good standing."[23] Membership records for the Aberdeen SUP are sparse, but according to the number of members receiving mail in Aberdeen—listed weekly in the *Coast Seamen's Journal*—we see that the number of unionized sailors visiting Aberdeen climbed dramatically between 1901 and 1905.[24] In late 1901 and early 1902, an average of only thirty-seven names appeared on the advertised letters list, while four years later that number nearly doubled to an average of more than seventy-three between April 5 and July 5, 1905.[25] The *Grays Harbor Post* commented on the union's progress: "Every vessel now leaving the harbor of San Francisco for this port is manned by union sailors. This . . . is the first time in the history of shipping there that this has been true."[26]

Gohl became branch agent of the Aberdeen SUP on July 6, 1903.[27] During the preceding year the local's affairs had been chaotic, as the job passed between four men. Once elected, however, Gohl held control of the local almost continuously between July 1903 and January 1910.[28] During Gohl's first period of labor leadership, Grays Harbor's labor movement grew in membership and influence at an impressive pace. In an address to the WSFL in 1905, longtime Aberdeen SUP agent John Gronow, then the fifth vice president of the federation, declared that "within the last few years unions on the Harbor have increased 300 per cent. till today Aberdeen and Hoquiam, the Grays Harbor cities, are of the best, if not the best, organized cities of the whole state of Washington."[29] With Gohl at its head, the local labor movement undertook an ambitious organizing program. Aberdeen and Hoquiam tripled in size between 1900 and 1907, but the labor movement outpaced even this furious growth.[30] By March 1904, in fact, the GHTLC represented twenty-three unions and well over a thousand members.[31]

Organized labor in Grays Harbor made its voice heard through a variety of media, including public speakers, leaflets, and a large and energetic union press. Local unionists established a series of trade union newspapers during the early twentieth century. Ranging in political orientation from conservative to socialist, the papers gave harbor workers—or at least their elected representatives—the ability to join in public affairs by expressing their interests to thousands of local subscribers and readers.

Labor newspapers were needed to build a counternarrative to that provided by mainstream papers, whose coverage of the labor movement was condescending and hostile. Editors from the Grays Harbor area's three largest local newspapers served as enthusiastic mouthpieces for capital. Ostensibly divided over politics—the *Aberdeen Herald* strongly supported the Democratic Party, while the *Aberdeen Daily Bulletin* (*World* after 1908) and the *Daily Washingtonian* in Hoquiam functioned as Republican organs—the papers were edited and published by men who came together to support business, champion economic growth, and to fight unionists and radicals. During a heated sailors' strike in 1906, one labor newspaper explained the need to publish labor's perspective: "The aim and object of this publication is to bring the sailors' and longshoremen's side of the present difference existing between them and their employers before the citizens of Aberdeen. The side of the employers has been fully explained, discussed, and eulogized in the subsidized *Bulletin* and *Herald*, of this city."[32]

The *Bulletin* and *World* certainly served as a voice of capital. Its first editor, Werner Rupp, purchased the *Bulletin* in 1908, renaming it a month later. Prone to self-righteousness, Rupp claimed to base his journalistic ethics around what he called his "Ten Commandments of newspapering," including one that read: "Be fair. Present both sides of any story. Remember, however, that being fair does not require you to permit either side to indulge in unlimited vilification and abuse."[33] But Rupp's words seem almost comically dishonest given the antilabor propaganda and massive abuse the *World* heaped on Gohl, his comrades in the maritime unions, and labor radicals of the era.

In 1904, unionists led by J. W. Clark, a union carpenter and trade union official, founded the *Grays Harbor Post*. Edited by Clark, the *Post* proved a boon to local workers who understood the need to publicly advocate for their own interests. Unionists published meeting notices, covered national and international labor stories, and analyzed economic and political issues in the paper, which was an important voice in the region. In February 1908, the Aberdeen City Council selected the *Grays Harbor Post* as the city's official newspaper. The city council voted unanimously for the *Post* to have this important honor over its antilabor counterparts, the *Herald* and *Bulletin*.[34]

Gohl's prominence in the labor movement showed in the *Post*. The Sailors' Union agent's name appeared regularly in its pages, including in the first issue, which reported that Gohl and others "were in Hoquiam last Thursday evening as a visiting committee in attendance at the Longshoremen's and Sailors' Unions of Hoquiam."[35] Gohl also used the *Post* to make proclamations regarding working conditions and union matters. In April 1904, facing a shortage of union sailors, the agent noted that ships were being forced to ship out with short crews, especially with the abundance of seamen flocking to Alaska for fishing season.[36]

In his study of the Sailors' Union of the Pacific, Paul Taylor discussed the unique structure of the union and the roles played by union agents. Unlike agents in locals of most other unions, SUP branch agents were elected by the entire SUP membership and represented the entire union. Thus, Gohl, who maintained his position as Aberdeen agent from 1903 until 1910, was elected by thousands of members of a union that comprised thirty-four hundred members as of August 1904.[37] Like other SUP officers, Gohl had to run for reelection twice a year and was also subject to recall, as the union's constitution made clear: "Any officer may be recalled at any regular meeting at Headquarters by majority vote of a supreme quorum."[38]

Gohl's importance in labor circles elevated his position in the Grays Harbor region's respectable working-class circles. Like other men around the country at the time, he joined a fraternal and mutual benefit society, in his case the Aberdeen lodge of the International Order of Foresters. In the early twentieth century thirteen million Americans were members of fraternal orders.[39] Many, including the Foresters, offered sickness and death benefits, functioning as a safety net in a country that at the time had no social security or welfare, which Gohl knew were needed. The Foresters' death benefits included arranging for members' funerals and announcing their deaths in local newspapers.[40]

The Foresters met regularly, providing the young single man with something to do in the evening besides patronize saloons. The group's leaders included several well-established men in the young city.[41] It was one of fifty fraternal organizations operating in Aberdeen and Hoquiam in the first decade of the twentieth century. But unlike the Elks and Hoo-Hoos, which were little more than fraternal wings of the chamber of commerce, the Foresters drew members from the working and middle classes, many of whom were unionists. In July 1904, Gohl took over office as subchief ranger of the Aberdeen Foresters, which placed him in close contact with several notable locals and helped bolster his place in the community.[42]

As a prominent labor and fraternal leader, Gohl had plenty of opportunity—and responsibility—when it came to planning large-scale celebrations. From his earliest time in the Sailors' Union office, he took a leadership role in organizing Grays Harbor's annual Labor Day festivities, daylong celebrations that included parades, picnics, sporting events, and evening balls.[43] A great deal of planning went into these events. On Labor Day 1904, with Gohl serving as president of the labor council (the GHTLC), members of the region's labor movement turned out in force on the streets of Hoquiam. Twenty-three Aberdeen and Hoquiam unions, representing fifteen hundred men, assembled that day to march through Hoquiam, making their festivity "the most successful celebration of its kind ever observed on the Harbor."[44] The parade included an impressive array of unionists, ranging from sawyers and filers to laundry workers, while the shingle weavers had the most men of any one trade. Floats included that of the longshoremen, whose entry was a fully rigged ship on wheels and loaded with lumber; that of the carpenters, who wheeled out a complete "house with yard, flowers in bloom"; and that of the bartenders, who manned a bar and played a piano on theirs.[45] The *Post* described the 1907 parade: "The gap at the end of the Hoquiam line was filled by Ralson's band, who were closely followed by the Sailors union of the Pacific, in their attractive uniforms, under the command of agent Wm. Gohl. 26 sailors in uniform, all the uniforms that are allowed in the local branch, were in line, and many sailors in plain clothes followed the procession."[46]

Labor Day events were produced by and for the labor movement, and, as a union leader, Gohl's participation would have been expected. Events on the Fourth of July each summer were larger and drew a more diverse crowd of celebrants. In June 1905, local elites chose Gohl as a member of the parade and transportation committee for the Independence Day celebration, no doubt because of his extensive experience during Labor Day events. Gohl joined Police Chief W. W. Anstie and attorney E. H. Fox (known as "Colonel") on the parade planning committee.[47] The parade, which drew an estimated twenty thousand spectators, drew heavy praise from the *Herald*, which noted: "The parade and morning exercises were in perfect keeping with the balance of the day."[48] It was a momentous day in the life of Gohl, a respected Aberdonian. With the others on the planning committee he had helped bring the region's population together for a celebration of America's birthday.

During Labor Day parades, unionized workers marched in uniform alongside floats such as this wooden lumber schooner built to demonstrate unionists' solidarity and pride in their craft. *Courtesy of Jones Photo Historical Collection, Aberdeen, Washington.*

Gohl's views and activism in the labor movement typified the wider union experience. Pacific Coast trade unionists unified around their commitment to goals defined largely by the early unionists' shared class position and racial and gender identities. Much of their effort centered on building and maintaining the closed shops (with work for union members only), preserving white men's control over union jobs, and securing decent wages necessary for a breadwinner to support his wife and children. Organized labor's vast cultural apparatus, militant workplace struggles, and forays into political activism all sprang from unionists' commitments to these goals.

By the time of Gohl's elevation into the labor bureaucracy, the SUP had already established contracts with the owners of most Pacific Coast vessels. Unionists used a variety of tactics to force employers to sign union contracts. These nearly always contained "closed shop agreements" dictating that employers only hire union members. Unionists issued "unfair lists" of businesses that refused to sign contracts with unions. Grays Harbor Trades and Labor Council officials were tasked with publicizing the unfair lists, which meant that, beginning in 1904, Gohl's name appeared when an Aberdeen union declared a business unfair. In April 1904, in Gohl's role as president of the labor council, he placed an announcement in the *Grays Harbor Post* declaring that a local plumbing company was unfair and should not be patronized by unionists or union supporters.[49]

With larger companies that did not rely on local business alone, unionists paired calls for boycotts with direct action on the job. The Hoquiam Lumber and Shingle Company mill proved to be ground zero for struggles between the shingle weavers' union and antiunion bosses intent on bringing the union to heel. The mill employed several socialist unionists.[50] After a sixty-day shutdown, mill manager Robert Lytle fired one of them, union leader J. G. Brown, saying that Brown was too much of an agitator to remain in his employ. The weavers responded by walking off the job, refusing to work until the discharged man was rehired. The mill was placed on unfair lists by the Hoquiam Shingle Weavers' Union. After a short strike, Lytle rehired Brown.[51]

Union auxiliaries, especially label leagues, provided an important way for working-class women and union supporters to use their collective purchasing power to support "fair" companies that hired union labor and punish "unfair" companies that used nonunion labor or otherwise had run afoul of unions.[52] Label leagues encouraged consumers to purchase goods featuring the union label. Between 1905 and 1912, women formed label leagues across Washington State. In 1912, Aberdeen and Hoquiam women formed their own branches of the Women's Union Card and Label League, although support for such endeavors was manifested as early as 1906 when *Grays Harbor Post* editor J. W. Clark suggested that "women should consider the benefits derived and unite with the label league, then use the purchasing power to better the condition of the community."[53] In spite of their late start in forming label leagues in the Grays Harbor area, female union supporters there had formed auxiliary labor groups much earlier. Expressing his approval of the auxiliaries, Clark stated: "The wives of the workers were and are a potent influence in the trades union movement." "[Women's auxiliaries] are not merely social clubs, nor are they sewing circles and pink tea clubs," he said. "They are practical from the word go."[54]

As a union of mostly itinerant workmen, the SUP lacked anything like a women's auxiliary to assist its members with workplace struggles and to do community outreach for the union. The person closest to filling this role was Bessie Gohl. In the years between her 1905 marriage to Billy and 1910, when they both left Grays Harbor, she provided support (often unpaid) through her work for the union. For example, she occasionally arranged flowers for unionists' funerals.[55] In her primary occupation—keeper of a rooming house—she blended home with work, providing care for her working-class patrons. Outside of making floral arrangements and tending to her rooming house, Bessie's union activities rarely qualified as "domestic." Indeed, a careful examination of Bessie's participation in Sailors' Union activities demonstrates the fluidity of working-class gender roles. She ran her own business and sometimes dressed in traditional male clothing—full Sailors' Union regalia, including a sailors' shirt and cap—and posed alongside dues-paying SUP members for photographs. Most famously, Bessie made waves during William's 1910 trial by verbally threatening state witnesses and challenging events in court when, in her view, they violated proper procedures.[56]

When negotiations, unfair lists, and boycotts failed to bring offending employers to the table, unionists (sometimes along with nonunion workers) declared strikes against them. Workers unionized and struck across many fields of work, including jobs in resource extracting, manufacturing, transportation, and the service sector. In March 1906, a crew of nine sailors quit the steamer *Coaster* to protest the poor quality of food served aboard ship. The crew demanded that the ship's cook be fired, but the captain refused to do this and instead fired one of the sailors. Quitting en masse, the seamen declared: "We are all one crew. If one goes, we all go."[57]

Despite its size and influence, the Grays Harbor labor movement of the early twentieth century did not represent a majority of the region's workers, nor was it built for that purpose. As with the entire United States, the harbor's workers organized trade unions, relatively small institutions that followed the narrow, restrictive boundaries of AFL craft unionism. Throughout the late nineteenth and early twentieth centuries, the American labor movement represented only a tiny minority of wage laborers. In 1913–14 the WSFL comprised 233 affiliated local unions and twenty thousand members in a state with 521,501 "gainful workers."[58] Aberdeen and Hoquiam unions contained few southern European immigrants or Native Americans, and practically no Asian American or black workers.

The Sailors' Union was a microcosm of the entire Pacific Coast labor movement. Its all-male membership fought for better hours, wages, and conditions and worked equally hard in an effort to stop immigration from Asia. Like the Knights of Labor, which organized thousands of members on the Pacific Coast, as well as the trade unions that succeeded the Knights in comprising the dominant labor movement in the region, the SUP was explicitly racist. Unionized sailors, nearly all of whom were born in the United States, Australia, Canada, or northern Europe, introduced and passed Asian exclusion resolutions annually at state labor conventions and fought to prevent Chinese seamen from working on American ships.[59] Nearly the entire SUP membership hailed from Scandinavia, Finland, and Germany. Union leaders believed in the inherent supremacy of northern Europeans. As Bruce Nelson writes, "Nordic racism would leave an indelible mark on the character of the Sailors' Union of the Pacific for many years to come."[60] In 1906 Gohl coauthored a resolution adopted at the WSFL convention that illustrated the union's deep-seated racism. The resolution complained: "Chinese having no certificate of domicile within the United States, nor being of the exempted classes, are employed as seamen on vessels of the United States." Gohl and his coauthors called "upon the President of the United States to instruct the Department of Commerce and Labor to cause this violation of the Chinese Exclusion Act to be stopped."[61]

As with many of his seafaring comrades, Gohl's racism knew few bounds. He and his union viewed Asian workers as synonymous with scabs. During the 1906 maritime strike, Gohl wrote: "Go to the merchants, gentlemen, and ask them how much money the five Mongolian parasites who now constitute the crew of the *Newburg* spend in their establishments, compare them with what a union crew would have spent, and you will find out that if these methods of employing Mongolian labor are to continue, some of you Mongolian-loving merchants will find yourselves up against the wall, and you will then join the sailors in their fight against cheap labor."[62] The Sailors' Union forbade its members to work with Chinese laborers. The union itself was fundamentally racist, as evidenced by its constitution: "It shall furthermore be the duty of every member to uphold and advocate the objects of Labor Organizations, to patronize all union-made goods, and in particular to shun all places or institutions where Chinese or 'scab' labor is employed."[63] The Sailors' Union supported racist exclusionary laws partly to create labor shortages, as employers could not pick freely from the "reserve army of labor" to fill positions. With much of the potential labor pool removed from competition via prohibitions on Chinese workers, those allowed to enter the industry possessed a relatively high degree of bargaining leverage with their employers, leverage used to exact greater gains.[64]

From its nineteenth-century origins, the Pacific Coast trade union movement was built on a firm foundation of racism. As historian Alexander Saxton argued, Chinese immigrants in California constituted an "indispensable enemy" for race-conscious white unionists as they built the labor movement. Denis Kearney's Workingmen's Party of California fought to restrict Chinese immigration. In an 1878 address Kearney argued that capitalists imported Chinese as "cheap working slave[s]" to "further ... degrade white Labor."[65] His party lobbied for restrictive policies at both the state and national levels, and Kearney declared, "The Chinese must go!"—a cry that echoed up and down the coast. In Washington, matters came to a head in Tacoma in 1885, when a coalition of city leaders and white workers pioneered the "Tacoma method" of deporting Chinese residents. They formed an anti-Chinese league, declared that all Chinese residents had to leave the city by a certain date, and then proceeded, with the complicity of the city's law enforcement, to round up and forcibly deport all those who remained. The 1886 Seattle sequel to the Tacoma expulsion was more controversial. It played out as a "brutal charade" in which those who wanted the immediate expulsion of the Chinese by force, which included a strong labor element, were opposed unsuccessfully by the "Opera House" faction of city leaders. The latter acquiesced to the anti-Chinese movement but sought to drive the Chinese out without violence or lawlessness.[66]

These anti-Chinese campaigns coincided with a period of increased joblessness and worker anxiety. In the 1880s, as the transcontinental railroads were completed and workers were laid off, white workers increasingly took up Kearney's cry and turned against Chinese workers, with whom they refused to identify. At least in its rhetoric, if not in its methods, the anti-Chinese movement of the era closely resembles the anti-immigrant movement of our own time. Chinese workers, their opponents argued, entered the United States illegally, refused to assimilate, sent their earnings home, and undercut white wages. In a time of economic dislocation, the Chinese immigrant minority proved an attractive scapegoat for workers' economic problems, and organizations like the Workingmen's Party and the Knights of Labor clearly exploited this in their drives to increase membership.

The case of the Sailors' Union of the Pacific provides one of the clearest illustrations of the racism endemic to Pacific Coast trade unions. Bruce Nelson argues that the union sailors were deeply dedicated to the idea of Nordic racial supremacy: "They simply took it for granted that whites, and Anglo-Saxon or Nordic whites in particular, stood at the summit of a hierarchy of races and nationalities."[67] The union restricted membership to US citizens and those eligible for citizenship, an unsubtle way to restrict membership to whites since only whites could become citizens.[68] Of the 3,441 members registered with the national union in 1904, all hailed from European, Australian, or North American backgrounds, and only 600 could be positively shown to have been born in southern or eastern Europe.[69] During the Labor Day parade in 1904, members of the Aberdeen SUP marched at "the head of the line because of being first on the Harbor." The sailors' leadership of the march, however, said just as much about whiteness of their unions as it did about their roles as the "first on Harbor."[70]

The *Grays Harbor Post* was a significant mouthpiece for working-class racism. In 1910 the paper warned of the formation of a Japanese "colony" near the harbor's beaches that would serve as a headquarters for the immigrants to "make maps of the entrance to Grays Harbor which is considered . . . a most strategic point for the Japanese in case of war with the United States."[71] Although racism against African Americans figured into the ideology of the harbor's labor movement, most of its members' and organizations' racism focused on Asian and southern European immigrants. For example, the Hoquiam People's Party, a short-lived political party formed in part by top local labor leaders to run candidates for the 1908 municipal election, included a plank opposing "the importation of Greeks, Dagos, Hindus, and all other Asiatic labor into this city, and we pledge our candidates to use all means within their power to remove all such undesirable persons from our midst."[72]

Sailors' Union members, including Gohl, were leading voices of racism in the late nineteenth and early twentieth centuries. During the 1906 maritime strike, the *Trades Council Gazette*, a short-lived daily that was published to aid the strikers' cause, sought to mobilize merchant support for the strikers by inciting hatred of the nonwhite, nonunion sailors in port at the time. "Does the merchant or business man believe that the Japs in the Newburg and the colored gents in the Santa Monica are more desirable to this harbor than union seamen, or does he believe that his business will increase with their advent into this community?" the *Gazette* asked.[73] Significantly, in February 1908 Gohl attended a meeting in Seattle of the Japanese-Korean Exclusion League. Days after his return to the harbor, the union agent founded and served as a leader of Aberdeen's Asiatic Exclusion Club in 1908. A notice in the *Grays Harbor Post* stated that everyone was "cordially invited" to the club's meetings held at Sailors' Hall. "These meetings are rapidly growing in importance and interest and all citizens who believe in a white coast should attend."[74]

Sailors had plenty of company in expressing their antagonism toward nonwhites. In December 1907, Hoquiam Shingle Weavers' Union secretary W. E. Willis publicly applauded the creation of the Japanese and Korean Exclusion Leagues, which he viewed as "a step in the right direction," saying that they "should have the moral and financial support of every Union in the Northwest."[75]

Unions, as noted, were also masculine institutions, with male membership, virile union rhetoric, and men's programs. As the labor movement expanded, more women entered its ranks. In 1902, Aberdeen's more than eight hundred unionists were almost entirely men. In addition to the sailors and longshoremen, the harbor's labor movement included shingle weavers, painters, blacksmiths, teamsters, printers, carpenters, and cigar makers. That five hundred workers showed up for the 1902 Labor Day parade shocked the mainstream press as, evident in this headline: "Number of Labor Union Men in the Parade Was a Revelation to Many."[76]

Two years later, Aberdeen's unions had grown dramatically. Although the labor movement remained a male bastion, for the first time its ranks included women wage earners. Twenty-eight unions marched in the 1904 Grays Harbor Labor Day parade, including the Laundry Workers' Union, whose members were mostly women. Much of the expansion of union membership, including among women wage earners, took place in 1904 during Gohl's first leadership term in the GHTLC. As historian Alice Kessler-Harris wrote, many early twentieth-century male unionists insisted on "women's primary function in the home and remained stubbornly ambivalent about their efforts."[77] Billy Gohl's work to aid wage-earning women to unionize suggests that he at least partially deviated from the patriarchal norm. Although it would be an exaggeration to describe Gohl as a feminist—a term gaining in popularity primarily among middle-class women in the early twentieth century—his actions suggest a commitment to using his male privilege to help working-class women unionize.

The clearest example of Gohl's work to aid wage-earning women came when he took a leadership role in founding Aberdeen's worker-run cooperative laundry. In 1905, Gohl was one of the incorporators of the Gloss Steam Laundry, operated by the Grays Harbor labor movement for the benefit of its members.[78] The laundry would become a stronghold for women's unionism on the harbor and one of many unionized laundries in Aberdeen and Hoquiam. By that year several laboring women had emerged as activists in the labor movement, hosting union fund-raisers, boycotting laundries that refused to sign union contracts or discriminated against unionists, and taking leadership positions.[79] Like male unionists, women laundry workers used the labor movement to condemn laundries that employed Asian-American labor, boasting in the labor press of their product's "whiteness and purity."[80]

Masculine language runs throughout the labor literature of the period. By acting as gendered codes insisted he act, a member was deemed a "union man," one of a group of "determined men," or a "worthy union man."[81] As historian David Montgomery remarked, craft unionists' "ethical code demanded a 'manly' bearing toward the boss," as union men "refused to cower before the foreman's glares."[82] Those who violated the prescribed manly working-class ethics became "responsible for everything . . . done wrong."[83] To follow the code meant to be expressly devoted to the union, to be someone who never missed a lodge meeting or allowed his dues to fall into arrears. The man who failed at these duties was labeled "the rottenest grape in the bunch. . . . He does more harm than all the other disrupters put together."[84] Unionists were men of action, the epitome of proletarian manhood. "To be a real union man," argued J. G. Brown, "requires not only the saying of things but doing things."[85] A pseudonymous *Grays Harbor Post* editorial (signed "Ex") compared a scab to "a human turtle," someone who "never learns by experience."[86]

Union men demanded "family wages" that would allow them to take care of their wives and children. During the 1906 maritime strike, the unionists' strike bulletin, the *Trades Council Gazette*, aimed its

columns at securing and retaining the family wage. It portrayed striking sailors as respected family and community members: "Our interests are here, our homes, our loved ones."[87] The wage increase they
demanded was fair because of shipping companies' increased profits,
but it was also necessary to further their union. "[The] organization
has made men of us, and as time goes on we hope to succeed in our aim
to make a sailor's life worth living, and we will have the same rights as
our fellow workmen on shore."[88]

The hypermasculine code also encouraged physical combat with
class enemies, and this was especially true during strikes.[89] Strikebreakers were sometimes subjected to beatings, verbal harangues,
and property destruction.[90] Unionists published scabs' names in the
local and regional labor press, and when someone crossed a picket
line their name was communicated far and wide to ensure a lifetime
blacklisting from sympathetic unionists. After scabbing on his fellow
unionists during a 1906 shingle weavers' strike, Jent Butler became
the subject of a sustained attack in the pages of the *Shingle Weaver*,
which stated, "Butler is absolutely devoid of even a shadow of princi-
ple, simply a slimy, crawling, unclean thing that is an eyesore to
decent people everywhere. A traitor is, and should be, ever regarded
with suspicion and treated with contempt."[91]

Although unionists fought scabs with some regularity, few men
were as active in this pursuit as William Gohl. During the maritime
strike of 1906, Gohl led armed attacks on scabs, imported strikebreakers, and deputized police. In September 1906 he broke his
right hand while giving a "genuine thrashing" to a scab who was trying to secure a job near the SUP offices. The *Aberdeen Daily Bulletin*
initially asserted that Gohl had been provoked by a man who had
"accosted" Bessie Gohl while she was doing some shopping downtown. J. McCoy, the scab in question, swore out a warrant against
Gohl for assault and battery, and Gohl pled guilty and paid a ten-dollar
fine.[92] But regardless of whether Gohl attacked McCoy for his scabbing or for accosting Bessie, it was clear that Gohl, the Sailors' Union
agent, viewed McCoy as a threat to his manhood. Victorian gender

norms dictated that William was duty-bound to protect "Mrs. Gohl," both from those who would physically accost her and those who would take food off the family table by scabbing.

One of the main benefits of union membership was the insurance program offered by many unions. Given the absence of a welfare state during the early twentieth century, unions, along with fraternal organizations and ethnic clubs, provided key support to working-class families in an era of unprecedented industrial accidents. Insurance benefits were extraordinarily necessary in the Grays Harbor area, where workers spent their lives with one foot in the grave. Having avoided early childhood deaths, they faced the real possibility that a spinning saw or falling logs would get them, and some were pushed to alcoholism and suicide by the depression-inducing conditions of capitalism. This collective misery, as much as anything, was the real ghoul of Grays Harbor.

Unions, however—workers banded together to improve their lot— addressed these conditions and their sometimes deadly result. The Sailors' Union provided a diverse array of benefits to members, including death benefits but also some specific to unique attributes of seaman's labor, such as shipwreck benefits. While hospitalized, members in good standing were eligible for up to one dollar per week for medical supplies. Also, many of the SUP locals ran reading rooms where members could relax together and read literature ranging from Jack London novels to the *Coast Seamen's Journal*. But, as SUP leader Andrew Furuseth noted, the union was "not running a Red Cross society," and the organization's leaders took pains to articulate that it did not bear responsibility for aiding members through all of life's vicissitudes.[93]

Some of Gohl's most pressing duties as union agent were patrolling the docks in search of missing workers, planning and paying for funerals, and hawking deceased sailors' goods and sending proceeds to their families.[94] During his career, Gohl planned and administered numerous union funerals. These were often elaborate events. SUP members dressed in formal union attire made up of sailors' cap and white blouse, while ministers preached and Gohl delivered tributes to his fallen comrades.[95] According to historian Michael K. Rosenow, union funerals became "a badge of honor that sent messages to the miners' families and to the broader community that the individual's life had meaning."[96] Funeral rituals likewise provided motivation for the labor movement to carry on despite oppressive conditions. When the Sailors' Union buried "their brother" Rudolph Pries, unionists acted as pallbearers, while Gohl served as master of ceremonies for the funeral. In a long editorial, the *Grays Harbor Post* paid tribute to Pries and complimented the union for providing a fitting funeral: "His brothers, in uniform, gave him a decent burial. . . . The baptismal certificate and the union card brought them all into one bond of brotherhood and sorrow. The lesson is not in vain. The men that pass out in the ships talk of it and are made better. It is well."[97]

A single statistic spoke to the dangers facing Grays Harbor seamen. In May 1909, Gohl estimated that thirty-nine sailors had found their graves in the waters of Grays Harbor during the previous five years.[98]

In providing death benefits to its members, Gohl's SUP was like most American trade unions.[99] On the face of it, this seems like a good use of union funds, given the number of seamen who died on the job. However, as Gohl's difficulties in this pursuit demonstrated, finding a sailor's next of kin was often difficult, given that few lived with spouses and children. In 1907 the *Grays Harbor Post* wrote regarding deceased union member Rudolph Pries: "The effects of the dead man were sold and Mr. Gohl notified the German consul at San Francisco, in order that he might notify the parents that the money is ready for their disposal."[100] Perhaps of more practical use for seamen were the shipwreck benefits, provided to any shipwrecked unionist. This benefit consistently proved to be a major financial outlay for the union. From 1891 to 1908 the SUP provided $33,423 in shipwreck funds out of total expenditures of $682,222, meaning the union allocated approximately 5 percent of its budget on shipwreck benefits.[101]

To build solidarity and encourage labor-based socializing, unions built halls and hosted social events as alternatives to the ritzy, see-and-be-seen social gatherings of capitalists in industrial America.

Several unions owned their own halls in the Grays Harbor cities. Twenty-first-century readers might be surprised to learn that in early twentieth-century "labor towns" like Aberdeen and Hoquiam, union-themed and union-sponsored cultural activities provided much of the area's entertainment. Indeed, although mass-market, popular, capitalist entertainments grew extremely popular in the Gilded Age and Progressive Era, workers clung tenaciously to their halls, union-sponsored sports, and a range of social activities including dances and parades.

Most local union events received attention in the *Grays Harbor Post*, which, especially during Gohl's early years on the harbor, was a reliable supporter of the labor movement. During strikes the *Post* became an especially useful tool for organized labor. For instance, during the 1906 maritime strike, unionists used the *Post*'s shop to print its short-lived *Trades Council Gazette*. That workers had the audacity to write and print their own newspaper so bothered the *Daily Bulletin* editor that he wrote, "They have ideas that are positively silly, yet in their very complete ignorance they persist in giving the widest possible publicity to their opinions. . . . The Trades Council Gazette, the free edition of the Weekly Post, has given these mental heavyweights a chance to 'go at it' like good fellows."[102]

Unionists also delivered speeches during meetings with their fellow workers and hosted national speakers, including perennial Socialist Party of America presidential candidate Eugene V. Debs.[103] In March 1906 Gohl addressed members on the twenty-first anniversary of the SUP, stating: "The day may be near at hand that you all will be called upon to put your shoulder to the wheel and help steer the good old ship safely to the goal of everlasting brotherhood."[104] Three months after this, the bonds of union brotherhood were put to the test, as the Sailors' Union faced down a group of organized shipping employers in what would be a long and violent strike.

4

BILLY GOHL AND THE 1906 MARITIME STRIKE

DOCKED AT THE S. E. Slade Lumber Company mill in Aberdeen on the night of June 12, 1906, was the steam schooner *Centralia*, one of the first nonunion ships to arrive in town during the 1906 Pacific Coast maritime strike. Since its arrival, the ship had encountered difficulties. Its captain, a man named Erickson, could not secure a scab longshoremen crew since no strikebreakers dared approach the *Centralia*. Erickson complained to Aberdeen mayor John Lindstrom and demanded protection from the unionists.[1] As the owner of a large local shipyard, Lindstrom sympathized with mill owners' plight. To aid fellow employers in their fight against the striking maritime unions, Lindstrom created an army of special officers, or "specials," to guard the ship, the docks, and the men who worked on them. He assigned the first of these specials, Deputy Frank Rattie, to protect the *Centralia*. While Erickson soon acquired enough men to unload the ship, the Sailors' Union boycott was still under way, so he couldn't find a crew to load and sail the ship back down the coast.[2]

Unable to leave port, Erickson was with Rattie and Slade mill manager W. B. Mack early in the evening of June 12, when a crowd of about two hundred men marched through the Slade mill and toward the docks. William Gohl led the unionists to the docks, along the gangplank, and onto the *Centralia*. In an interview with the *Bulletin*, Mack

summarized the confrontation that followed: "Agent Gohl of the seamen's union and a number of other men jumped onto the deck, disre-
garding the orders of the special police officer, Captain Erickson, and
myself. When I saw that the mob would not heed the instructions
given, I went to the side of the vessel and fired a shot." Mack continued, stating that after a heated exchange of words between himself
and the union agent: "Gohl drew a revolver from his pocket and fired
it into the air. I was standing with my hands behind my back when this
incident occurred. After firing Gohl pointed his revolver at my body,
saying: 'If you make a move, you'll get yours.'"[3] As the two men traded
threats and discharged their guns, crowds of workers watched from
aboard the ship and from the docks.[4] According to Gohl in subsequent
newspaper reports, unionists had mustered the offensive against the
Centralia because they had heard that its crew had been shanghaied
in San Francisco.[5] Other sources cited by the papers suggested that
union men were being held on board against their will and that the
local SUP wished to interview the ship's fireman about the conditions
of his employment. Whether those on board were shanghaied scabs
or imprisoned unionists, it is apparent that the crowd marched to the
Slade dock with overtly political goals and believed that a show of
force would be enough carry the day. The strength and passion of the
marchers indeed proved irresistible, and they forced their way aboard
ship and laughed at Mack's orders to remain away.[6]

   According to the *Grays Harbor Post*, the standoff between Mack
and Gohl inflamed the crowd, whose members demanded the strikebreakers' blood.[7] Although Gohl would soon be labeled "bloodthirsty,"
the antiunion *Aberdeen Daily Bulletin* described Gohl as a restraining
influence on the "mob." When Gohl escorted one of the nonunion sailors off the ship, the union agent ignored shouts of "Kill him!," "Throw
him into the river!," and "Lynch him!" and reassured the man of his
safety. In this case, from all available sources it appears that Gohl's
leadership allowed the sailor to depart the ship safely.[8]

   The 1906 confrontation over the *Centralia*, and the 1906 maritime
strike of which it was a part, epitomized early twentieth-century class
relations in marine transportation, as organized labor and organized

capital waged sometimes violent struggles to protect their class interests. By the early twentieth century, Grays Harbor's longshoremen and sailors were thoroughly organized.[9] To enforce workers' rights on the job and in their communities, local maritime unions took militant stances toward employers, striking frequently during the first two decades of the century. The 1906 strike stands as the pivotal event in Gohl's life, as his defense of workers' rights infuriated the region's employers and their allies, turning them into his vocal enemies. Gohl foresaw this shift coming, as the conflict boiled over into open class warfare in the cities of Grays Harbor. During the strike, he led small contingents of unionists into armed combat with scabs, imported strikebreakers, and police. Perhaps of greater importance, Gohl verbally threatened employers, men whose wealth and power kept them isolated from the brutality of industrial capitalism.

Before the strike, the need to rebuild San Francisco after the twin disasters of earthquake and fire in April 1906 had set in motion a massive reconstruction project that presented fantastic opportunities for shipowners and lumbermen to profit from others' loss. These men greeted the disaster as an economic opportunity and a chance to prove their mettle by providing the materials to reconstruct the largest city on the West Coast. Boasting of the industry's capacity, the *Pacific Lumber Trade Journal* opined: "By working double time the Pacific Coast mills can furnish enough lumber in sixty days to meet all requirements [of the reconstruction project]."[10] While Aberdeen's leading lights trumpeted the generous role they would play in providing San Franciscans lumber, working people argued that the "new city of San Francisco" would be "the product of the workers' hands and brains, not of the financiers' credit in the money markets of the world."[11] An illustration of working-class generosity came in the days after the disaster when Grays Harbor teamsters voluntarily transported relief supplies to the docks where longshoremen loaded a ship bound for San Francisco. Given that the Harbor's teamsters were on strike at the time, this act was exceptional.[12]

In the strike, sailors demanded a wage hike of five dollars per month, a raise they argued was necessary to keep up with the increased cost of living. Some shipowners appeared willing to grant the raise, but the United Shipping and Transportation Association (USTA), an organization of shipping employers, ordered its members to resist the union's demand, a move designed to provoke further conflict. According to unionists and many subsequent historians, the shippers' unwillingness to bargain had little to do with the SUP's demand for a pay increase of sixteen cents an hour.[13] According to Gohl, the USTA provoked the strike in order to destroy the union.[14] Angered by the shipping association's intransigence, the SUP instituted a new wage scale on May 29, incorporating the raise, and during the subsequent week many steam schooner owners agreed to adhere to the new scale.[15]

The strike began in early June when negotiations between sailors and owners broke down. At that point, sailors at ten West Coast ports officially struck against the USTA, which had refused to budge on the wage increase.[16] With the headquarters of both the SUP and USTA based in San Francisco, the city took center stage in negotiations, and headlines there focused on the strike and related violence. Scab sailors aboard the schooner *National City* there shot at a boat carrying twenty-five unionists as the latter attempted to board the schooner, killing one man and wounding three others. But threats and violence between picketers and scabs, strikers and police, and union activists and employers occurred all along the coast. In Portland a group of SUP members armed themselves and boarded the nonunion lumber schooner *Paulson*, which arrived from San Francisco carrying a crew of longshoremen to unload the cargo. After failing to drive off the scabs using threats alone, the unionists opened fire on the men, shooting and seriously injuring three of the nonunion workers.[17]

Heading the shippers' and lumber manufacturers' side in the strike was W. B. Mack, dedicated organizer for united employers' interests. During Gohl's years on the harbor, Slade (formerly West and Slade Mill Company) frequently led Aberdeen mills in lumber production and coastal shipments. The Slade mill lay at the confluence of the harbor's two great rivers, the Wishkah and Chehalis. Longshoremen, sailors, and mill hands kept busy, moving lumber and loading the many vessels, both steam and sail, docked at the mill. It wasn't unusual for several lumber schooners to be docked at the Slade mill at the same time, and delays could be costly. Mack was tasked with keeping shipments running as smoothly and cheaply as possible, two goals that occasionally led to conflicts with Gohl and his fellow union members. Whether in his office or walking through the mill yard, Mack would rarely have been much more than a stone's throw away from the Sailors' Union of the Pacific office, and the Slade superintendent and Sailors' Union agent had frequent contact.

Born into a Rhode Island farm family in 1862, Mack was the unquestioned leader of anti-unionism on Grays Harbor during the early twentieth century. Skillfully cultivating political and business ties, he had served as ticket agent for the Northern Pacific Railway as it was extended into Aberdeen and had gained election to city and county office during the 1890s.[18] Much of his career would be spent as a Slade mill manager in Aberdeen, a position that made him "probably the highest salaried manager on the harbor."[19] Besides managing the largest mill in the city, with its more than three hundred employees, and a mill for the Slade-Wells Logging Company, which in 1908 employed nearly four hundred loggers, Mack concurrently held management positions at several lumber, banking, and stevedore companies. Mack was also one of the most active members of the Aberdeen Chamber of Commerce.[20] An avid joiner, Mack belonged to several elite fraternal, commercial, and cultural organizations.[21]

A number of times, the rabidly antiunion Mack stated his preference for shutting down operations rather than recognizing a union or bargaining with workers.[22] The Slade mill, easily the largest in Aberdeen, was also the most strike-prone. Workers struck Mack's mill at least five times between 1904 and 1912.[23] Mack, however, avoided trying to pacify workers through paternalistic programs or incentive schemes. Instead, he sought to force Slade employees to submit to his will. Described by one booster as "the man . . . with the energy that never ends," Mack stood on the front lines of the class war.[24] He carried a gun to ward off picketing unionists, clubbed left-wing immigrant laborers during a 1912 lumber strike, and spewed derogatory nativist comments about Finnish employees at the Slade mill.[25]

At Mack's back stood a small army of employers drawn from both lumber manufacturing and small business. By 1906 Aberdeen had thirty-two manufacturing firms, including eleven sawmills and three shingle mills, and with the adjacent towns of Hoquiam and Cosmopolis it comprised the largest lumber port in the world.[26] Maritime transportation unions threatened lumber manufacturers because of the unions' strength and history of generating working-class solidarity, and union agents such as Gohl were especially threatening. Agents assigned union sailors to vessels, and it was their job to ensure sure that employers followed the letter of the law and abided strictly by their contract. The most effective agents—including Gohl—found a bevy of methods to make business difficult for employers who failed to follow laws and contracts.

In Aberdeen and in San Pedro, California, union longshoremen struck in sympathy with the SUP, owing in part to the high level of joint union membership by sailors and dock workers in those localities—many Grays Harbor unionists held cards in both organizations.[27] Maritime unionists were linked by work culture, union membership, and social standing, and scholars have noted the cultural similarities between dock work and ship work.[28] Sailors and longshoremen frequently lived in the same parts of town, socialized in the same groups, and faced similar levels of work regimentation from their bosses. And the two sometimes did the same sort of work, according to SUP historian Stephen Schwartz, who writes, "On the lumber ships the sailors worked cargo, in contrast with deepwater ships which were increasingly loaded and unloaded by 'men along shore,' or longshoremen."[29]

The importance of this marine transport alliance showed in San Pedro when eight nonunion sailors came into port on a lumber schooner: the lumber remained unmoved as employers could secure no longshoremen to unload it. The *Los Angeles Herald* summarized the shipowners' predicament in Southern California: "The longshoremen will stand by the sailors in the trouble, making it practically impossible to discharge a cargo while the strike is on."[30]

A similar standoff took place at Grays Harbor, where the sympathy strike put the two oldest, most-entrenched, best-connected unions on strike together against shipping employers. As in San Pedro, this made transporting materials virtually impossible. Grays Harbor lumbermen and shippers issued a resolution noting, "We understand that the mills of the Columbia River and Puget Sound are not meeting with the same difficulties, owing to the fact that the stevedores at those points are not refusing to load vessels manned with non-union crews."[31]

The unwillingness of employers to concede to sailors' demands figured prominently in the sailors' tactics to halt coastwise shipping in June 1906. But it was more than that. Beyond the wage dispute boiled years of frustration among the sailors. As historian Bruce Nelson wrote, "The provisions of the Thirteenth Amendment and subsequent legislation barring involuntary servitude did not apply to the seafarer. In other words, he was still subject to arrest and imprisonment for desertion and absence without leave."[32] Facing the reality that their existence resembled chattel slavery, seamen seethed with hostility toward their employers. Maritime unionists instituted armed patrols of the streets in the harbor towns, providing an effective counterforce to the bosses' company guards and "specials" hired on the city's dime. Gohl led armed groups of local workers in raids on scab-operated lumber schooners. These raids served a dual function: they coerced scabs into quitting work and liberated the unfortunate men who had been shanghaied by unscrupulous ship captains. He also led armed patrols of streets and docks, looking for known scabs on streetcars and riverboats, searching them for weapons, and interrogating men about their intentions regarding the strike.

On July 14 Gohl joined a group of fellow unionists as they verbally and physically assaulted scab longshoreman and special policeman James Beckey as he attempted to reach the South Aberdeen docks.[33] Charles R. Sauers, a foreman at the Union Mill, who frequented the steamers across the Chehalis River, swore that this harassment had been "frequent and occurring every day" since the strike began.[34] Aberdeen police officer R. F. Cox wrote in an affidavit: "Gohl . . . went part way down the next block to meet the car and commenced searching the men, who were employees of the Gray's Harbor Stevedore Company [sic], and about that time the car got to the corner and there was a gang of Sailors and Longshoremen standing on the corner . . . there was a general mix up in which the Sailors and Longshoremen, headed by Gohl, assaulted the employees of the Stevedore Company, and we arrested several of them."[35] Several scabs, foremen, and employers swore out affidavits echoing the words of C. F. Drake and H. Van Tassel, managers of the Grays Harbor Stevedoring Company, who stated, "[Picketing unionists call] them vile names, scabs, etc., and threaten the said employees with death, and in every way impress upon the said employes [sic] that unless they desist from their labor on behalf of the said Grays Harbor Stevedoring Co., that they will not only be assaulted but their lives will be in imminent danger."[36]

According to some accounts, Gohl was the main instigator behind this sort of "mix up" and the man most willing to insert himself into the center of a fight. Learning that the notorious Beckey was aboard one streetcar, Gohl climbed on, proceeded to search each passenger, then forced the scabs out at a street corner where they received a beating from armed sailors and longshoremen. Beckey, who was something of a scab foreman, acknowledged, "It has been very difficult for me to secure men who will remain in the employment of the company, or in fact engage in the work of the company." That, of course, was precisely Gohl's objective.[37]

As seen in these confrontations, Gohl was known to have carried a gun and was seemingly unafraid of confronting and even provoking nonunion workers, but it would be a stretch to claim that picket line fights and harassing scabs equated to the crazed, antisocial violence attributed to him by writers claiming to know of the man's life. Most of the militant acts that can be legitimately attributed to him— with even the slimmest of evidence—were committed as part of class struggle. During the 1906 maritime strike and other times he did not mindlessly choose his targets. He acted as a sort of counter to the special police, recognizing the state's interests in protecting capital and extending protection to working-class and poor people (and filling a tremendous void by doing so). Moreover, Gohl's combative acts were not unusual in US labor relations prior to World War II. Employers, unionists, professional strikebreakers, police, and the military—to name only the most frequent participants—routinely engaged in acts of picket line violence during this time.

As an example at least of the threat of violence, on June 2, as the schooner *Fearless* set out to sea, a gasoline launch approached the ship without its customary lights showing. The small launch, the *Water Boy*, contained approximately sixteen men, including Gohl, "armed to the teeth," whose mission was to stop the *Fearless* from leaving port with its nonunion crew.[38] Questioned nearly three months later at his trial for organizing the raid on the *Fearless*, Gohl recalled some of his comrades' names. Among the names, three stand out: Captain H. E. Hanson, who captained the launch and received a fine of $250 for running the *Water Boy* without lights; Gohl's longtime friend and creditor, Sam Jacobson, owner of an Aberdeen saloon; and John Vance Thompson, a longtime Sailors' Union official, union newspaper editor, and future president of the California State Federation of Labor.[39]

The union sailors' grievance was with the *Fearless* captain C. W. Liljequist and what they saw as his improper dismissal of a union crew, their replacement by "mill hands and others," and his refusal to pay the union crew their customary day's wage for being assigned to work a ship. Subsequent investigations revealed that a sailor was being held on board against his will and forced to work.[40] A member of the union launch's crew demanded that the cook aboard the *Fearless* show himself. Liljequist responded by threatening that "he would shoot, and shoot to kill"—before noticing the heavily armed unionists on the launch. After a few more choice words, a shot was fired, and this was followed by an eruption of gunfire estimated to have been at least one hundred shots.[41] Upset, the crew of the *Fearless* returned the ship to dock and abandoned her, while members of the *Water Boy* crew returned to shore under the cover of darkness. The next day, the *Fearless* sailed to Mexico, unloaded its cargo, and returned to the harbor in mid-August. Upon its return to Aberdeen, authorities examined the ship and found it to be riddled with holes.[42]

Rumors of Gohl's involvement in the unionists' shootout with the *Fearless* circulated for weeks, until mid-August when Captain Liljequist confirmed this upon his return from Mexico. Angered that the

Schooner *Fearless* and crew loaded with lumber during the early twentieth century. At left is Captain C. W. Liljequist, who commanded the nonunion vessel during the 1906 lumber strike. *Courtesy of Polson Museum, Hoquiam, Washington.*

unionists had not been arrested, Liljequist swore out a warrant for Gohl's arrest and produced five bullets dug out of the ship's woodwork as evidence of the attack.[43] In statement after statement it became clear that the sailors had approached the *Fearless* in an attempt to induce scabs to leave the schooner, using force if necessary.[44] Given the involvement of so many armed men, including a captain, a saloon owner, and union activists, it is perhaps surprising that Gohl alone was arrested and prosecuted for the attack. In particular, it is surprising that prosecutors failed to charge Thompson with any crimes, considering that he had written incendiary articles in the *Trades Council Gazette* during the strike accusing the editor of the *Aberdeen Daily Bulletin* of being "willing to sell his manhood and honor for the pecuniary benefit derived from those who would purchase the service of such a contemptible fraud."[45] More relevant to the case, Thompson was the only unionist who admitted in court that members of the launch fired guns during the shootout. Still, Thompson remained free while the state and mainstream press fixed its fire on Gohl. On August 22, the *Aberdeen Daily Bulletin* greeted Gohl's arrest by running the headline: "Wm. Gohl in Toils."[46] At a preliminary hearing at the Aberdeen Justice Court on August 25, Judge E. H. Fox transferred the case to the Chehalis County Superior Court.[47] The law firm Marquis and Shields ably defended Gohl in court, while saloon owner Ed Dolan and undertaker James Bowes acted as sureties for Gohl's $500 bail.[48]

Condemned in the mainstream press as an "anarchist" who committed "piracy," Gohl felt the weight of the law bearing down on him. In October, he appeared in front of Chehalis County Superior Court judge Mason Irwin, charged with the felony of "unlawfully maintaining, organizing and employing an armed body of men." On October 10, the jury began deliberations. In a preliminary vote, eleven jurors voted to convict, with one supporting acquittal. After six more hours of deliberation, the majority convinced the holdout to join their side and declared the union agent guilty. For this crime, Judge Mason Irwin fined Gohl $1,200, with no imprisonment.[49] Gohl appealed the decision to the Washington State Supreme Court on several grounds, including his right to bear arms. In *State of Washington v. Gohl* (1907), the court struck down each of Gohl's appeals. The justices decided: "A constitutional guaranty of certain rights to the individual does not place such rights entirely beyond the police power of the state." In other words, the state had the right to regulate an individual's right to bear arms.[50] The court further found that Gohl had violated the statute prohibiting the organizing of an armed body of men, "although he did not 'hire' them."[51]

Although Gohl had to devote time to carrying out his legal defense, he and his union still had a strike to win. On June 18, 1906, Aberdeen mayor John Lindstrom, a loyal ally of local business interests, purged the police force of any man with connections to the labor movement. While he didn't fire Police Chief Peter Christensen, he did force

Christensen to resign from the longshoremen's union and publicly renounce ties with the organization.[52] His former labor comrades responded by mocking the chief in their *Trades Council Gazette* (and thus illustrating the gendered constructions of working-class respectability):

> In walking the street, should
> You happen to meet
> With a pair of beautiful eyes,
> Don't lose your feet, they belong to Pete
> The chum of non-union guys—oho!

> [*Chorus*]
> Beautiful Pete
> Officer Pete
> The man who threw up his card.
> He held on his job
> Did this beautiful snob
> And let his old playmates down hard,
> Sweet Pete.[53]

The *Gazette* sarcastically offered a reward for "the individual who will sign an affidavit that he respects Mr. Peter Christensen, ex-unionist."[54] The Aberdeen municipal government, on the other side, authorized "Sweet Pete" to deputize as many "special" police officers as he felt necessary to protect the docks.[55] The city's police force quickly ballooned from six officers to a force of thirty. The "specials" cost the city $65 per day.[56]

Local governments across the United States in this era regularly aided employers, providing strikebreaking services, for example. The business-friendly Aberdeen government was a case in point, hiring strikebreakers and labor spies to combat unions. In May 1909 lumber workers, led by Finnish socialists, would strike at several Aberdeen mills. Quick to respond to the mill owners' needs, Aberdeen mayor E. B. Benn, elected to office two months prior, appointed twenty-five strikebreakers as special police officers. When picketers marched to the A. J. West mill to encourage more laborers to join the strike, former Aberdeen mayor A. J. West, the mill owner, would meet them with a rifle and threaten the strikers with deadly harm if they didn't leave promptly.[57]

Attacking unionists and strikers in the press and hiring special police officers were among the mildest approaches to union-busting in the period between the Civil War and World War II. Nearly every corner of the United States experienced epic labor struggles during this period, as employers maintained nonunion shops by organizing "businessmen's associations," hiring labor spies and strikebreakers, and using state and vigilante violence against union organizers, picketers, and other "troublemakers." By the time of the 1906 maritime strike, employers in cities across the country had banded together into hundreds of so-called citizens' alliances and citizens' committees. These organizations ranged from formal institutions with headquarters and elected officers to informal clubs formed spontaneously to "deal with" a strike or radical uprising. In Colorado, more than thirty thousand people took part in that state's citizens' alliance movement, formed to roust the Western Federation of Miners (WFM) from Colorado mining communities. In response to a 1903–4 WFM strike in the labor stronghold of Cripple Creek, Colorado, the region's citizens' alliance swept into action. Its members published antiunion pieces in newspapers, assaulted pro-strike journalists and elected officials, forced pro-union public officials to resign under the threat of death, and deported union activists from the mining district. The campaign was ruthless, as the alliance "forced more than thirty officials to resign, imprisoned many of them, and replaced them with opponents of organized labor," in the words of historian Elizabeth Jameson.[58] While this was far from the only successful antiunion drive coordinated by so-called citizens' groups, the Colorado Citizens' Alliance served as a model for future union opponents to emulate.

In the Grays Harbor area, the "specials" used clubs to break the strike—and occasionally strikers' heads. One striker sued Officer J. F. Myles for viciously beating him over the head with his club.[59] The

SUP and longshoremen issued a joint resolution condemning an attack on union sailor Emil Bratman, who "was assaulted and brutally beaten by a hired thug."[60] The special police also worked as scab-herders for their employers. G. F. Moyer, a Hoquiam carpenter, swore in an affidavit that one of the specials approached him and "persistently urge[d]" Moyer to work as a scab stevedore.[61] The type of "law and order" protected by the specials was made crystal clear when two imported "thugs" assaulted and robbed union longshore-man Oliver Garapee and were then allowed to escape from the Aberdeen jail four days later.[62] Two resolutions, each signed by every member of the Grays Harbor Trades and Labor Council, condemned Chief Christensen for his role in precipitating the violence.[63]

On July 2, harbor employers escalated the conflict by importing armed strikebreakers into Aberdeen to intimidate picketers. Bringing in professional strikebreakers was a common tactic bosses and local governments used to defeat unions throughout the United States. Strikebreaking services were often based in a single location, but their reach was truly national. Writing of the strikebreaking firm Berghoff Brothers and Waddell of New York, historian Stephen J. Norwood states that it "promised it could supply 10,000 strikebreakers to a corporation within seventy-two hours, mobilizing probably more men more quickly than the federal government could."[64] The presence of these imported thugs proved to be a source of anxiety for strikers and their families, who were concerned both for their personal safety and for the moral affront that came with having hired ruffians, a group widely known for their abuses, occupying their communities. The *Trades Council Gazette* reacted with horror to the importation of strikebreakers: "Citizens, what do you think? About six weeks ago a man was escorted out of town and told if he came back again he would be put in jail and kept there. The same man (save the mark) was employed as one of the specials on the *Centralia* and the city has to pay him."[65] Unionists' worst fears came true on August 31 when John Jones, a hired gunman, shot and killed union longshore-man Alexander Wahlgren, then unloaded his gun on Grant Wilson, a union bartender who tried to apprehend the killer.[66] In February 1907, Wilson died from complications of the gunshot wounds.[67]

Much to the employers' chagrin, the state-funded private guards, scab-herders, and thugs were still overmatched by the union forces well into the strike. For a month after the introduction of the special police force, Gohl still swaggered about town, revolver in hand, willing to search for and pistol-whip scab stevedores.

Gohl's leadership of the strike, and more specifically of the street patrols, would give his enemies in the press and the ranks of local employers a convenient target for future campaigns. Throughout the strike, much of the local and national press expressed outrage at the audacity of a transport union striking during the crisis in San Francisco. According to many in the mainstream press, a tyrannical and greedy union was capitalizing on the misfortune of others.

Local reporters, particularly those at the *Aberdeen Daily Bulletin*, depicted strikers as an unthinking mob of subhumans. (According to the *Bulletin*, "to call them human would be to do an injustice to the rest of the people.")[68] The paper heaped scorn on the maritime workers for "working incalculable damage to the trade of the states of Washington, Oregon and California," and one of its headlines practically screamed an alarm: "Widespread Disaster May Follow Strike of Coast Seamen."[69] Trying its best to divide the local working-class citizenry, the *Bulletin* worked to pit "independent-minded" loggers against the striking sailors and longshoremen. Hoping to create a self-fulfilling prophecy, the *Bulletin* predicted, "Clashes are likely to occur at almost any time, and if large bodies of men meet the probability of bloodshed will not be at all remote." Acting on the same impulse, employers induced loggers to leave the woods and load ships for increased wages. W. B. Mack, who managed both the Slade sawmill and logging camps, informed loggers that the strike had ended (it had not) and that it was thus safe to come to Aberdeen, and he offered them large pay increases to work as longshoremen once they arrived in town.[70] But the unionists' *Trades Council Gazette* mocked employers' presumption that they could turn the loggers into scabs: "The loggers came in this afternoon and raised hell with the longshoremen—but it was with the scab longshoremen on the *Newburg*. The Shipping Association are not getting the help of gallant loggers to defeat the men. . . . YOU ARE GOOD BOYS!"[71] One group of unionists was so outraged by the efforts of "the little curly-haired" editor of the *Daily Bulletin* that they vandalized the *Bulletin* building, covering it in red paint.[72]

Unable to secure sailors, and with scab stevedores frightened for their lives, Grays Harbor employers turned to the courts for an injunction. On July 12, Chehalis County Superior Court judge Mason Irwin issued a temporary restraining order that prohibited the maritime unionists and their agents from "in any manner interfering with, attempting to interfere with, placing obstructions in any way of, using vile epithets or opprobrious names, or aiding, abetting or seeking to procure the performance of any and all of these aforesaid things towards the plaintiffs, their employes [*sic*] and associates in the discharge of the business of said plaintiffs."[73] Nonunion plaintiffs made a great deal of the verbal abuse that the unionists had leveled against them. They introduced no fewer than six affidavits complaining that, among other things, the sailors and longshoremen were "calling the employees of the Stevedore Company all sorts of vile names and applying the epithet of 'Scab' and 'God damned sons-of-bitches.'"[74] The affidavits decried—and demonstrated the wide scope of—the "preventing [of] these plaintiffs and all other persons not affiliated with said Unions from engaging in the business of loading and unloading vessels" and made this a simple case for Judge Irwin.[75] The complaint named the two maritime unions and specified their agents and officers by name, but five days later, when the hearing for a permanent injunction opened, it became clear that the state had its aim set primarily on one man, William Gohl.

Judge Irwin labeled Gohl "a man deliberate in action, energetic, aggressive and courageous" but said he lacked "good judgment and discretion." In rendering his decision in favor of the injunction, Irwin focused special attention on the sailors' agent and distinguished him from the other defendants. Unlike the agents of the longshoremen's union, who "conducted themselves with singularly good judgment and discretion," Gohl "was not so discrete. He gave his members very good and proper instruction when talking to them at their meetings, but violated his instructions himself when on the street."[76] Predictably, the *Bulletin* celebrated, running the headline "Union Men Enjoy No Special Privileges," and interpreted Irwin's decision as a "stand that membership in a union does not extend to a man legal privileges not enjoyed by other men."[77]

Sailors had a long history of defying injunctions, a practice openly supported by union leadership. Longtime SUP official E. Ellison penned a letter to Gohl encouraging the Aberdeen agent to break the law if it meant winning the strike: "Officers would welcome a month of rest in jail to emerge at the end of that time as the idols of the labor movement." Ellison more than hinted that the rewards for jail time were well worth the sacrifice.[78] Gohl and others took this advice to heart and maintained armed patrols throughout the conflict.

To varying degrees, other maritime workers followed the SUP's lead and kept most scab ships from loading through the summer. On September 1, the union announced it had reached a settlement with coastwise sailing vessels, with employers agreeing to the demand for a raise of five dollars per month.[79] The steam schooner strike persisted until the end of October, when Sailor's Union president Andrew Furuseth negotiated a contract providing the union seamen engaged in the coastwise lumber schooner trade with their demanded monthly wage increase. Gohl notified local news organs: "All has been settled satisfactorily."[80] In September 1906, after most harbor employers had acceded to the union's demands, Grays Harbor mills shipped over twenty-nine million board feet of lumber.[81] According to a lumber trade journal later in the fall, these shipments were heavy, "but the demand was heavier." Grays Harbor shippers raised production and were responsible for more than 35 percent of all Northwest lumber shipments to Northern California during the following month.[82]

Following the maritime workers' victory in the 1906 strike, sailors and longshoremen built on their solidarity by forming an alliance of the region's most militant labor organizations. In September, Gohl led the sailors into an institutional alliance with Grays Harbor longshoremen, teamsters, caulkers and joiners, ship carpenters, and shingle weavers from some of the harbor's most militant unions, formalized as the Grays Harbor Waterfront Federation (GHWF). The new federation's four hundred members elected Gohl, its chief architect, as president.[83] The federation was an ambitious project designed to respond to structural changes in American capitalism. As the union newspaper *Shingle Weaver* explained, "Individual craft organizations are no longer able . . . to cope with the growing power of organized capital." Workers, it continued, were "awakening to the need of united political action [that] has been brought about by the tyranny of the heads of great industrial institutions on the one hand and the very partisan way in which the ruling class has been lashing the struggling workers with the whip of governmental power on the other."[84]

But while Gohl's activism won real victories for working people, it also earned him powerful enemies. For the next three-plus years he would be the target of a concerted campaign by Grays Harbor employers, labor spies, and mainstream newspaper editors acting in concert to drive him from the harbor. The strike marked a real transition in Gohl's life and in the region's labor history. Defeated in a bitter labor struggle by organized workers, employers unified around their class interests and brought in outside support from allies. While the labor movement, particularly its most militant elements, celebrated its victory and moved to extend its community influence, organized capital fixed its gaze on Gohl, who they rightly saw as a powerful threat to employer profits and control over the community.

5

STRUGGLING FOR
RESPECTABILITY

THE THIRD WEEK of October 1908 was a lot like most others for William Gohl. Most evenings, after attending to union business around the office and assigning union members to ships, Gohl attended meetings of one or another of the several labor, reform, and fraternal organizations he belonged to. For a few months in 1908, after his election as president of the Grays Harbor Trades and Labor Council, Gohl simultaneously held three local union offices: SUP agent, secretary-treasurer of the Grays Harbor Waterfront Federation (GHWF), and president of the GHTLC. With Grays Harbor ranking as the most densely unionized part of Washington State, Gohl's many positions established him as one of the Northwest's most notable working-class residents. That same year, the union agent joined the Fraternal Order of Eagles, the largest fraternal organization in the region and one composed of a cross-class combination of white unionists and small employers. The local Eagles' membership likely resembled that of another all-white fraternity, the Asiatic Exclusion Club, founded by Gohl, who also hosted its meetings at his office in 1908.[1]

Between his official duties as a union leader and his fraternal engagements, Gohl was busy. On Monday nights he attended the weekly meeting of his own union, the SUP. The next night, the Foresters, one of his fraternal orders, held meetings. Wednesdays took him to meetings of the Grays Harbor Waterfront Federation, and on Friday nights he oversaw the proceedings of the GHTLC and went to meetings of the Fraternal Order of Eagles. Many Thursdays saw the agent attend meetings of the International Longshoremen's Association, which regularly had dealings with his own union.[2] Mixed in with these official gatherings were informal celebrations hosted by one of his organizations or allied groups.[3] Given all these activities, it is difficult to comprehend how the union agent had time for leisure or assisting his wife Bessie with her small business, a rooming house located on East Heron Street amid mills, docks, and saloons.[4]

The preceding eight years had brought wave after wave of changes to Gohl's life. In 1900 he was an itinerant seaman lodging with dozens of other men in San Francisco. He worked aboard ships and spent nearly all his time around men. His earliest years on Grays Harbor were somewhat similar, as Gohl divided his time between boardinghouse, saloon, and union hall. But, within a few years of his settling in Aberdeen, he was pursuing the life of a respectable working-class man. He married, purchased property, joined organizations, and got involved in politics. He wrote letters to newspapers, attended city council meetings, and formed relationships with like-minded residents. He sometimes described his occupation as "clerk" or "cigar merchant," white-collar jobs bearing little resemblance to that of seaman. Gohl saw organized labor, and specifically the Sailors' Union, as the lynchpin of his changing life course. Writing to a union newspaper in 1906, Gohl hailed the successes of moral reform initiated by the union: "Properly considered and weighed, it will be seen that these achievements amount to more in the real advancement of the seaman than all the efforts of all other movements in all the years gone by."[5] In 1906 a Grays Harbor seaman wrote: "Ten years ago, sailors at mess could talk of nothing but women, whiskey, and tobacco. Today, they talk of the union, maritime law, and brotherhood."[6] Gohl believed that the union had helped him to achieve "real advancement" and "brotherhood," and in the years ahead he resolved to work at advancing other seamen, even if he had to push them grudgingly to adopt changes in their lives.

As illustrated in his writings, Gohl yearned for working-class respectability and its trappings, including a living wage, a stable and sedentary life, and influence in the local community. Scholars have long viewed the characteristics of respectable working-class manhood as marriage, stability within a community, proficiency in a craft, and involvement with a trade union.[7] Someone acquainted with Gohl at the turn of the century would likely not recognize his life and work a decade later, as the man pursued a life of family, camaraderie, and stability.

Before Billy married Bessie Hager, he rented a room near the Aberdeen docks. Following their nuptials, the Gohls did not buy a house but continued to room, albeit at the Capital Rooming House that Bessie

Bessie and William Gohl. After marrying in 1905, the Gohls remained one of the most prominent working-class families on Grays Harbor until William's arrest in February 1910. *Courtesy of Southwest Washington Archives, Olympia, Washington.*

owned and operated. With this role, Bessie was one of the few women business owners on the harbor. If William was a fine union leader, then Bessie excelled at running her small business, which she advertised in newspapers.[8] Shortly after the Gohls' marriage, Bessie set up her business, including making $900 in furniture purchases from the Aberdeen Brewing Company to outfit the rooming house.[9] Located at the corner of Heron and F, the Capital Rooming House stood near mills, docks, saloons, and riverfront shacks. Its location allowed those sailors who preferred to not face the many dangers of working-class Grays Harbor to come into port, meet their union agent, attend a union meeting, get a bite to eat at one of the nearby restaurants or purchase a cigar from William, and fall asleep at the Capital, all without walking more than a few steps.[10] Marketed to "gentlemen," the Capital housed at least a handful of long-term residents, including Fred Hewett, proprietor of the Humboldt Saloon. With rates between ten and twelve dollars per month, the Capital was a mid-priced housing option.

For the Gohls, the Capital was an asset, providing a stable income. Since Bessie was its owner, newspaper ads listed her name ("Mrs. Wm. Gohl") as its "proprietress," and she paid considerably more in taxes than did her husband.[11]

Several issued faced William Gohl in his struggle for respectability. Though Bessie owned a small business, the Gohls lived in a rooming house, surrounded by saloons, brothels, and lumber mills—an area known as "the restricted district" in the press. Although the Capital Rooming House lay less than a mile from the middle-class residences on the hill, the social distance between Broadway Hill and the waterfront could hardly have been greater. But beyond it all, Gohl could never become a respectable member of society because after 1906 he would be a working-class felon convicted of a violent crime, which the most powerful men on Grays Harbor would never let him forget.

If middle-class respectability in the United States comes from home ownership, then the Gohls never reached this sought-after status. In January 1909 Bessie and William began renting a house on Broadway Hill. They did not live alone: at the time of Gohl's arrest in early 1910, two of Bessie's relatives lived with them. To supplement their skimpy family earnings, working-class women regularly took in boarders, both family members and strangers. In 1909 the Gohls rented a room to sailor Charles Hadberg.[12] The Gohls also took in two of Bessie's siblings: Josephine, her much older sister, and Robert, a disabled logger. The dependence of these extended family members caused Gohl significant anxiety, and when he was arrested for murder in February 1910 he expressed concern. As a local paper noted, "He has no income but has been living from week to week on his salary and now that that source of revenue has been cut off he does not know what to do."[13]

Both William and Bessie understood the precariousness of single workers' lives in the early twentieth-century American West. In both San Francisco and Aberdeen, William had rented rooms in houses owned by others. This was the standard life for single working-class men in industrializing America. In 1910 R. L. Polk's *Grays Harbor Cities Directory* counted seventeen boardinghouses, thirty-two rooming houses, and twenty-seven hotels in Aberdeen.[14] But this was only the tip of the iceberg. Scores of Aberdeen and Hoquiam homeowners rented out rooms to workers. To make ends meet, several generations of working-class families often lived under one roof. One such structure belonged to the Johnsons, a Finnish-American family, on Marion Street in South Aberdeen. Evret Johnson, the father and "head" of the family, worked as a sawmill laborer, as did the seven male Finnish-American boarders who lived in the Johnson household.[15]

The Pacific Coast provided opportunity for some white working-class men to accumulate property. Bolstered by the availability of cheap land and high wages, unionists like Gohl bought and sold inexpensive lots of land and acquired diverse forms of property.[16] Most notably, Gohl purchased shares in local cigar stands. Decades before the image of the heavy-set, cigar-chomping union official in the mold of George Meany pervaded Americans' perceptions of the labor movement, unionists spent much of their time in smoke-filled rooms. As historian Barbara Wertheimer described the early twentieth-century union meeting: "Cigar smoke filled the hall, which was located as often as not above a saloon."[17]

In fact, cigar making was one of the most highly unionized trades in the late nineteenth and early twentieth centuries, producing such labor luminaries as AFL cofounders Samuel Gompers and Adolph Strasser. On Grays Harbor, cigar making contributed many of the region's most notable labor and leftist political leaders, including socialist city council member Emil Milette. As with other US cities, Aberdeen boasted several cigar stands.[18] Unionists indulged liberally in smoking cigars at social events. Indeed, get-togethers called "smokers" were among the most common types of union gatherings. At one mass 1906 union celebration hosted by the SUP, the evening ended by passing around cigars: "a social hour spent as the climax to a successful and enjoyable gathering," noted the *Aberdeen Daily Bulletin*.[19]

Gohl co-owned two of Aberdeen's cigar stands with Lars Kingstad, a longtime harbor area resident and former mill worker. Like many laborers at the time, a workplace injury forced Kingstad out of the mills—he became "permanently disabled from doing any manual labor." But during 1902, in a tremendous act of beneficence, area residents contributed funds to support Kingstad, raising more than $275, which he used to start a cigar and confectionary business.[20] Gohl bought a stake in the enterprise, and by 1905 Kingstad and Gohl Cigars operated two stands. Surrounded by saloons, mills, and boardinghouses, the stands were in good position to serve a steady flow of working-class customers. Gohl helped maintained the stands for several years until financial hardship convinced him to sell his stock to his partner in 1907 for $100.[21]

If Gohl concerned himself with the condescending views of Grays Harbor's upper crust toward him and his family, he never let on that their opinions bothered him. He had far too much to get done, including work with the Grays Harbor Waterfront Federation (GHWF).[22] Following his 1906 arrest for leading the raid on the *Fearless*, members of his union local awarded him an expensive "magnificent silver set."[23] This required a major outlay for sailors, whose low wages made it difficult to purchase even basic goods. Gohl also played an increasingly prominent role at the annual WSFL conventions. During the 1907 convention, the first since the great maritime strike, Gohl gained a convention chairmanship, overseeing the work of the constitution committee.[24] Later the same week Gohl was one of the nominees for the position of fourth vice president of the federation but was outvoted by the incumbent.[25] In January 1909, Gohl and his fellow Grays Harbor delegates won a second WSFL convention for the harbor cities the following year. Upon their return from the 1909 convention in Walla Walla, Gohl served as the delegates' spokesperson, announcing that the 1910 convention was to be held in Hoquiam.[26] That January 1910 event would see three hundred delegates descend on the harbor, making it the largest labor convention in state history. It also proved to be Gohl's last official duty as a union agent. On the one hand, he seconded the nomination of President William Blackman for a new term to head the WSFL. But the sole resolution he introduced called for the "extension of Chinese Exclusion Act to include all Asiatics," an ignominious end to a generally impressive career in the labor movement.[27]

Gohl's career was marked with a strong commitment to white supremacy. But he also fought for changes in laws and workplace practices that promised to improve the lives of maritime workers. Knowing well the dangers of seamen's work, he was a vocal advocate for the establishment of marine hospitals in the United States. At the 1906 WSFL convention in Aberdeen, with his fellow Sailors' Union delegates, Gohl introduced a resolution condemning the actions of the US secretary of the treasury, who had "recommended the abolishment" of twelve marine hospitals, including one located at Port Townsend, Washington. The resolution noted, "Such service [the hospitals provide] is necessary for the care of those engaged in the maritime industry; . . . the abolition of those establishments would involve the farming out of sick and disabled seamen, a custom now prevalent in certain localities, and one that leads to great abuses, both in neglect of the patients and in imposition upon the Government."[28] Two years later, at the WSFL convention in Tacoma, Gohl joined two harbor unionists in writing a resolution that "earnestly request[ed] and urge[d] upon congress the establishment of a permanent United States marine hospital on Grays Harbor for the further reason that the present system of farming out seamen to some private hospital invariably tends to the degradation of the seamen themselves."[29]

Gohl also tried his hand at lobbying. During the 1907 Washington State legislative session Gohl accompanied other SUP officials to Olympia where they convinced a state assemblyman that many of the state maritime laws were "slave laws," and the legislator "expressed his surprise that they were still on the statute books, and agreed to introduce a bill to have them repealed."[30] The sailors' agent was also knowledgeable about the law more broadly, having studied it some and having acted as an attorney for union members in court and paid unionists' fines when they ran afoul of the law.[31] In June 1906, after the captain of the steamer *Grace Dollar* refused to pay the crew following their arrival in Grays Harbor, the sailors sued the steamer's owner for back pay. Gohl represented the Sailors' Unionists in court.[32]

From his earliest days on the harbor, Gohl was a registered voter. This placed him in a small, privileged minority of area residents, as the ballot was restricted to folks based on gender, age, race, citizenship, nationality, itinerancy, and other factors. Elections were small affairs featuring only a small group of English-speaking adult males with US citizenship or who had taken out first papers in their citizenship applications. The extent of these restrictions can be seen by looking at voter turnout. Although Aberdeen's 1910 population was more than 13,000, as of March 1909 only 12 percent of its population registered to vote.[33] In April 1909 city elections, only 539 persons voted, about one-third of the city's 1,552 registered voters, and just 4 percent of the population.[34]

Gohl's status as registered voter was one of many things that distinguished him from those he represented in the Sailors' Union. Sailors, in the words of historian Leon Fink, labored on the "sweatshops of the sea."[35] Seamen had very little voice in public affairs. As a workforce composed almost entirely of first-generation immigrant workers who migrated between port towns, sailors rarely voted. In Aberdeen, the largest lumber port in the world and Washington State's largest coastal city, where dozens of seamen regularly plied their trade, only four sailors registered to vote in the 1909 elections.[36]

Gohl's role in the 1906 strike briefly thrust him into the world of electoral politics. In a front-page editorial published in the *Aberdeen Daily Bulletin*, he argued that many of the problems experienced by unionists could be remedied by greater involvement in politics. "The union men of Grays Harbor have in the past been easily led and bamboozled by political bunko-steerers, and they have now a chance to see that they must go into the political field themselves and select such men as will do their best to enact laws that will protect their interests," Gohl forcefully concluded.[37]

In September 1906, up-and-coming Chehalis County deputy sheriff Ed Payette nominated Gohl to be a delegate to the county's Republican convention.[38] Amid a months-long crusade to taint Gohl's reputation among its readers, the *Aberdeen Daily Bulletin* commented: "The feature of the Seventh ward caucus was the nomination of William Gohl, agent for the Sailors' union at this port. Mr. Gohl, so rumor has it, aspires to become a member of the city council from the Seventh, and it is said that he had been nominated for delegate to the convention as a sort of a starter." Although Gohl quickly withdrew his name from consideration, this marked a sign of his potential influence in local politics. But it also exposed the disdainful view many employers and newspapermen held of him in the aftermath of his arrest during the strike. The *Aberdeen Herald*, a leading anti-Gohl voice, criticized Payette for having had the gall to nominate a "gentleman [who] was under a criminal indictment on a charge, [which,] if proved, may remove him for an indefinite period from political scenes." Gohl's indictment and eventual conviction for a felonious crime tainted him in the eyes of the harbor's elite. Ed Payette's nomination of Gohl as Republican Party delegate was so scandalous that Payette, the soon-to-be victorious candidate for sheriff, felt he needed to publicly deny that he had made such a nomination.[39]

Even with the unrepresentative nature of early twentieth-century US politics, workers and unions did exert some influence at the polls and with elected representatives. Most of Grays Harbor's eligible working class voted for Republicans or Democrats at the county, state, and national level, with their party allegiance owing a great deal

to ethnicity, occupation, and religion. But in local elections residents of Aberdeen and Hoquiam formed a variety of local third parties, so-called citizens' and working men's parties, as well as branches
of the Socialist Party of America (SPA).[40] Between their fellow fraternal lodge mates and unionists, the "labor vote" in cities with sizeable
union movements like Hoquiam and Aberdeen could be considerable.
Unionists won several positions to the Aberdeen City Council in the
first decade of the twentieth century.[41]

Labor proved even more successful at mobilizing around individual issues.[42] For example, in response to Police Chief "Sweet Pete"
Christensen's resignation from the longshoremen's union, the local
labor movement launched a concerted attack on the chief. Unionists
accused him of disloyalty and of using the police force as a violent
strikebreaking operation, and they lobbied the Aberdeen City Council
to remove him from office. On July 25, 1906, a little more than a month
after Christensen withdrew from the union, the city council voted
unanimously to remove him from office.[43] Representing union labor's
perspective, the *Grays Harbor Post* celebrated Christensen's ouster
with the headline "Chief 'Pete' Had to Go."[44]

A lengthier labor political campaign came in 1906–7 during discus-
sions around building a Carnegie library in Aberdeen. Built in the late
nineteenth and early twentieth century through a combination of
public funds and donations from a foundation set up by industrialist
Andrew Carnegie, Carnegie libraries dotted—and continue to dot—
the United States. Although these Carnegie grants appeared to many
to be benevolent, they struck others as attempts by Carnegie, a notorious robber baron, to revive his good name and place tributes to
him in public spaces across the country. Speaking to this, socialist
leader Eugene V. Debs described Carnegie as one of "the philan-
thropic pirates of the capitalist class."[45] In cities with strong labor
movements across the country, unionists mobilized and stopped the
construction of Carnegie libraries, replacing his "blood money" with
public funds. In Carnegie's home state of Pennsylvania, six communities rejected his money.[46] The *Aberdeen Daily Bulletin*, which in 1903
was edited by the muckraker H. D. Crawford, slammed the idea of

paying for a Carnegie library: "Those who believe that it is a good thing to have the city assume the role of a pauper prostrate before the Carnegie millions should vote for the resolutions. Those who believe that the city can afford to spend $1,000 a year to maintain a Carnegie monument in perpetuity should vote for the resolutions."[47]

The local effort against construction of a Carnegie library indicated the power of the harbor's labor movement. In December 1906, the Aberdeen City Council passed a resolution to accept Carnegie's offer of $15,000 to the city for building a library. As with other Carnegie offers, Aberdeen was required to allocate 10 percent of that amount—$1,500 —annually to maintain the library.[48] In response, the local labor council unanimously approved a resolution opposing the library, laid out reasons for their opposition, and protested against the city council for favoring "the Carnegie library scheme." Unions opposed the library as "a needless burden upon the taxpayers of the city," given that Aberdeen already had a public library. But they also stood "opposed to a gift from Mr. Carnegie," with a lengthy article in the *Grays Harbor Post* explaining why this was so problematic, quoting English novelist Marie Corelli: "In every Carnegie library there should be placed a history of the Homestead strike." This referred to the 1892 strike at the Carnegie steel mills in Homestead, Pennsylvania, where armed Pinkerton guards attacked the strikers, and eighty-five hundred National Guardsmen descended on the mills and surrounded the region. Federal involvement at Carnegie management's request succeeded in breaking the strike and the local steelworkers' union.[49]

The labor council's opposition succeeded at delaying the library project. Two months after the council's resolution appeared in the local press, the newly elected Aberdeen mayor Eugene France joined all twelve city council members in voting unanimously to rescind the previously passed resolution accepting the Carnegie library proposition.[50]

In late 1907 support for the library remained strong, especially among middle-class residents whose thirst for an impressive library outweighed any commitment to labor. Still, opponents to accepting

Carnegie's "blood money" refused to back down, with the *Grays Harbor Post* leveling consistent criticism at the proposal.[51] Ultimately, however, the proposal carried: in January 1908, the Aberdeen City Council accepted the Carnegie library money by a vote of ten to two. The harbor's unionists had delayed acceptance of funds from the Carnegie Foundation for more than a year and temporarily convinced the city council to reconsider its support for the proposal. Still, the Carnegie library would be built in Aberdeen within the year.[52]

The multiyear fight over the Carnegie library in Aberdeen effectively divided residents by class, with organized labor standing in strong opposition to the building. A similar conflict took place in the latter half of 1906, as residents of Chehalis County wrestled with the question of whether to relocate the county seat and its courthouse from the small town of Montesano to a plot of land between Aberdeen and Hoquiam. Gohl took center stage in the courthouse removal project, which divided the harbor's unionists and furthered Gohl's infamy in the eyes of the region's employers and newspapermen.

Gohl's entanglement in the courthouse removal campaign escalated into a major political fight. His opposition to moving the courthouse outraged local power brokers.[53] Most of Aberdeen's leading citizens vigorously supported the move. The *Bulletin* led the cheers with a series of front-page stories and headlines like "Removal Proposal Will Surely Carry" and "Every Man Must Help: County Seat Demands Support."[54] More thoughtful comments about economic benefits, including those for workers, accompanied the bold headlines.[55] Employers and newspapermen formed committees to solicit funds from businesses to support the county seat removal "vigorously . . . till the polls close on election day." Aberdeen's newspaper editors publicized the move while wealthy locals raised funds for it.[56]

Years later, Gohl remembered this political fight as having been the turning point in his life on Grays Harbor. He saw himself as "the victim of a ring of Aberdeen politicians, who [had] been pursuing him persistently in an effort to effect his downfall, ever since the county seat fight of three years [earlier], when he took a firm stand against its removal."[57]

Leading the charge for removal was the son of Aberdeen founder Samuel Benn, Edmund Burke Benn, a real estate speculator and theater owner who from 1909 through 1911 was mayor of Aberdeen. If Aberdeen had a first family, surely the Benns were it. E. B. Benn owed his social standing to his father's importance and laid claim to being the "first white boy" born in Aberdeen. His footprints are all over the early history of the Harbor.[58] Inheriting his family name, wealth, and the land he used to make his own money, E. B. Benn had an easy road in life. He enjoyed moneymaking and fraternal activities, but his primary interest was in politics, and the Republican Party was his vehicle to elected office. Through the first decade of the twentieth century, he stood atop the Grays Harbor Republican Party.[59]

Opposing the courthouse removal project was a large segment of the local labor movement, with Gohl at its head.[60] Controversy erupted after the *Chehalis County Vidette* of Montesano printed a resolution from the Grays Harbor Waterfront Federation and its president (Gohl) and secretary (J. G. Brown): "Resolved—That the Grays Harbor Waterfront Federation in regular meeting assembled at Hoquiam, Wash., on October the twenty-first, 1906, hereby places itself on record as being unalterably opposed to the removal of the county seat, on the grounds of the self-evident graft in connection therewith."[61] The *Vidette*, which as the central news organ of the county seat, stood to lose much should the courthouse move, could barely contain its gushing praise for "the laboring man," "the small taxpayer," and "organized labor," all of whom "by hard work [know] how to appreciate the value of money [and dread] a raid upon the public treasury."[62]

The reaction against Gohl came fast and furious, and the attacks centered on three points. First, many wealthy Grays Harborites contended that Gohl was dishonest, claiming he had accepted money to support removal but was lending his influence only to those who opposed removal. E. B. Benn served as point man in the attacks on Gohl's character during this affair. Benn swore in an affidavit published in the *Aberdeen Daily Bulletin* that he had secretly paid Gohl $25 to round up labor votes in favor of removal. Gohl swore out an affidavit of his own, calling Benn's statement "absolutely without any foundation whatever" and "false and untrue." In what cannot have been simple coincidence, the *Bulletin* published the opposing affidavits right next to an article reporting that Gohl faced charges for stealing "a valuable bulldog."[63] That a dognapping charge became front-page news during a heated political fight had everything to do with discrediting the union agent.

Second, Aberdeen newspaper editors proclaimed that the GHWF, particularly its leaders, had no right to claim they represented the opinions of the working class or even the local labor movement. The right-wing *Bulletin* lectured to the "laboring element": "You have placed your confidence in them by electing them to office in your unions, and they have sold themselves to the Montesano gang under the representation that they CONTROL YOU BODY AND SOUL."[64] The *Grays Harbor Post* questioned Gohl and Brown's judgment, noting: "We cannot understand why an Aberdeen or Hoquiam man should fight for Montesano."

Third, beyond its provincial concerns, the *Post*, the ostensible voice of Grays Harbor organized labor, was mostly angered over the Waterfront Federation's use of newspapers, such as the *Vidette*, that did not use "the union label and . . . has [never] shown any sympathy or interest in the union labor movement."[65]

Still, the Waterfront Federation's support proved decisive, pushing the anti-removal vote over the top. The *Aberdeen Daily Bulletin* mourned the defeat of a plan so ardently supported by the energy and wealth of the area's upper crust, and vented: "Fraud was employed in the east end of the county is the opinion of politicians here. However, loss of the issue is charged to traitors at home."[66]

Much of the boosterism surrounding the removal proposal referred to the desirability of a unified harbor.[67] Aberdeen and Hoquiam, then divided spatially by a short stretch of land, had in the minds of many residents morphed into a single entity. As historian Richard Brown noted, "Except for their separate municipal governments, the twin cities were virtually one unit."[68] But behind ostensibly altruistic reasons for removal was division over whether workers or bosses would be at the center of the unification process. For years prior to the courthouse removal election of November 1906, Grays Harbor area employers had played the leading role in the fight for removal.[69]

Local workers had a different vision for the space, one in which they played a central role in building the harbor cities. The *Grays Harbor Post* announced plans for a grand labor hall in mid-June 1908, announcing that "organized labor will have the credit for driving the golden spike uniting the two cities."[70] Local unions unveiled plans for the first building ever constructed between Aberdeen and Hoquiam, a massive structure with a sixty-by-ninety-foot assembly space.[71] Local laborers signed articles of confederation with the State of Washington for the Grays Harbor Labor Temple Association on July 9, 1908, and by April 1909 construction was under way.[72] Unfortunately, the labor unions never completed the temple, abandoning it "for lack of funds," according to a March 1911 issue of the *Aberdeen Herald.*[73]

In the years after the strike, Gohl had plenty of personal experiences with personal, legal, and financial hardship. As often happens with working-class families who lack the financial and social resources to recover from major setbacks, trouble for the Gohls snowballed from arrest and trial to unemployment and bankruptcy. Making it even more difficult, William's actions during the maritime strike led the region's major power brokers to view him as a troublemaker. From 1906 until 1910, employers, police, and newsmen scrutinized Gohl's every action, looking for any excuse to discredit the man, and state authorities watched him with constant vigilance.

In September 1906, as described in chapter 3, Gohl pled guilty to charges of assault on one J. McCoy and paid a ten-dollar fine.[74] To twenty-first-century readers, ten dollars might seem a paltry sum, but it amounted to approximately 20 percent of Gohl's monthly salary. The fine could hardly have come at a worse time. It exacerbated the family's financial stresses when he lost his position as union agent. By October 1906, Gohl was under felony indictment for employing an armed body of men (in the attack on the *Fearless*) and facing the possibility of a long prison term. Despite his popularity in the SUP and the Grays Harbor area labor movement, Gohl had no friend in longtime Sailors' Union leader Andrew Furuseth, who criticized his recklessness during the strike.[75] Rather than elect Gohl, a man under indictment, in November 1906 the Sailors' Union chose a new union agent, Charles Hammarin, for its Aberdeen office.[76] By late 1906, Gohl faced a serious criminal case that threatened his freedom and the challenges of poverty as an unemployed worker.

As the autumn of 1906 stretched into winter, the Gohls' lives grew desperate. Although his post as union agent had not been a high-paying job, it had provided the Gohls with a steady income: $50 per month, approximately $600 per year. To make ends meet, the family must have scrimped and saved, while seeking sources of potential income. E. B. Benn claimed he paid Gohl $25 to work on the 1906 courthouse removal campaign.[77] In September 1906, building on his fierce reputation as a labor leader, Gohl had founded and become the first president of the GHWF. Union records and newspaper accounts don't note whether this was a paid position, but Gohl's comrades may have used this new position to create a salary for their leader, who sacrificed so much to stand toe to toe with bosses, strikebreakers, and police during the harrowing summer of 1906.

As the Gohl family's financial situation worsened, William suffered health problems. In July 1907, after returning to work as a Sailors' Union officer, he needed a long time off work as he recovered from what the *Coast Seamen's Journal* called a "case of bad blood poisoning" that caused him to lose twenty-five pounds.[78] The *Grays Harbor Post* ran an article mentioning that Gohl had been admitted to a hospital and stating: "An operation will be performed, amputating the middle finger of the right hand. Dr. Watkins has decided that this step is necessary in order to save the hand. Mr. Gohl is enduring his misfortune with heroic fortitude." As noted above, Bessie drew praise from the *Post* for aiding William's recovery: "The swelling extended from the hand to the shoulder and only the most careful nursing by Mrs. Gohl and excellent surgical care by Dr. Watkins prevented the loss of the finger, if not the hand. Mr. Gohl has been reduced from 175 to 153 pounds weight."[79]

The Gohls had long aspired to a middle-class lifestyle. But even with William's return to work he and Bessie were forced to make do with less. During his years as a working sailor, Gohl would have certainly experienced slack periods, perhaps even finding it difficult to afford necessities. As it was, the burden of debt forced him to declare bankruptcy, surely a tremendous blow to him and Bessie.

In March 1908, William Gohl petitioned for bankruptcy in the US District Court for the Western District of Washington, represented by Aberdeen attorney Elmer E. Shields. According to the petition, "[Gohl swore] that he owes debts which he is unable to pay in full; that he is willing to surrender all his property for the benefit of his creditors except such as is exempt by law, and desires to obtain the benefit of the Acts of Congress relating to bankruptcy."[80] Gohl further swore that he had no debts due to taxes or debts owed to the United States, State of Washington, or local governments; debts due to wages owed to workmen, clerks, or servants; or other debts "bearing priority by law." However, the debts Gohl *had* acquired were massive. As an individual, he had taken out more than $1,500 in loans to operate the cigar stands. Additionally, he swore to be jointly liable with his partner in the cigar business, Lars Kingstad, for another $523.[81] All told, Gohl owed more than $2,000, producing a crushing burden that, by early 1908, he could no longer bear.

The US District Court judged Gohl bankrupt on March 30, 1908. As per the 1898 US bankruptcy law, bankrupted individuals needed to hold and attend a meeting with creditors so they might "prove their claims, appoint a trustee, examine the bankrupt and transact such other business as may properly come before said meeting."[82] The court required Gohl to advertise that meeting in a local newspaper and attend it to resolve matters with his creditors. In April 1908 the *Aberdeen Daily Bulletin* ran a notice of Gohl's bankruptcy and advertised a meeting of his creditors in Tacoma later that month.[83]

Despite Gohl's bankruptcy, debtors continued to come calling. In April 1908, Sam Jacobson, a Norwegian-born saloon owner, sued William and Bessie for an unpaid loan the Gohls took out in October 1905, likely for the purposes of opening the Capital Rooming House.[84] The civil case filed by Jacobson against the Gohls contained considerable detail about the family's finances, detail showing persistent economic troubles for the couple. The Gohls contended that they could not pay the debts to Jacobson, citing William's recent bankruptcy as evidence. But unfortunately for them, the Grays Harbor Superior Court found that William, rather than the Gohl family ("a community" composed of William and Bessie), had been declared bankrupt. In May 1908 Judge Mason Irwin of the Chehalis County Superior Court found William and Bessie Gohl liable for the family's debts and ordered her to pay $220 to Jacobsen for the loan and an additional $19.50 in fees.[85]

Understandably, this decision angered Bessie, a businesswoman and taxpayer. In response, she petitioned the Chehalis County Superior Court to vacate the decision because William had taken the loan from Sam Jacobson "without the knowledge or consent of this defendant and in violation of her rights as a member of the said community and of her individual rights."[86] Represented by A. E. Cross, Bessie Gohl further charged that she "was never served with any manner of legal process in said cause whatsoever; that she never received a copy of the alleged summons or complaint in said cause," and that the court made an "irregular and void" judgment by ordering her to pay William's debts.[87]

Few things in the early twentieth-century American patriarchal society were fair or equitable toward women. Bessie Gohl, for example, was heavily taxed without representation, having no right to vote. She was subject to the jurisdiction of the courts, and forced to pay fines by those courts, but had no right to serve on juries. She owned and operated a business for several years but would have never been accepted into the region's business organizations, which were made for men by men and reserved for businessmen during her career in Aberdeen. The superior court's decision to hold her liable for William's debts was thus only the most recent of a string of insults and injuries to Bessie Gohl's independence and property.

Some of William Gohl's troubles were financial, but some stemmed from threats and violent actions during the 1906 strike. Gohl certainly used physical force and threats, wielding a pistol and raiding nonunion ships, fighting fire with fire in labor's struggle with capital. But direct action represented only one end of a wide range of tactics that Gohl, like many union activists, used in an attempt to improve working conditions. If anything, he preferred to deal with conflicts outside of the workplace in more societally acceptable ways, especially by involving the police.

Charges that Gohl was a violent brute were belied by ample evidence, as the union agent defused plenty of explosive situations by using compromise or the legal system. In August 1907 Gohl filed a complaint against soapbox orator Charles Buck for "using language fit to provoke an assault," a charge stemming from Buck's public harangues of Gohl, in which he dubbed Gohl "a thief, grafter, and labor faker." The *Aberdeen Herald* reported: "The old-time grudge between Wm. Gohl and Chas. M. Buck was aired again in the police court Tuesday, when the latter was sent to jail, to serve out a fine of $20 and costs for carrying a concealed weapon." Although "Mr. Gohl was strongly tempted to use physical force," noted the *Post*, "he wisely decided to place the matter where a peaceful solution of the case could be had."[88] After the sentence, Buck made sensational charges against Gohl and was again sent to jail, spending several days there. Dubbing Buck "a general nuisance," Aberdeen police chief Adam Schneider "invited" Buck to leave town, which he did, in October 1907.[89]

Similar dealings with the law followed over the next two years, as Gohl, a resident of the toughest neighborhood in the region, had a close relationship with some members of the police. Only a few months after Gohl's run-in with Buck, the union agent reported to police a disturbance made by a man named Henry Johnson, who had apparently drunk too much tanglefoot. A local prosecutor charged Johnson with disturbing the police, although the *Herald* noted the case was dismissed, with Johnson receiving nothing but "a lecture."[90] In March 1908, Gohl was the victim of a violent crime, when E. Donaldson assaulted him. Appearing in Aberdeen's justice court for assault and battery, Donaldson escaped punishment when Gohl refused to press charges.[91] In sum, William Gohl frequently found himself targeted, but, unlike in his dealings with employers or scabs, he appears to have preferred peaceful and law-abiding methods for seeking justice.

At times William seems to have been, if anything, overly reliant on the police and courts, turning to law enforcement for even the most trivial reasons. On the morning of January 8, 1910, Gohl intervened to stop a group of boys from sledding down Broadway Hill in front of his home. According to the *Aberdeen Herald*, Gohl "objected to the amusement, and scattered ashes on the walks. The boys removed the ashes and went on with their play, when Gohl nailed slats across the walks." Undaunted, the kids pulled off the slats and proceeded to play. In response, Gohl—described by the *Herald* as an "abused sailor"—called the police. As anyone who grew up on the Washington Coast knows, a day where enough snow sticks for it to be suitable for sledding is a rarity, a treat enjoyed only a few times in a person's youth. In this respect, Gohl seems to have been mean-spirited, a mixture of a stressed-out grump and a doddering fool hollering "Get off my lawn!" rather than a criminal mastermind.[92]

In 1906 Gohl even dealt nonviolently with E. B. Benn, future mayor and ringleader of a local citizens' committee, when Benn went on a very public smear campaign against Gohl for his opposition to the Montesano courthouse removal. Instead of assaulting Benn, Gohl preferred to write letters to the local newspapers engaging Benn in dialogue, contesting his accusations, and more importantly worked double-time to defeat Benn's political program.[93] That Gohl found himself provoked and attacked in public but did not lash back with violence reveals a good deal about his character.

As a labor leader and representative of the Sailors' Union in the Grays Harbor area, Gohl understood that the tactics he used during the 1906 maritime strike only went so far to advance his fellow unionists' interests. To protect seamen's safety and advance the cause of unionism, Gohl used the tools available in the political and legal systems. Although he had allies, including attorneys, Gohl took a good deal of this work upon himself, studying the law and engaging directly with police and elected officials. As the winter of 1906 stretched into the early months of 1907, his ability to use available legal resources would be tested as sailors and other workingmen were found dead, floating in the waters of Grays Harbor.

6

THE FLOATER FLEET

THE MAY 11, 1907, issue of the *Grays Harbor Post* carried a story that in the spring of 1907 was familiar news. Under the front-page headline "Two More Floaters," readers learned of J. B. Meers and Connie Lockett, whose bodies had been found floating in local rivers. Meers, a timber cruiser (a logging company employee who estimated the amount of standing timber), had disappeared in March while carrying an estimated $700 in wages owed to employees of the Continental Timber Company, but that money was not found on his person. Lockett, a sailor, was described by the *Post* as "a powerful young man," and he too had empty pockets when discovered floating in the bay. In Meers's case, a coroners' inquest was unable to determine the cause of death. A coroner's investigation into Lockett's death recorded that the deceased sailor had been found with no marks on his body indicating violence, and he was "supposed to have been accidentally drowned."[1]

In early 1907 the front pages of the local newspapers carried stories featuring headlines like "Another Body Found" and "The Floater Fleet." Perhaps feeling that its readers had grown tired of reading these grisly stories, the *Grays Harbor Post* dedicated a mere three sentences to "floater" John Anderson, whose "body had been in the water so long that the flesh had entirely disappeared from the skull."[2]

Harborites had plenty of experience with these front-page accounts of injury and violent deaths. For more than a decade they had read reports of saws lopping off workers' arms and trees falling and crushing loggers. Men died along the Grays Harbor waterfront due to a wide range of causes. Most common were so-called industrial accidents, the all-too-common deaths in the region's mills, camps, docks, ships, and other workplaces.[3] Speculation ran rampant that the "floaters" were evidence of murders committed by notorious saloon keepers who had then dumped the bodies into the water. In May 1907, coroner A. C. Girard, the man tasked with examining many of these dead bodies, proclaimed: "As long as Aberdeen allows the saloons and dives in which the worthless element carry on their nefarious practices, it may expect to find the bodies of murdered men at any time."[4] Notably, Gohl publicly condemned these sources of danger and sought to remedy those sources of violence.

A close look at the primary sources produced in Grays Harbor during the first decade of the twentieth century leads to several questions about the so-called Floater Fleet and about Gohl's supposed involvement in helping to launch it. First, do we have any indication that there were more suspicious or violent deaths than usual during Gohl's time on the harbor, especially from 1906 to 1909, when he is said to have committed his criminal deeds? Second, was there any sign that the men who died were murdered, or did their deaths come about by accidents resulting from their working and living conditions? Third, what involvement, if any, did Gohl have with these deaths? Fourth, given that Gohl strongly and repeatedly condemned the conditions that he viewed as responsible for creating the Floater Fleet, why did blame for the deaths end up on him?

In 1910, local and regional newspapers reminded readers about this spate of deaths and, without evidence, laid them at Gohl's doorstep. But at the time of the deaths, Gohl went unmentioned in the press as a suspect, although police arrested other "questionable characters" and forced them to leave town. Recall that some of Gohl's most pressing duties were patrolling the docks looking for missing workers, planning and paying for funeral expenses, and hawking deceased sailors' goods to send the proceeds to their families. As with other working-class port towns, residents of Aberdeen and Hoquiam (and visitors too) drowned with some frequency during the early twentieth century. Aberdeen and Hoquiam boasted many saloons, and its waterfronts were unlit and unguarded, making a treacherous trek for saloon patrons as they walked along the riversides.[5]

After a night out at the saloons, any number of dire fates could befall someone walking through the waterfront district. The paths from saloon to home for a seaman docked in Aberdeen contained several potentially deadly obstacles. Drunken brawls and shootings contributed their fair share of bodies to the Floater Fleet.[6]

Beatings and robberies were practically routine, with sailors frequently the victims. In September 1908 sailors Frank Hamburk and Peter Rood accused Peter Swanson, bartender at the Phoenix Saloon, of robbing them at the bar.[7] In February 1909, after a night of drinking at Aberdeen saloons, sailor Lars Jorgensen was beaten by unknown assailants and left "unconscious and . . . in a position to have been fatally injured, killed instantly, or maimed for life had a train passed over the track before he was found." Jorgensen survived the assault and made his way to the Sailors' Union office, where he worked with Gohl, to report the assault to police. But police weren't always friendly. A police officer named Lesnick brutalized sailor J. McGoldrict when the seaman arrived in town intoxicated. Arresting the sailor for public drunkenness, the cop tried to march McGoldrict to jail. When the sailor stopped and refused to march any farther, the cop beat McGoldrict so brutally with a billy club that "blood flowed freely" from the man's face. "There are blood clots on the roadway today," noted the *Aberdeen World*.[8] After an evening of drinking in August 1907, a Norwegian-born sailor named Nilson passed out on the trolley tracks in Cosmopolis. As a result, a trolley rolled over him, tearing off a leg and his scalp.[9]

Swimmers, fishers, and young children likewise drowned in the region's waterways. In November 1908, authorities discovered the boat of a young man named Ray Burke, turned bottom-up in the water, leading authorities to conclude: "probable drowning."[10] Each winter, as itinerant workers swelled the population of the Harbor towns, the number of floaters increased. The January 25, 1908, issue of the *Grays Harbor Post* described the drownings of two men.[11] A pile-driving crew laboring at the C. E. Burrows mill in Aberdeen discovered the body of Finnish-American fisherman and SUP member Matt Simi, which had been in the water for five weeks.[12] In August 1908, union sailor G. A. Backman drowned in the river near the West and Slade docks as he returned to his ship from a night on the town drinking. As his position commanded, Gohl took control of the funeral, and Reverend Charles McDermoth of Aberdeen officiated the event.[13]

Most commonly, workers fell into the water after a night of drinking in one of Aberdeen's nearly forty saloons. Victims had few sympathizers in the press, as newsmen appeared to have delighted in mocking at least those who survived. The *Aberdeen Herald* commented, "[Andrew Devine] tried to drown himself in the Chehalis river Tuesday, and was rescued by Councilman Stalding. He was given ten days in jail, to give him a chance to sober up."[14] Grays Harbor's other towns presented similar difficulties. In early June 1907, a drunk sailor fell overboard from a schooner docked in Hoquiam. According to a press account, he "was too intoxicated to seize the sling that was thrown to him."[15]

Clearly, the harbor's waterfront was unsafe. Built on the Chehalis, Wishkah, and Hoquiam Rivers, the harbor towns developed haphazardly, with residents' safety considered as an afterthought. In its early history, Aberdeen had plank streets and boardwalks. People in other cities had long understood the hazards of plank streets. Historian Matthew Morse Booker wrote of nineteenth-century San Francisco's streets : "Numerous persons drowned after falling through the city's unfinished and treacherous plank streets and wharves. An unsuspecting walker might suddenly find the sidewalk giving way, or a sailor weaving drunken back to his ship would slip and plummet to his death through a gap in the planking."[16] Aberdeen's streets were no better than those in San Francisco. In a January 1904 accident, three elite Aberdeen residents broke through the sidewalk and fell into the "muck" below, with one woman receiving serious injuries. The *Aberdeen Daily Bulletin* opined: "The sidewalks in Aberdeen are in an extremely dangerous condition and many accidents would result were it not for the fact that people are always expecting to be turned down and are more cautious than people are expected to be in well regulated cities."[17]

Thus, by 1907, both grisly industrial deaths and floaters were well known by Grays Harbor residents, but their increase during the early part of that year put the region on high alert. According to one estimate, between January 15 and March 31, 1907, ten bodies emerged in local rivers, roughly one per week.[18] Again, such deaths were already familiar, so common that by June 1906 locals read of a quasi-scientific formula to determine when the drowned bodies would resurface: "It is not expected that the body of Surveyman Scheive . . . will be recovered at least until the nine-day limit, after which bodies generally come to the surface."[19] The death toll grew, and in August 1907, the GHTLC passed a resolution granting its secretary the power to purchase flowers without union approval, recognizing that they could not meet regularly enough to allocate funds to send flowers for deceased workers' graves.[20]

Many of the 1907 floaters were bodies of sailors.[21] Frequently, the dead had no money on their person, and while it has never been unusual to find a working person without money, the press and police alike considered this the best evidence of foul play.[22] Local police proceeded cautiously, but in early May that year they carried out a "clean-up," which forced "questionable characters" from town.[23]

Two archival collections—the Record of Deaths for the City of Aberdeen and the Chehalis (Grays Harbor) County coroner's record—provide the most detailed information about the Floater Fleet. The date range of the Aberdeen Record of Deaths is August 1, 1890, to July 18, 1907, and the records contain significant information about each person who died in Aberdeen during that period, including name, age, occupation, and cause of death. Unsurprisingly, given that the city's population was quite small until after the turn of the century, the city experienced few deaths during the 1890s.

Beginning in 1900, the annual death rate increased each year. More relevant here, the number of drownings also increased beginning in 1900. The US Census only records population every ten years, so for Aberdeen's major decade of population growth, 1900–1910, when the city grew from 3,747 to 13,660 inhabitants, we don't know its annual population. But, if we average out the 9,913 growth in population over the ten years, we get a rough estimate of the city's population each year between 1900 and 1907. Although writers didn't start using the term "Floater Fleet" until late in the decade, between January 1, 1900, and July 18, 1907, fifty people are said to have died by drowning in Aberdeen. The annual number varied:

YEAR	NUMBER OF DEATHS BY DROWNING
1900	5
1901	0
1902	7
1903	4
1904	7
1905	5
1906	13
1907	9

Adjusting for population increase, the highest rates of drowning in Aberdeen took place in January–July 18, 1907, followed closely by the rate of drowning in 1906 and 1900 when the rates were virtually identical. Thus, while there was an unfortunate spate of drowning deaths in 1906 and 1907, adjusted for population, those years had only slightly more such deaths per capita than in 1900, long before Gohl settled on the harbor.

Perhaps of greater importance, the Aberdeen death record lists only a handful of homicides between 1903 and 1907. Although the record does not separate murders from other types of death, it includes few deaths said to have been caused by gunshot or otherwise at the hands of another. In 1906 Aberdeen experienced three deaths from gunshot wounds, including the case of union longshoreman Alexander Wahlgren, who was shot to death by a scab during that year's maritime strike. Other than mourning Wahlgren's death and attending his funeral, Gohl had nothing to do with any of these murders.[24]

Writers about Gohl have been principally interested in the years 1906 and 1907. In the latter year, according to one account, "forty-three men were found floating in Grays Harbor," between February and September, and "fourteen bodies were pulled out of the harbor" in "one month alone."[25] These figures are wildly incorrect. Fortunately, the Chehalis County Coroner's Record provides a detailed examination of deceased persons throughout the early twentieth century. The county tasked its coroners, Horace Campbell and A. C. Girard, with determining causes of death. In especially difficult cases, coroners called inquests, investigations aided by a jury called to assist with identifying the bodies and determining causes of death.

From January 1, 1906, to December 31, 1908, the coroner's office conducted investigations for 145 deaths.[26] The number of investigations increased each year over the period: 31 in 1906, 54 in 1907, and 60 in 1908. More important than the numbers of investigations, however, are coroners' findings. In reading the coroner's record, the overwhelming impression one has is that the harbor's logging camps and docks were terribly dangerous places, ones where "accidental" drownings took place and deaths occurred due to workers being "accidentally hit" by a falling tree. Campbell and Girard determined that most deaths they investigated were accidental, as intoxicated men had drowned after slipping and falling into a waterway or perished from industrial accidents.

The year 1907 has long proved to be key for Gohl mythologists, who view it as an especially dark period in local history. Examination of the coroner's fifty-four investigations that year sheds light on the sources of the Floater Fleet. In 1907 the coroner determined that twelve deaths—22 percent of the cases—were the result of "accidental drowning." On at least one occasion, Gohl aided coroner Girard during an inquest for a drowning victim. After J. Edward Jacobbsen fell from the schooner *J. M. Weatherwax* and drowned, his body did not surface until four months later, in June 1907. By then the body was "badly decomposed," but Gohl, familiar with itinerant seamen, was able to identify it.[27]

An even larger share of the investigated deaths in 1908 were said to be accidental drownings. Girard determined that eighteen out of sixty—30 percent—were in this category. For example, in January, Adel Lileng fell off the Northern Pacific Bridge into the Wishkah River and drowned. On August 25, 1908, according to Girard, one intoxicated man fell into the Wishkah and drowned. Two months later, a man "accidentally drowned" at Copalis, a small coastal community northwest of Aberdeen, while duck hunting. On Christmas night that same year, Girard determined that sailor Barney Dougherty had come to his death after drunkenly stumbling while trying to board a steam vessel.

During 1906–8, Chehalis County's two coroners rarely called juries to help with the inquests. Of the 145 deaths investigated by their office, Coroners Campbell and Girard deemed only 5 worth an inquest.[28] Moreover, although the coroners' office investigated dozens of drowning deaths in that period, it conducted only one inquest in the case of a drowning victim. In fact, the two coroners provided ready explanations for the overwhelming majority of drownings on the Harbor.

Although the county coroners rarely determined (or even speculated) that any of the city's drownings resulted from murder, at least one body in the Floater Fleet was a murder victim, although there is no reason to believe the killer was Gohl. In June 1907 Girard and a local physician determined that Gabrielle Auested, whose body had been found floating in the Wishkah River, had died before entering the river. Authorities learned that on the last night Auested was seen, he had been in a bar fight prior to his disappearance.[29] Grays Harbor area saloons played leading parts in this murder investigation and in the cases of most of the other Floater Fleet victims. Coroner Girard was not subtle in his reports, frequently declaring the cause of deaths to be "excessive use of alcohol." This was Girard's determination when, in September 1908, a man died after jumping from a window of the Hoquiam hospital.

Authorities did classify some local deaths at the time as murder. In October 1907 Edward Gardner shot and killed his wife, Annie, before turning the gun on himself, and in November police arrested Ralph Steele for the murder of Frank Todd, who had been beaten over the head with a blunt instrument. Placed in the Chehalis County jail, Steele also committed suicide, hanging himself.[30] Notably, as in other clear murder cases of this type, authorities did not arrest Gohl or question him as a suspect.[31]

Gohl was not charged with any murders during 1906–8. There is good reason for that: public officials didn't state that the Floater Fleet deaths resulted from murder. The coroners' office records provide the best evidence that local authorities did not believe the region was experiencing a violent crime wave or served as the home of a serial killer. Untimely deaths took place on the harbor during these years, but the cause was societal, a vicious system of industrial capitalism that killed workers on the job with unsafe working conditions and even in the streets. It was the same society, after all, that furnished laborers with booze to escape the realities of their brutal lives and did nothing to safeguard the city's red-light district from kidnappers and thieves or ensure safe boardwalks. If there was a Ghoul of Grays Harbor, then he wore a top hat and frequented the halls of the chamber of commerce and state legislature.

Although public officials and journalists did little to prevent most of the real causes of the Floater Fleet, some of them joined other Aberdeen residents in curbing what they saw as one of the main causes of drownings in the region: drunkenness. City officials' preferred method for regulating alcohol consumption was to arrest and jail people for public drunkenness. Police and sheriffs routinely arrested and jailed persons on "drunk" charges and housed dozens of men in city and county jails for this. Not surprisingly, police and courts used laws against public intoxication as a cudgel to punish the poor. In 1906 the *Grays Harbor Washingtonian*, published in Hoquiam, criticized Aberdeen's police and courts for using the law to attack workingmen and -women:

> The city of Aberdeen, under its present police court justice, is building up a dangerous and reprehensible policy with regard to its petty offenders.... For the month of March the collections for fines under the new justice, who came in with this year's administration, amounted to nearly, if not quite, $1,400. The fees of the justice were nearly $300. These fines came largely, if not entirely, from drunks and the women who reside in what is commonly known as the "red-light" district. Now, most of the men arrested for being drunk are working men. One rarely hears of a business man being arrested in Aberdeen, no matter how drunk he should be. These working men or "lumber jacks" and the women of the tenderloin paid very large penalties, it is said by the justice not only to help the city, but also to increase his own fees.[32]

The efforts by the *Washingtonian* to explain the class-based nature of Aberdeen's policing stood in sharp contrast to most local reporting, which mocked the hardships experienced by poor people. In side-by-side front-page articles, the *Daily Bulletin* condemned the "vagrants who want work but are afraid they will be offered some" and the "bad men in the county jail" who showed that "Aberdeen is fully represented in the category of evil doers." "The usual grist of drunks and vags were before Judge Bush to receive judgment for their sins," continued the *Daily Bulletin*. And indeed, the treatment afforded poor people by the harbor's legal system was quite usual, as authorities prosecuted scores of "vags" each year.[33]

A more systematic critique of saloons and the liquor trade existed in the United States decades before the Floater Fleet appeared on the harbor. In the late nineteenth and early twentieth centuries, a massive, well-organized, and well-funded temperance movement spread across the country. Long before the imposition of Washington State and federal prohibition measures in 1916 and 1920 respectively, temperance activists encouraged individuals to abstain from drink and advocated for local, state, and federal laws curbing alcohol consumption.[34] Debates around prohibition stretch back well before Washington's statehood in 1889, with organizations such as the Women's Christian Temperance Union and Anti-Saloon League (ASL) advocating such limitations.[35] During the 1890s, the Anti-Saloon League grew to become a leading temperance organization. Washington members founded a state branch in 1898, which by 1909 received pledges of support from a majority of state legislators. As its name indicated, the ASL marked the saloon rather than liquor as the enemy. The league's position reflected that the "national temper was increasingly antisaloon but not yet antidrink," in the words of historian Norman Clark.[36]

In the years leading up to the enactment of prohibition in Washington in 1914 (it took effect in 1916), the state passed a host of saloon regulations. In the years around 1910, temperance activists, newspapers, and lawmakers all spent much time debating questions of liquor.[37] On the harbor, some politicians distinguished themselves for their support for temperance and struggle to control the most notorious "dives" in Aberdeen. Aberdeen mayor Eugene France (elected in December 1906) oversaw a reform administration that worked to regulate saloons, brothels, and gambling houses. In 1908, the City of Aberdeen closed the city's dance halls. France oversaw a "general cleaning up in the city along moral lines," which, in this instance, meant imposing new regulations on women's lives. Toward that end, in June 1908, the Aberdeen City Council voted unanimously to ban women from saloons. The city ordinance mandated a fine of $50 or revocation of the saloon keeper's license for violating the ordinance. France's municipal administration even earned praise from the temperance advocates in the Anti-Saloon League. In March 1908, an Anti-Saloon League periodical praised France for enforcing the Sunday closing law. It also threatened the future of saloon men: "For violating the Sunday closing law, Aberdeen saloon men are commencing to feel the lash of the law. Fighting stubbornly every step of reform progress, the saloons at last are being driven into the corner which has been so dreaded and it is but a matter of time until Aberdeen, along with Hoquiam, will be held in the control of the moral forces."[38]

The council also reduced the number of saloons allowed to operate. In September 1908 the city council limited the number of saloons in the city to forty, with council members John O'Hare and Ed Dolan, both saloon owners, voting in favor.[39] Support for reducing the number of these establishments was self-serving for saloon men like O'Hare and Dolan. But the policy also provided authorities with the ability to let the "good" businesses to remain open, while closing the "dives" that had developed reputations for violence and criminal mischief. John Kahle, a onetime owner of the Pioneer Saloon in Aberdeen, argued the need for further regulation and reduction in the number of saloons. He contended that Grays Harbor saloons offered thousands of loggers "some place to go when [they come] to town" but also stated that there were too many of these businesses in operation.[40] Kahle's reasoning was revealing. He argued that some area bartenders and saloon proprietors used knockout drops to drug saloon patrons, with the intention of robbing and killing their victims. These accusations, made by a former saloon owner in a good position to know about these matters, elicited horror from some harbor residents. The *Elma Chronicle*, for one, demanded that a grand jury be called to investigate whether saloon owners were indeed responsible for drugging, robbing, and killing men on the harbor and thus to blame for "so many floaters being found in the bay."[41]

Gohl, who for several years lived near Kahle's saloon, shared many of Kahle's concerns. Those who only think they are acquainted with Gohl's biography will be surprised to discover that he was perhaps the most public opponent of dives, "knockout drops," and fall-traps. In fact, he used the pages of local newspapers to condemn saloon keepers for drugging and robbing men. The union agent had lived in the heart of the saloon district long enough to be unsurprised by *any* violence against workers. Stopping violence against sailors remained central to Gohl's life throughout his time on the harbor, but the historical record clearly establishes that William strengthened his resolve to protect workers' safety in the years after the 1906 maritime strike.

It is a damning oversight that previous Gohl writers have ignored this important part of William's life, intentionally or not.

After burying Johan Johnson in June 1907, one of several Sailors' Union members to perish in the first half of that year, Gohl chastised city authorities for the lack of streetlights along the wharves in Hoquiam.[42] Angered at the lack of progress on the issue, at a 1909 Aberdeen City Council meeting Gohl made an "eloquent plea for the lives of seamen," arguing that some of the dozens of sailors lost in the waters of Grays Harbor could have been saved had the many wharves and docks been lit. Gohl's proposed to have lights installed on the docks and wharves and approaches to the vessels and "also that vessels be required to keep lights at their gang ways." In support of this proposal, Gohl said, according to the *Grays Harbor Post*, that "thirty-nine" seamen "had been drowned at the docks and wharves in Aberdeen and Hoquiam in the past five years, and of this number eighteen had gone into the Wishkah."[43] The editors of the *Post* agreed with Gohl, writing: "The sailors union is right in asking for lights on the wharves and docks. Life is more sacred than the cost of lights and the council committee in charge of the matter will doubtless so decide." Despite Gohl's persistent agitation on his fellow workers' behalf, the dives, dark streets, and floaters persisted. That the police shortly thereafter turned their attention toward the agitator rather than the problem should give us a good idea of the political motivations of those controlling the police agenda.[44]

In late 1908 and early 1909, another rash of workers turned up as floaters. In a February 1909 letter to the *Aberdeen Daily World*, Gohl asked if there was a relationship between the "dives," their "falltraps," and his many fallen friends: "Are they [traps] there for the purpose of giving the janitor a chance to get rid of the refuse? Are they there in order to evade the officers on Sundays so that booze may be lowered into a skiff through the trap? Or are they there to accommodate some poor sailor or logger by giving him a free ride along the Wishkah?"[45] Certainly he had seen far too many of his comrades drink themselves to death or drunkenly fall victim to violent predators for Gohl to vigorously support the saloon interests. But it is also worth noting that

Gohl's accusations echo those of Kahle, a man who, like Gohl, spent a life in position to observe the difficulties experienced by working-men along Aberdeen's waterfront.

Gohl also came out publicly in his attacks on some individual local saloon keepers. Never a teetotaler, William had spent a good deal of time in saloons during his early years on the Harbor, leading one sailor to write: "I remember the time when you yourself were a constant visitor at various periods to those same dives."[46] But Gohl drew a line. Writing to the *Aberdeen World*, the Sailors' Union agent drew upon his years on the waterfront: "My experience on F street has been of a sort that certainly was sufficient to convince me that there are good and bad saloons. The fact remains that we will not lose anything should the 'dive' be killed and with it the parasites that fosters within. Everything in our power will surely be done to help bring about the extermination of the 'falltrap' and the 'dive.'"[47] In a letter to the editor of the same paper a week earlier, Gohl wrote: "Wonder if those saloon keepers who induced [an alcoholic] to spend his hard earned money for their rotten stuff will attend his funeral and say: 'There is another victim?' No, sir, there will be no one of that brigade there because, forsooth, they are ashamed to acknowledge that the poison administered by them has brought the man to his early doom."[48]

In Gohl's commentary in local newspapers on the harbor's dives and their keepers, shipowners, and the sailor's life at sea, he argued that the rough working-class culture of the waterfront district made Aberdeen an unappealing place for seamen to settle. In a long opinion piece for the *Aberdeen World*, Gohl wrote: "How many sailors are settling down in Aberdeen in our days? But very few, I believe. There are some, but these are exceptions, and the ones who do not indulge to the extent that they have become slaves to liquor." Adopting a paternalistic view, Gohl commented: "How many sailors are voting? But few, also, because booze prevents them from thinking clearly so that they may understand that [their] ballot should be cast at every election."[49] Gohl's life course took him from itinerant seaman, living the roughest forms of masculinity, to the life of a white-collar sailor ashore. He publicly mourned that Grays Harbor's living conditions made that transition unappealing and difficult for his fellow unionists.

Gohl was also a strong advocate of the "local option" and hoped "that each and every one of the working men of this community will put forth their very best efforts in promulgating the movement for 'local option.'"[50] "Local option" was the central legislative plank of Washington's temperance movement and its most important legislative achievement prior to the 1914 passage of the state's prohibition law. Passed in 1909, the Local Option Law allowed municipal and county governments to hold elections so voters could decide whether to allow liquor consumption locally.[51]

Gohl's fight for the local option, and perhaps even support for the temperance movement, had complex roots. A working-class alcoholic, argued Gohl, was a bad unionist who wasted what little money he had on booze, failed to pay his union dues, and was often penniless, with little more than "bottles to console him in his last hours."[52] Some labor leaders agreed with AFL president Samuel Gompers, who asserted: "The time has come when the saloon and the labor movement must be divorced."[53] But temperance never represented more than a minority position within the American labor movement. Thousands of union members labored in jobs that produced, transported, and served alcoholic beverages. An even larger number of unionists found comfort in the saloon and deeply resented reformers—ranging from middle-class teetotalers to paternalistic union leaders and bosses worried about the lost productivity of drunken workers—telling them how to live their lives.[54]

The conflict over labor and the saloon affected Gohl's personal life and his relationship to other Sailors' Union members. During his career as union agent, he had consumed alcohol and smoked cigars, two habits he shared with much of the nation's working class. In 1908 a physician recorded that Gohl imbibed "one or two drinks" per day.[55] But the union agent never descended into alcoholism. Given the responsibilities of his job, alcohol addiction would have been wildly out of line and in violation of his union rules. Gohl was an advocate for restraint when it came to the bottle, and upon his arrest in 1910 would make this clear, stating that in 1909 he had ceased consuming liquor and within a year had even dropped beer: "Of late only 'Puritas' water has been my beverage."[56]

When Gohl attacked saloon owners as "divekeepers" who had "beaten" sailors out of their wages and kicked them off the wharf, he made enemies among this powerful group.[57] In 1910 there were fifty-three saloons in Aberdeen and Hoquiam. That year two saloon keepers held positions on the Aberdeen City Council, and saloon men turned out in droves to vote. In 1909, at least thirty-six saloon owners and bartenders registered to vote in Aberdeen, making it one of the largest occupational groups to participate in that city's franchise.[58]

Gohl and his wife were close to several of the harbor's most prominent saloon men. Until early 1909 they lived in the Capital Rooming House, sharing space with boarders such as saloon owner Fred Hewett and bartender Stewart Barber.[59] Moreover, at times Gohl turned to prominent saloon owners when he was in desperate financial straits. In August 1906, saloon owner and soon-to-be Aberdeen city councilman Ed Dolan acted as one of the sureties for Gohl's $500 bail during the union agent's trial for unlawfully and wrongfully organizing and maintaining an armed body of men. Dolan's act of support allowed Gohl to remain free and carry out his union duties during the maritime strike and subsequent formation of the Grays Harbor Waterfront Federation.[60] In 1908 Aberdeen city councilman and saloon man John O'Hare sponsored Gohl's application to join the Fraternal Order of Eagles. Gohl was also a longtime acquaintance of John Gronow, founder of the Aberdeen local of the Sailors' Union, owner of the Union Saloon, and longtime officer in the Aberdeen Eagles.[61] O'Hare and Gronow likely held sway, as the Eagles accepted Gohl's application, making him a member of the region's largest fraternal order.[62]

Gohl's attacks on "dives" and advocacy for the local option aggravated long-standing tensions between him and some of his neighbors in the restricted district. But in his critiques of saloon owners and the workingmen who visited saloons, Gohl struck a nerve in many of his union comrades. In a long letter to the *Aberdeen World*, six

Sailors' Union members took the union agent to task for a patroniz-
ing letter published just one day earlier. Echoing the prevalent views
expressed by societal elites, Gohl's letter suggested that many seamen suffered from alcoholism and said that their habits with the
bottle prevented them from acting as good union members and citizens. In a justifiably angry response, the sailors, writing as one, said:
"I would kindly ask you to permit me to answer that article by Mr.
Gohl. I am not a friend of any saloonkeeper, which I can prove, yet I
believe in a fair and square deal, to tell the truth, and shame the devil.
And if I want a drink, I go and have it. I do not care who sees it." The
letter continued: "Of course, I am willing to agree to the gentleman
when he says that a clear brain is necessary to know the law, but
allow me to say this, too, that some of our best lawyers in this country
do not know the law."[63]

In early 1909 Gohl and saloon owner Sigvald Jacobson had a major
falling out. Jacobson had a letter published in the *Aberdeen World*
that Gohl considered to be an attack.[64] Gohl wrote to the paper in
response, saying that "in compliance with requests of [his] friends"
he needed to respond publicly to Jacobson's attack: "At first, I believed
it would be useless to answer the expressions of a man who would
sign his name to most any old thing as long as such would further
the interest of his damnable business." Gohl went on to blame Jacobson for Sailors' Unionist Matt Simi's death: "The circumstances surrounding the drowning leave little doubt but that bad socza [liquor]
of the kind distributed by Sig. Jacobson and his cohorts and given
since for a Christmas present, was responsible for this man's end."
"Verily, it is true," continued Gohl, "that the dead sometimes will rise
even out of their watery graves in order to attest the damnable methods used by these human sharks in order to get rich quick. Matt Simi
had in his possession two bottles full of that rotten stuff that sent him
to his early grave."[65]

Gohl also reported on illegal activities in the saloons. He even
allowed local police to use the Capital Rooming House to surveil
alleged cattle thieves and saloon law violators.[66] Specifically, William
and Bessie allowed police to use the rooming house to investigate

violations at the Club, Sigvald Jacobson's saloon.[67] After using the views provided by the Capital's location, they brought charges against Jacobson for violating the Sunday closing law. After two hung juries in the Aberdeen Police Court, a third trial resulted in Jacobson's conviction, resulting in a $50 fine and costs.[68] In a February 1910 interview from his jail cell at Montesano, Gohl reminded all those who cared to hear that he "was the first man to go to the police and county officials to tell them of crimes committed and the possible doing away of some person."[69]

Gohl's actions make it clear that he saw himself as a patriarch providing guidance and protection to those lacking the privileges of a settled life. As the local representative of the Sailors' Union, Gohl had responsibility for the preservation and safety of union records, the union hall, and other union property. Given the propensity for fires to break out in Aberdeen's waterfront district, guarding union property was a major concern, one that Gohl clearly took seriously. In 1906, when an earthquake and fire ripped apart San Francisco, Gohl received word from Paul Scharrenberg from SUP headquarters that the fire had "badly damaged" Sailors' Union headquarters. "[The headquarters] will be useless for business transactions," Scharrenberg said.[70] From 1903, when he took over as union agent, until his February 1910 arrest, Gohl remained worried about the Aberdeen hall's location. Twice Gohl moved the SUP office because of his concern about building safety.[71]

Gohl also understood that some of his comrades at sea worked for ship captains who viciously beat, locked up, and even shot sailors. In March 1908, captain Tom Stream of the schooner *G. W. Watson* shot sailor Albert Hellig because, according to Stream, Hellig had shown "insolence" toward the him. The son of a captain and himself a co-owner of a ship, Stream was a wealthy young man and doubtlessly resented Hellig's uppity attitude. The two men came to blows, after which Stream shot Hellig. Placed on trial for assault with the intent to kill, Stream got off when a jury declared him not guilty after deliberating for only twenty-four minutes.[72] In an obscene illustration of its sycophancy toward those in power, the *Aberdeen Herald* gushed about the captain, writing a front-page biographical article praising the "bright young commander" and detailing his "thrilling experiences although he is not much over 25 years of age."[73]

Two years earlier, in early 1906, the full range of shipboard horrors experienced by sailors (including union members) at the hands of masters and mates came to public attention when the barkentine *Kolhala* arrived in Aberdeen. Captain Dedrick made headlines then after seamen complained about his cruel treatment on their voyage to Grays Harbor from Central America. When union sailors had refused to perform labor not covered by their contract, Dedrick had locked the seamen in the hold, placed them in irons, and refused them food and sufficient water. Worse, Dedrick hung one of the sailors over the side of the ship, pulling the man back onboard before he died. The *Aberdeen Daily Bulletin* compared Dedrick's acts to "the days of the Black Flag, and the imperious tyrannical rule of Captain Kidd and other pirate captains." The sailors reported Dedrick's cruelty to federal authorities, and the captain was arrested on April 14 for his alleged criminal acts. Dedrick was tried in federal court, but the court dismissed the charges of cruelty and inhumane treatment once they determined that the crew had mutinied.[74] Like Stream's, Dedrick's violent behavior was not illegal, in part because his class gave him privileges, including access to quality defense counsel, a jury drawn from his peers, and a judge hailing from his own social class.

This *Kohala* decision infuriated Gohl and his fellow sailors. The fact that an abusive master would not be punished for his acts of violence against workers at sea was simply too much for the unionists to stomach. In the weeks after the ship's arrival in Aberdeen and the publicity Dedrick's cruelty received, the Sailors' Union placed a boycott on the *Kohala*. Union sailors refused to work the ship, and Gohl refused to even set foot on the vessel. In a letter to the *Daily Bulletin*, Gohl harked back to the dark history of seamen's servitude to explain why unionists refused to serve on his ship:

> The reputation of Captain Dedrick is bad, so bad that men who [know] him will avoid his vessel, with the natural result that but very seldom a union crew leaves port in the *Kohala*. Sailors in our

day refuse to be sold with body and soul, and the sailors of this port especially have no desire to make any further acquaintance with Captain Dedrick. The sooner the *Kohala* leaves this port the better we will like her; her appearance in this port has marred our peaceable course, and we hope that we will never have occasion again to meet her.[75]

Gohl called on law enforcement officials to investigate abusive, law-breaking, or careless ship masters. As with the *Kohala*, he reported to the federal government other cases of captains' abuses. On March 31, 1909, the *Charles. E. Falk* wrecked on the beach near Copalis, causing a total loss of the ship's cargo. The ship had no insurance, making it difficult to pay off the crew after the wreck. Gohl found the circumstances of the wreck "peculiar" and contacted the US Justice Department to investigate. In his typical plodding, thorough manner, Gohl first collected statements from the ship's crew. They testified that the mate had refused to leave his quarters even after a seaman reported that the ship had hit rocks. After the wreck, the captain had refused to pay for lodgings, instead marching the cold, wet crew to an old barn where they stayed.[76]

Gohl's dogged pursuit of lawbreakers, paired with his support for workers' rights, infuriated some local elites. Many captains were deeply arrogant and authoritarian men who demanded to be called "Captain" or "Master" and who resented assertive unionists. Assessing Gohl's union leadership skills, "Captain" Hugh M. Delanty, longtime boss of the Grays Harbor Stevedore Company, one of the most notorious scab-herding agencies in the region, wrote that Gohl "tried to rule the local waterfront with an iron hand. Especially did he delight in trying to make the masters of the sailing vessels eat out of his hand, the latter naturally resenting his very offensive and overbearing manner."[77] Indeed, after several years on the harbor, Gohl developed a reputation for being "difficult" toward ship masters, especially those who refused to obey the law. It would be difficult to fault Gohl for hating shippers and captains, men who tried to break his union, abused sailors aboard ship, and benefited from shanghaiing Gohl's fellow seamen.

Employers saw Gohl's efforts to protect workers' rights as being bad for business. In November 1909, shipping agents W. R. Grace and Company ceased its business on Grays Harbor after Gohl refused to secure union sailors for the schooner *Wilbur Smith* because of its owners' violations of the union contract. Grace's Seattle agent stated that Gohl's attitude made it difficult to do business on the harbor.[78]

Gohl's militancy had long outraged harbor employers and their allies in the press and local government. But his threats remained confined to the lumber mills and docks, spatially distant from the large hillside homes occupied by those opposite Gohl on the class divide. All that changed in early 1909. After several years living among the noise, crime, and violence of Aberdeen's waterfront, the Gohls moved from the Capital Rooming House to the Broadway Hill neighborhood. It's difficult to know for how long Bessie and William had planned the move, but William's bankruptcy alleviated the family of most of its of crippling debt. In January 1909 the family sold the Capital Rooming House to James Mulikah, a tugboat engineer. A notice of sale appearing in one Aberdeen newspaper noted that William sold the property, which was Bessie's, because he was "preparing to leave for an extended visit in Germany."[79]

The Gohls relocated to a neighborhood filled with single-family homes owned and rented, primarily, by employers, middle-class families, and unionized laborers.[80] Like in many Pacific Coast cities, as Aberdeen grew in population, builders constructed new homes on the hillsides rising from the riversides and waterfront development that comprised the oldest parts of the towns. In Aberdeen and Hoquiam, as in so many places, elevation closely followed socioeconomic status, with wealthier individuals and families residing on the hills, de facto class segregation. By 1906, Aberdeen's Broadway Hill sported magnificent luxury homes, including the "magnificent mansion" of mill owner Charles R. Wilson's family.[81] Journalist and amateur historian

Ed Van Syckle captured this segregation when he recalled that those who lived on the hill referred to Aberdeen's saloon district as Down There.[82]

This move marked a major change in the Gohls' lives, a shift from the poverty and brutality of Grays Harbor's roughest neighborhood. Still, they were hardly middle class, and to supplement the skimpy earnings that had led William to bankruptcy only months earlier he and Bessie took in a series of boarders, including sailor Charles Hadberg and members of the Gohls' extended family. Moving up the hill took the Gohls into a different social sphere, one where they were not welcome. For years prior, employers and newspaper editors had done battle with Gohl on the harbor's picket lines and publicly made snide comments about his life. "Billy Gohl" represented something malicious in the eyes of many elites. He showed up at city council meetings to demand better protections for sailors, wrote long letters to newspapers to expose wrongful practices of ship captains and lumbermen, and hindered commerce when employers failed to abide by law or contract. But he had always confined that activity to the harbor's restricted district, a place full of saloons and mills and bawdy houses. With his 1909 move uphill, Gohl had invaded the sacred space of "better" classes. It is possible that he did not grasp the strength of the barriers American elites placed in front of working people who tried to achieve social change or upward mobility. But Bessie, who had spent much of her life dealing with poverty, recognized the spite of elites when she saw it. A little over a year after the Gohls moved to Broadway Hill, her husband would reside in a prison cell. Bessie did not mince words, proclaiming the case against William to be "[an effort] to get rid of us on Broadway Hill."[83]

7

SOLIDARITY REPRISE

ON SEPTEMBER 24, 1904, members of the Aberdeen branch of the Benevolent and Protective Order of Elks (BPOE or Elks) celebrated the completion of their new hall. Dubbed "one of the finest in the country" and "admired by all visitors," by the *Daily Bulletin,* the home of the Elks exuded wealth and prestige. Secluded within their $22,500 clubhouse, members could partake in poker or billiards, play cards, eat a fine meal, or walk along the velvet red carpets to retire to the steam baths. The interior was all "finished in weathered oak," and furniture was "made to order by Carpen of Chicago."[1] Founded in 1900 and 1907 respectively, the Aberdeen and Hoquiam Elks included as members most of the major lumbermen and boss loggers of the two cities.[2] The list of Aberdeen's founding Elks provides a veritable who's who of Grays Harbor social life. The conservative *Aberdeen Daily Bulletin* boasted that the Elks comprised "the most prominent commercial and professional men in this section of the state" and said the lodge "enjoyed remarkable freedom from undesirable characters."[3]

The article heralding completion of the Elks hall carried the headline "The Best People on Earth."[4] A play on the Elks' initials—BPOE—the fraternal order's use of the nickname Best People on Earth also spoke to its members' belief that they, as wealthy employers, deserved special recognition for their achievements. The Elks hall was an important structure, the center of employer culture and antilabor planning on the harbor.[5] Because of the harbor's importance as a lumber center, Aberdeen and Hoquiam manufacturers were thrust into prominence in the club, which enabled locals to host meetings, participate in rituals, and forge business relationships with men near and far.[6] But the clubs also served as expressions of employer class unity, places where businessmen could come together and complain about employees, and, as often as not, they found they shared the same complaints. Given this context, there can be little doubt that William Gohl, the region's most important union activist, was sometimes a topic of discussion for these "best people."

Seven years later the Elks would again make headlines, and this time it would be national news. In November 1911 Aberdeen businessmen would meet at the Elks hall to form a citizens' committee, an employers' vigilante group to do battle with local members of Industrial Workers of the World (IWW or Wobblies). The IWW was (and is) both an industrial union and revolutionary organization with members across the globe, and it grew dramatically in Aberdeen during the summer and fall of 1911. Five hundred men, "numbering among them the most prominent business and professional men in the city," attended the November 1911 Elks meeting. They adopted several resolutions, one of which pledged "service until such a time as the invading force of Workers shall be quelled or run out of town."[7]

Efforts by Wobblies to establish a stronghold on the Harbor would trigger a six-month-long coordinated attack on the radicals by Grays Harbor employers and agents of the state. Employers formed citizens' committees in Aberdeen and Hoquiam, with members from local chambers of commerce, to disrupt and remove the IWW presence on the harbor. Over the next two months, hundreds of men from the citizens' committees engaged in violent crime, including kidnapping, assault with a deadly weapon, attempted murder, organizing of an armed body of men, and other felonies.

The news coverage of the citizens' committees' actions resembled the 1904 "Best People on Earth" article, as reporters praised the violent direct action used by Grays Harbor employers. John Carney,

A group of Grays Harbor lumbermen and boss loggers meeting to plan tactics during a strike in the early 1910s. Local elites held meetings like this one to fight unions and labor activists like Gohl. *Courtesy of Jones Photo Historical Collection, Aberdeen, Washington.*

editor of the *Aberdeen Herald,* left little doubt as to his stance, writing in January 1912, "The issue is not free speech; it is not whether or not street speaking be permitted or denied, but who shall control Aberdeen, its resident citizens or a bunch of irresponsibles gathered under the red banner of anarchy by a small coterie of grafting officials parading under the high sounding name of the Industrial Workers of the World."[8] Not to be outdone, the crosstown *Aberdeen Daily World* praised the good work of the Aberdeen citizens' committee, saying, "It was inspiring to see the law-abiding men of this city—hundreds of them—rise in Elks' hall yesterday and pledge their aid to the preservation of order in this community."[9] The *Daily World* complimented the citizens' committee for its vigilance, writing, "The city will not place them [the IWWs] in jail, nor will meals be furnished them. They will be shipped out by the carload or train load, if necessary, and as soon as enough of them have been collected to make up a shipment."[10]

The 1911–12 attacks on the IWW would occur more than a year after Gohl's arrest and imprisonment. But both the intense forms of violence used against the Wobblies and glowing reception the vigilante businessmen received from local journalists indicated their depth of support for the Grays Harbor employing class, no matter what their actions. Employers' actions also indicate a willingness to closely coordinate their activities to combat unionists who stood in the way of the smooth functioning of commerce. There is no question that in the first decade of the twentieth century, no figure in the local labor movement so threatened Grays Harbor employers as did Gohl.

Beginning in 1906, employers waged a series of open shop campaigns against the harbor's unions. In 1906 all of Washington's major shingle manufacturers banded together into the Shingle Mills Bureau, an employers' organization dedicated to imposing the open shop in their industry, the sole union outpost in the Pacific Northwest lumber industry. After a long but unsuccessful general strike waged by the International Shingle Weavers' Union of America (ISWUA), employers declared victory in no uncertain terms. In the Grays Harbor area, the largest shingle companies published newspaper ads stating their commitment to the open shop—no unions. Demonstrating that a new era of employer solidarity was at hand, Grays Harbor shingle manufacturers issued a statement threatening united action against the "menace" of labor activism: "Any discrimination against any of the undersigned [all large Grays Harbor mills] shall be considered as a menace to all."[11]

Employers in other industries followed suit, declaring their commitment to the open shop. On June 1, 1908, the thoroughly unionized Matthews shipyards posted a notice to that effect, and, in response, unionized shipbuilders—the Pacific Coast Maritime Builders' Federation, Local 7, struck at the shipyards.[12] Even the region's carpenters, a bastion of trade union conservatism, cautioned against the growing open shop campaign, which, they worried, could encompass their trade. In September 1908, the carpenters, comprising the region's largest union, with close to four hundred members, declared that they would "handle no lumber hauled by . . . Johnston Transfer [an antiunion company]." In the face of the carpenters' unity, mill managers met and repeatedly declared their commitment to the open shop. One *Aberdeen Herald* article captured the standard antiunion rhetoric used by the harbor's mill men, who, it noted, expressed concern that to "submit to union dictation as to the delivery of their product would leave the path open for the interference of unions in other branches of their operations." The *Grays Harbor Post*, a strong supporter of building trade unions, declared the mill managers to be locked in a "closed shop" of employers. "The unions of the harbor are inclined to believe that the action of the millmen is a move to disrupt unions on Grays Harbor, and inaugurate the open shop method," contended the *Post*.[13]

The antiunion drive was part of a coordinated campaign by capital to reassert control over the local labor market and workplace. But the harbor was a lumber port, and its leading lights were lumbermen. Until the IWW created a mass industrial union movement in 1911, no group of workers so threatened these lumbermen as did the militant maritime unions with Gohl at their head.

Gohl's militancy during the 1906 strike and its aftermath helped local unions win important concessions. But it also earned him numerous adversaries, and for many years he was the target of a concerted campaign by Grays Harbor employers, labor spies, and mainstream news editors to drive him from the harbor. Antiunion newspapers portrayed the strike as harmful to the entire community and Gohl as an irresponsible ruffian. Many journalists, particularly editors, had little sympathy for unions or their members. In response to union protests over the use of injunctions to break strikes, the *Aberdeen Daily Bulletin* claimed that unions were little

more than criminal conspiracies, saying: "If union men must be permitted to commit outrages in order to maintain their organizations
and the principles of their unions, then the unions are illegal." Only
lawbreakers would oppose injunctions, the paper said. "We can not
see that there is anything in the order which will make one iota of
difference to the law-abiding laboring men of this city."[14] During
strikes, the harbor's primary newspapers criticized unions. All of
these newspapers' editors belonged to local business organizations
and had close connections to Pacific Northwest lumber and shipping companies.

After 1906, employers and news editors no longer viewed Gohl as
a tough but successful union leader but instead as a nuisance at best
or a piratical thug at worst. Summing up elite opinion, the *Aberdeen
Herald* called him "notorious" and dishonestly stated that he had
been convicted "of the crime of piracy."[15] In a few nasty hit pieces,
the *Aberdeen Daily Bulletin* referred to him as "Billy Gohl," a dimin-
utive that would stick, though Gohl rarely, if ever, referred to himself as "Billy."

In his memoir, Hugh M. Delanty, head of the Grays Harbor Stevedore Company and a noted scab-herder, told of an attack against
Gohl and the Sailors' Union. In 1909 Captain Michael McCarron
navigated the schooner *Sophie Christenson* up the Wishkah River
and speared Gohl's privy. The *Sophie Christenson* was a large vessel,
measuring 180.6 feet in length, capable of navigating between Grays
Harbor and Australia. In Delanty's words: "The result of this maneu-
ver was to carry away the flimsy structure and in the collapse of the
old fashioned two-holer, the seat landed so that the end of the jib-
boom stuck out of one of the holes and swung merrily back and
forth, much to the amusement of the crowd of citizens who usually
overlooked the movements of the lumber vessels." Fortunately for
him, Gohl was not using the toilet, and the attack resulted in property
damage alone. Finding humor in what many would see as attempted
murder, Delanty wrote that the captain got "a little revenge on the
Sailors' Union agent in a way that caused considerable levity along
the front."[16] Understandably, Gohl found little humor in the attempt

at "revenge" and threatened to move the union hall from Aberdeen to Hoquiam, citing "the antagonistic spirit displayed toward union men in Aberdeen."[17]

Editors of mainstream newspapers had long been critical of Gohl for his union activism, strike militancy, and successful efforts to thwart the county courthouse plans. But an editorial published on February 4, 1910, shortly after Gohl's arrest for murder, provides a useful glimpse into the depths of elite hatred of the Sailors' Union agent. The editorial suggested that Gohl should be removed from the city, regardless of his guilt in the murder case. The editorial read, in part: "He may not be guilty of murder—his innocence at present must be presumed—but he has been guilty of other offenses that have shown his utter contempt for authority." Tellingly, the *Aberdeen Daily World*, organ of the wealthiest residents on Washington's coast, concluded that because prominent Aberdeen residents were frightened by Gohl, he should be locked in prison: "Certain it is that he has been free with his threats, and certain it is that there has been a general opinion that he would not hesitate to make good his threats. Per se, such a man has forfeited all right to liberty."[18]

Given Gohl's large base of labor support, bringing about his silencing and quashing his liberty would take a massive outlay of resources. Building on several years of steady employer class collaboration, Grays Harbor's wealthiest bosses and news editors joined select politicians to weave an impressive coalition dedicated to removing the man who would become known as the Ghoul of Grays Harbor.

By October 1908, area employers had achieved remarkable unity in their strategies for combating working-class activism.[19] Bosses learned lessons from the waterfront strike and their courthouse election defeat and shortly thereafter put into place a united front to attack the maritime unions. Gohl, as their main target, was initially the focus of vigorous and selective enforcement of local laws and attacked in the press, both with the intent of forcing him out of the region. Employers made a more traditional attack against the Aberdeen longshoremen, with their second-oldest union in the region, the source of much of the rank-and-file militancy during the summer of

1906. At the heart of the attacks on the maritime militants was a new organization under a name nearly identical to that of one of Gohl's oldest nemeses: the Grays Harbor Stevedore Company.

Capital's campaigns against the harbor's sailors and longshoremen were part of a wider regional movement to defeat or defang Washington's waterfront unions. From 1906 to 1907, Seattle's trade union membership grew by four thousand, topping out at nineteen thousand workers enrolled in 110 unions. Feeling their strength, the city's waterfront unions pushed for improved wages and working conditions. In response, in 1907, waterfront employers attacked, forming the Puget Sound Shipping Association. "If longshoremen persisted in demanding the closed shop," wrote historian Ronald E. Magden, "employers would fight to a finish." And fight to a finish they did. In May 1907, the association locked out the city's union longshoremen and promised to not rehire any unionists except under the "open shop." After a two-week lockout, during which employers failed to secure sufficient scab labor, the two sides met and reached a compromise. Still, waterfront employers made their point clear as day: they stood united in pursuit of total control over the workplace. In Grays Harbor, the lumbermen who ran the waterfront pursued a similar, and ultimately more successful, strategy for combating labor.[20]

On September 18, 1908, ten major mill owners signed articles of incorporation for the Grays Harbor Stevedore Company. The articles stated that the owners had formed the firm to "engage in the stevedoring, brokerage, and vessel agents' business on Grays harbor, Washington" and to "load and unload vessels, and do a general brokerage, vessel agents', and contracting business with relation to the handling of vessels."[21] But the company's real purpose was to break unions. The firm promised to operate on an open shop basis, hiring nonunion workers to perform work previously done by union longshoremen. Shortly after incorporation, the Grays Harbor Stevedore Company began an eighteen-month lockout of union longshoremen who refused to load alongside scab workers supplied by the new company. The new firm hired nonunion longshoremen, bringing the open shop to a former union stronghold.[22]

During October 1908, longshoremen and sailors jointly protested the Grays Harbor Stevedore Company, as it hired nonunion workers to labor on the docks. As employers acted in concert to pursue their class interests, the harbor's maritime unionists, divided by craft, followed a cautious path. The longshoremen struck, but the sailors', firemen's, and cooks' unions refused to strike in sympathy. Visiting Aberdeen during the struggle, SUP president Andrew Furuseth made it clear that the sailors had no intention of striking alongside the dock workers.[23]

The stevedore company's implementation of an open shop regime decimated the longshoremen's union. The *Aberdeen Herald* greeted the union's defeat with joy and played immigrants against native-born Americans: "The Longshoremen's Union that was superseded by the open shop three years ago, was the neatest little trust on the face of the earth. A Scandinavian labor trust that had refused admission to its membership every American born applicant for more than four years."[24] The *Herald's* comment is a reminder that employers have ideological weapons to deploy when recruiting scabs and setting workers against one another. In this instance, the press deployed nativism to claim that unionized immigrants enjoyed "special privileges" and took away native-born Americans' jobs. Divided by craft, between 1908 and 1910 the harbor's maritime unionists suffered repeated defeats at the hands of employers who acted in accordance with their class interests.

The stevedore firm crippled the union, delivering a major blow to the region's labor movement. According to the *Grays Harbor Post*, from late 1908 until January 1910 the longshoremen's union loaded no ships in Aberdeen. The first ship to be loaded by the union was the schooner *Churchill*: "This is the first vessel to be secured by the union longshoremen under contract for fifteen months, their lockout on the docks having been complete."[25]

For employers to silence Gohl permanently, they required state assistance, and installing a pliant businessman as Aberdeen mayor was a logical step. An Aberdeen citizens' committee recruited a replacement for mayor Eugene France from among their own ranks.[26] We know next to nothing of the proceedings of this shady organization except that banker, politician, and booster W. J. Patterson stood at its head. Beyond Patterson, the most likely member was lumberman W. B. Mack, a leader in the Aberdeen Chamber of Commerce and the man who had traded fire with Gohl aboard the *Centralia* and accused him of trying to dynamite his home, and who would work with Thiel Detective Service spies to secure witnesses during Gohl's murder trial.[27]

The citizens' committee raised somewhere between $7,000 and $10,000 to fund a pro-business candidate and to pay for the vigorous investigation of Gohl that was to follow.[28] The committee quickly settled on thirty-five-year-old Edmund B. Benn, who, in his own words, ran because of "the solicitation of several hundred of the best men of the city who signed a petition asking me to file my intentions."[29] Adding to the wealth acquired from his family, Benn made his money in real estate and as manager of the Grand Theatre. He had also served terms in the Aberdeen City Council and the Washington state legislature.[30]

Benn's mayoral campaign began in mid-January 1909. He fronted an imposing political machine that included a following among employers and the trumpeting of the *Aberdeen World*, the chief Republican Party organ.[31] Benn pledged himself to a "business administration," and that was certainly what his supporters desired.[32] The backing of Aberdeen's businessmen was decisive because of Benn's lack of support among working people. In 1908 Benn had run for city council against Ed Dolan, a popular saloon owner whose constituency included saloon enthusiasts, union members, and the minority of workers who enjoyed the privilege of voting. In that election Dolan had handed Benn a decisive defeat. A year later, with most of the region's employing class and pro-business media at his back, Benn had won in a landslide, taking over two-thirds of the votes cast.[33]

Many employers disliked Gohl, but "first son" E. B. Benn despised the union leader and wasn't shy about expressing his opinion. In fact, Benn stood as a useful counterpart to Gohl, two regionally prominent white men of a similar age who shared virtually nothing in socioeconomic background, worldview, or life course. While Gohl endured

E. B. Benn, longtime Gohl opponent and mayor of Aberdeen during the Gohl investigation, arrest, and trial. *Courtesy of Jones Photo Historical Collection, Aberdeen, Washington.*

shipwrecks and split time between boardinghouse and forecastle, Benn endured parliamentary debates and divided time between his Broadway Hill home and the Elks hall. In an era when ship provisions ran low and seamen sometimes starved, Benn was an obese man who clearly indulged in life's treats. His weight was often the subject of none-too-subtle digs, including by fellow elites (an *Aberdeen Daily World* headline: "Big Candidate Apparently on Heavy Side of Scale").[34]

Both Gohl and Benn stood near the pinnacle of regional prominence. However, the two men's constituencies differed greatly. Benn, as a mover and shaker in Republican Party and chamber of commerce circles, gained election to public office from the votes of the small number of resident men deemed qualified to vote. The US Census recorded 13,660 residents of Aberdeen in 1910, but a year earlier Benn had won the mayoral election though he received only a little more than 500 votes. On the other hand, as a Sailors' Union agent, Gohl had gained his position in the union by winning elections among the entire union membership, which counted close to 4,000 men. He had also been elected as vice president of the Grays Harbor Trades and Labor Council and twice as president, and he was the founding president of the Grays Harbor Waterfront Federation. As Benn allied himself with the interests of regional employers and Gohl stood firmly in the corner of militant labor, it became increasingly clear that the two men were on a collision course.

Benn's attacks on Gohl were personal, but they also reflected his antipathy toward unions, especially those that dared to disrupt commerce through strikes or demonstrations. As a Washington State representative in 1903, Benn had joined legislators in passing the Criminal Anarchy Act. The law made it a felony to advocate the doctrine of "criminal anarchy"—"that organized government should be overthrown by force or violence, or by assassination of the executive head or any of the executive officials of government, or by any unlawful means."[35] Like its successor the Criminal Syndicalism Act, it was a clear-cut attack on the freedom of speech. More specifically, though, employers and the state used these laws to criminalize leftist political beliefs and activism, outlawing membership in revolutionary working-class organizations such as the Industrial Workers of the World. Like the criminal anarchy law, the Criminal Syndicalism Act received massive support from Grays Harbor lumbermen and Republicans.[36]

Benn's mayoral administration, especially the police department, fixed its gaze on Gohl. True crime writer Hollis Fultz wrote that the city's employers demanded that Aberdeen police chief George Dean "run Billy Gohl out of town."[37] According to the myth of Gohl as ghoul, Dean was the man most responsible for bringing him to justice, and he looms largest among Gohl's foils.[38] Details of the elaborate part supposedly played by Dean are outlined below, but it is a mistake to think that Dean was a major protagonist in Gohl's story. Prior to 1910, Dean had impressed neither the county's voters nor Mayor Benn. In

the 1908 Chehalis County sheriff's election, Dean finished behind
two other candidates, including future sheriff Ed Payette.[39] Dean was
also not Benn's first or even second choice as chief of police; rather, he
was appointed to this post in May 1909 after J. M. Birmingham and
then F. R. Archer left the position in quick succession.[40]

Where Dean did not fall short, however, was in his connections to
the top tier of the local Republican Party and a willingness to look the
other way as morally and legally questionable law enforcement practices were followed. Long after Gohl went to prison, Dean proved a
reliable ally of business. In 1917 Dean traveled to Chicago to testify
in a federal trial against members of the Industrial Workers of the
World. Capturing some unionists' views of Dean's relationship with
employers, two Aberdeen Wobblies wrote to IWW attorney George
Vanderveer, warning about Dean, "If he confined his statement to
facts it will be of no use to them, but from what we know of him we
think he said or will say what he is told."[41]

Benn had long-standing personal animosity toward Gohl. Early in
his mayoral term, he took decisive action to rid the harbor of the union
agent. Like many other state authorities and leaders of employers'
organizations, Benn turned to labor spies—euphemistically known
as "private detectives"—to coordinate the investigation into the local
"labor problem." Indeed, the critical component in the citizens' committee scheme to get rid of Gohl "and his gang" came in its hiring of
several labor spies, employees of the infamous Thiel agency, known
for its leading role in helping to break miners' strikes in the US West.[42]

Labor spies, particularly those from private agencies, have a
long and troubling history in the United States. Their continued use
throughout much of the nineteenth and twentieth centuries can be
attributed to spies' successful infiltration of unions, their implication
of unionists and radicals for real and imagined subversive activities,
and ultimately their ability to destroy workers' organizations.[43] A key
to their success was operation in secret, free from the public scrutiny
that sometimes hinders public officials from abusing their power. In
Washington State, from the turn of the century, the most prominent
of these agencies was not the Pinkerton National Detective Agency

but the Thiel Detective Service Company. Gus Thiel, the agency's founder, had worked as a Pinkerton agent during the 1860s before setting out on his own in 1873 when he moved to St. Louis.[44] Within a decade his agency was thriving, with branches scattered throughout the country, particularly in the West, where the Thiel agents became the dominant force in their industry.[45] Six agencies, including the Thiels and the infamous Pinkertons, maintained headquarters in Seattle.[46]

Although unionists and labor allies hated labor spies, employers would no doubt have been impressed by private detectives' efforts to thwart union campaigns. By 1909, Grays Harbor area employers relied on the detective services. For example, in early 1909 area logging firms hired private detectives to disguise themselves as loggers and report on log theft.[47] Mill owner Charles Wilson hired a detective to dig up information related to a steam schooner accident that threatened to cost the company big bucks.[48] Clearly, by the end of the first decade of the twentieth century, harbor elites were comfortable relying on private detectives as a supplement to public police forces for all their antiunion needs.

In the public-private investigation into Gohl's alleged criminal activities, the first and most important spy engaged was Patrick J. McHugh, sometimes known as Paddy. McHugh had a long, storied career on the harbor. He was one of the region's early loggers, working in the woods alongside his brother Neil for fourteen years. Between 1895 and 1902 he owned at least a piece of no less than four independent logging operations in the Grays Harbor area, a feat of social climbing that was achieved by local loggers during these early years.[49]

McHugh also tried his hand at politics and law enforcement. In 1904 he unsuccessfully ran for county sheriff as a Democrat.[50] By 1907 he lived in Aberdeen, owned a home on East Wishkah Street, and operated a saloon with his brother Neil.[51] Paddy McHugh was on the radar of local police as far back as the summer of 1907. Prior to becoming a labor spy, he had achieved something of a notorious first on the harbor. In August 1907 police arrested McHugh and charged him with violating the Sunday closing law. Four Grays Harbor residents purchased liquor at McHugh's saloon on a Sunday and then reported him to the police. These residents testified to that fact in Aberdeen Justice Court in a jury trial. McHugh's defense offered no witnesses, but his attorney questioned the constitutionality of the Sunday closing law. After deliberation of twenty-five minutes, the jury declared McHugh not guilty. The *Hoquiam Sawyer* condemned Aberdeen's municipal government and the jury, saying, "It hardly seems possible that the Aberdeen saloonkeepers can successfully defy a law that has worked successfully in Tacoma, Seattle, and other cities of this state."[52]

In mid-1909, after months of trying but failing to incriminate Gohl, a citizens' committee, with Dean as its point man, hired McHugh.[53] The committee served as a nexus of public and private concerns. It collected money from both businessmen and the Aberdeen City Treasury and channeled it to the Thiel Detective Service. Perhaps illegally, the committee would keep its actions—including its use of municipal funds—secret from the Aberdeen City Council until more than a year after Gohl's trial. R. J. Hilts, a member of the council's police committee, which oversaw the city's law enforcement budget, would then demand an investigation. In response to the investigation, W. J. Patterson, head of the Aberdeen Chamber of Commerce, addressed the council, laying out the efforts of local business interests and Thiel spies to investigate Gohl.[54]

Mayor Benn and the citizens' committee had good reason to keep the appropriation of public funds to pay labor spies secret from the city council. Working-class residents of the harbor were familiar with the Thiel agents' role in antilabor activities in the Mountain West and beyond. Labor newspapers roundly condemned these private detectives. In May 1909 William "Big Bill" Haywood, the socialist and industrial union leader who had been framed for murder by labor spies, toured the Grays Harbor area. He delivered a speech to inform listeners about socialism and labor struggles but primarily to thank supporters for defending his life against the machinations of mine owners and spies: "Without the aid of the workingmen of this country, instead of standing here tonight, I . . . would be occupying a bed of quick lime in the vault of the Idaho penitentiary." Railing against labor spies like those whose actions had nearly led to his execution, Haywood stated: "Of all the men on earth, I consider the detective the most despicable."[55]

Haywood was among the most beloved labor leaders in the country, and his speech drew a massive audience. Its content provides important context to help explain the secrecy around the employment of private detectives to investigate Gohl. Certainly, labor allies on the city council and the reading public would have known about the notorious reputation of labor spies and might have issued stern protests against mingling public and private funds to investigate a prominent Aberdonian. In this instance, it appears clear that Mayor Benn and other members of the citizens' committee understood that it was easier to ask for forgiveness than permission.

In his position as a spy posing as a legitimate saloon keeper, McHugh befriended Gohl, and it appears that the union agent had genuine feelings of affection for him. But the two men's reasons for the relationship were drastically different.[56] While awaiting trial in the Chehalis County jail, police would ask Gohl to name his friends. Gohl replied by listing names of twelve people, one of whom was McHugh.[57] McHugh, though, was a mercenary. He had supplied Gohl with drinks and apparent friendship, gaining the union agent's trust. Gohl must have been surprised and hurt when McHugh testified against him during the murder trial, testimony that related illicit stories of years of murder.

As companions who shared time drinking alcohol, it is perhaps unsurprising that Gohl shared intimate details about his life with McHugh. The spy alleged and later testified in court that a drunken Gohl had bragged to him about his long history of committing crimes, including murder.[58] According to Gohl, the two men also shared a financial relationship. Gohl's defense relayed to the court that the local SUP regularly left money at McHugh's saloon for safekeeping and that just prior to his arrest Gohl had deposited $325 with the saloon keeper. Although impossible to confirm, the possibility of an additional \$325 in blood money must have seemed a nice tip for McHugh's services.[59]

Blessed with large coffers, the citizens' committee hired approximately ten more Thiel agents, including Billie Montyee, otherwise known as Billie Montana.[60] Shortly after Gohl's conviction, newspapers broke the story that a "corps of Thiel detectives [had] worked on case all winter."[61]

Gohl's suspicions of this campaign against him surely peaked in the summer of 1909 when police arrested him because of the report of "a prominent citizen" who claimed that Gohl had stolen his bicycle. The union agent quickly proved that the bike was his own, but the accusation led police to search one of the waterfront shacks Gohl helped maintain for itinerant seamen. In the shack, police discovered two automobile robes stolen three months earlier from mill manager Arthur L. Paine.[62] At a late July 1909 trial, Gohl's friend and roommate Charles Hadberg, a union sailor, testified that he had bought the robes at a secondhand store.[63] Given Hadberg's testimony, a jury found Gohl not guilty after deliberating only a few minutes.[64] According to the *Tacoma Daily Ledger*, "Gohl says he is a victim of spite."[65]

Gohl was no fool, and he was right to be suspicious considering the libelous attacks in local newspapers and the destruction of his union hall privy. The *Daily Ledger* reported, regarding Gohl's trial for the theft of the auto robes, "Detectives who have been working on the case promise revelations." Since we now know that a citizens' committee of wealthy employers ("prominent citizens") had hired detectives to spy on Gohl, his paranoia was reasonable, if too late. According to one newspaper, Gohl was determined to respond to the harassment and brought a \$10,000 lawsuit for malicious prosecution against "prominent business men of Grays Harbor" whose false allegations led to his arrest and trial.[66] Considering the lack of publicity this incident received, either this newspaper report was incorrect or Gohl's lawsuit never made its way to court. Still, that Gohl felt that his prosecution had been "malicious" was an indication that Gohl understood the dangers he faced from the prominent residents of Grays Harbor.

Gohl's list of enemies had grown long by 1909. Angered by the attacks on longshoremen, in December 1909 Gohl threatened a general strike, hoping to revive the labor solidarity of 1906. While the general strike never materialized, it proved a vivid reminder of the potency of maritime solidarity on the harbor and its central proponent, William Gohl.[67] A month after Gohl issued the threat, local elites ensured that this would be the last flash of maritime militancy to originate from the office of the Sailors' Union.

8

GOHL ON TRIAL

ON THE MORNING of February 2, 1910, William and George Lightfoot, two Hoquiam brothers, discovered a man's body while they towed a rowboat across mud flats near Indian Creek. Tied down in eighteen inches of water and held there by a fifty-pound anchor, the body had two bullet holes in the head.[1] Six weeks earlier, Aberdeen chief of police George Dean had been told that the body of sailor Charles Hadberg, along with that of local cigar dealer John Hoffman, could be found in Indian Creek. Shortly after receiving this information, Dean had traveled to Indian Creek in search of the bodies. Six months later, in May, covering William Gohl's murder trial, the *Herald* would detail his efforts: "The chief of police and an amateur officer proceeded to Indian creek, looked about the beach and on top of the water for the body they had been told was held to the bottom with a 50 pound anchor; questioned some men in the vicinity—who had they been members of the Gohl gang would have removed the body— and came home with report that there was nothing in the story."[2] Dean would not correspond or talk with the county sheriff or state authorities during the investigation, and Gohl would attribute this to "personal grievances and pettifogging strife between the police department and sheriff's office" resulting from Ed Payette's runaway victory over Dean in the 1908 election for sheriff and both men's desire to be credited with solving the case.[3]

With the discovery of the body, the allegations of labor spy Paddy McHugh, and the pressure coming from city elites to remove Gohl, Aberdeen police immediately secured a warrant for Gohl's arrest. Carrying the warrant firmly in hand, Aberdeen police officer K. Y. Church traveled the five blocks from the Aberdeen police station to the office of the Sailors' Union of the Pacific on the morning of February 3, the day after the body was found.[4]

Earlier that morning, Gohl had walked up the stairs to his office, hoping to get a little paperwork done before making his daily rounds. He likely had no idea this would be his last morning as a free man. At 10:00 a.m., Church entered the Sailors' Union office and arrested Gohl as a murder suspect.[5] By now well accustomed to arrests, Gohl remained composed, and the two men returned to the police station, where Gohl first heard the ghastly and startling charges against him. "My God," he responded. "Please notify my wife and my attorney, Wilson Buttner."[6] Justifiably "unnerved," Gohl spent a "miserable night" in what was to be the first of thousands of nights behind bars. The next day, two officers transported him to the county jail at Montesano. By all accounts, Gohl was "determined to fight" for his freedom, demonstrating the characteristic defiance toward authority that had earned him so much support from his fellow workers.[7]

Shortly after Gohl's arrest it became clear that he faced two sets of charges. He had been arrested as a suspect in the murders of Charles Hadberg and John Hoffman. A week after Gohl's arrest, Chehalis County prosecuting attorney William Campbell charged Gohl with murder in the first degree for killing Hadberg.[8] But in the eyes of local elites, he faced trial for his role in the entire bloody history of Grays Harbor. On the day of Gohl's arrest, the *Daily World* blamed him "for many of the members of the 'floater fleet,' comprising more than 40 bodies."[9] Attempting to turn the SUP's documented history of violence against sailors on its head, the *Grays Harbor Washingtonian* ran the headline "Red Record of Crime on Grays Harbor Charged to William Gohl."[10] The press laid every crime that had occurred in the region during the previous seven years at Gohl's door, whether that crime was real or imagined. He became variously a "fire bug," rapist, thief, labor racketeer, and most importantly the man behind the Floater Fleet.[11] Reporters alleged he "kept a large number of hangers-on to do his bidding and swear him out of trouble," a reference to Hadberg, whose testimony during the summer 1909 auto robe theft trial had vindicated Gohl.[12]

Throughout the legal process, the many local newspapers declared that this trial was "the most important in the annals of criminal history of Chehalis County," and indeed it was, since it provided an explanation—no matter how far-fetched—for the violence the region had experienced for years.[13] In one fell swoop, Gohl became the personification of all that violence and enabled local citizens to purge themselves of the terror they had ostensibly experienced. "The days of which he is typical have gone forever, not only in Aberdeen but in the West," asserted the *Aberdeen Daily World*. "No man has a right to liberty in this or any other community when his liberty becomes a constant menace to law-abiding citizens." Threatening that Gohl's enemies might take the law into their own hands, the *World* continued: "So if he shall escape the courts, he may as well know at this time that he cannot continue to make Aberdeen his place of residence. We want no more of him here or of his kind. They [Gohl and his 'gang'] can all take notice."[14]

After the discovery of the body on February 2, Aberdeen police moved it to the Aberdeen morgue, where four doctors performed an autopsy. They announced that the death had come from "two gun shot wounds at the base of the skull, ranging upwards, and from that cause alone." Within the week it was reported that "[since an] indictment of Wm Gohl has already been made by the Prosecuting Atty, no inquest was held [other] than the establishment of the mode of death and identification of the body."[15] In what looks in retrospect like something out of a crime drama, authorities refused to allow Hadberg's coworkers—members of the Aberdeen local of the Sailors' Union—to view or identify the body. Not so easily cowed, these men, the people in town most likely to be familiar with the itinerant sailor's appearance, forced their way past security, viewed the body, and stated unequivocally that it did *not* belong to Hadberg. The unionists were so certain that the body was not Hadberg's that they refused to grant the body a union burial.[16] The *Daily World* stated that a "steady stream of curiosity seekers" had viewed the body, with "many of the men" stating that it belonged to Hadberg.[17] Official identification of the body fell to Aberdeen mayor E. B. Benn and Judge J. M. Phillips, who declared that the body belonged to Hadberg.[18] How these wealthy elites could be expected to provide an accurate identification of a sailor who split his time between lumber schooners and a riverside shack is difficult to imagine.

Once he learned of his comrades' finding, Gohl tried hard to view the body of the man he had allegedly murdered, but he was denied this opportunity.[19] At trial months later, however, the state would marshal the testimony of saloon owner Emil Olson, who claimed to have served aboard ship with Hadberg. Unlike SUP members, Olson stated that the body was Hadberg's.[20] Still, Gohl maintained that the body could not possibly belong to Hadberg. Following his arrest, Gohl claimed that Hadberg had moved to Alaska. In May, at the murder trial, Gohl's acquaintance Waldemar Neilson testified that in December he and the union agent had gone to the cabin where Hadberg lived to collect his possessions. Hadberg didn't need them any longer, according to the story Gohl told Neilson, because he had moved to Alaska to work for a lighthouse contractor. After Neilson, police chief Dean testified that in late December or early January, Gohl had visited the police station to report that Hadberg had stolen Gohl's money and fled to Alaska.[21]

The controversy stemming from the identification of the body provides a useful reminder that Gohl saw Charles Hadberg as a person, a comrade, and "my best and truest friend."[22] In contrast, the state, employers, and the reporters who were so interested in Gohl's prosecution saw Hadberg as little more than flesh, a piece of evidence useful in a murder case with political implications. Hadberg had spent considerable time on the harbor and been close friends with Gohl. Like many seamen, Hadberg lacked a permanent residence, a place to call home. Responding to his comrade's precarious situation, Gohl had offered Hadberg a place.[23] Although local elites publicized Hadberg's death, they rarely, if ever, mentioned his name while he was alive, and Hadberg had till death received little mention in local newspapers. He was little more than a common workman to those who profited from his labor. The public's main source of information about Hadberg came in the occasional details Gohl dropped about him in his jail cell interviews.

Gohl stayed busy behind bars. In fact, he exhibited a defiance that surprised both state authorities and members of the press. The union agent was a self-taught student of law, and he proclaimed that he had "adopted the American flag," saying, "It has changed some of my ideas of life—and has caused me to love this grand old nation and its stars and stripes." But he had little time for a system that enabled what he dubbed powerful "interests" to control and ruin the life of someone like him.[24] He asked the authorities to give him "the celebrated 'third degree' or sweating process" and proclaimed that it would not take him five minutes to vindicate himself: "I do not fear a trial, because I have nothing to fear."[25] The Portland *Oregonian* reported that Gohl had responded to a comment about the serious nature of the crime by stating: "It's a fairly serious charge, all right: but then you know a man is never guilty until you prove it." The paper added, "He spoke in a nonchalant voice, and dismissed the subject as if discussing the weather."[26] Gohl's defiant attitude toward authority, nurtured in his years at sea and in fighting on the front lines of the class struggle, never diminished during his four months in county jail.

There in jail Gohl occupied himself with the many tasks necessary to prepare for his trial. For most of his time, his only access to the outside world came through his wife and lawyers (Wilson Buttner and later A. M. Abel), whom he could visit for only short periods of time.[27] Bessie headed fund-raising efforts. Between February and May, she sold her valuables and traveled to Puget Sound, seeking assistance there from labor unions, and led a variety of crusades to get financial and legal assistance from SUP headquarters in San Francisco.[28]

Early during his jailing, Gohl spoke with members of the press, which provided the lone source of positive publicity.[29] The interviews all occurred during the first week after his arrest, which he blamed on a conspiracy by "a ring of Aberdeen politicians." These politicians, the *Chehalis County Vidette* said, reporting Gohl's views, "have been pursuing him persistently in an effort to effect his downfall, ever since the county seat fight of three years ago, when he took a firm stand against its removal."[30]

The interviews demonstrated the prisoner's shock at the ludicrous nature of the charges and his sadness at the possible death of his old friend Hadberg. According to the *Daily World*, Hadberg was Gohl's "true and loyal friend who had lived at his home and who was for a long time as one of the family."[31] Gohl's professed certainty that the body was not Hadberg's was no doubt bolstered when SUP members declared as much.[32] It was significant to Gohl that he was not allowed to identify the body.[33] During each interview, Gohl condemned the notion that he could have killed Hadberg, telling a *Washingtonian* correspondent, "The idea of me harming one hair on his head is repugnant to me."[34] But with the sadness was mixed an equal amount of anger at being blamed for numerous murders around the harbor during the preceding decade, crimes he was at the vanguard of efforts to prevent. Gohl asked A. C. Girard, a reporter for the *Washingtonian*, whether it was "reasonable that [he was] guilty of these alleged crimes, or that the entire story was fabricated by the unscrupulous and fiendish machinations of [his] enemies."[35] As far as Gohl was concerned, Girard was an ideal choice for the interview. Earlier in the decade he had served as county coroner and had on several occasions worked with the man who now sat behind bars, charged with murder.

After the interviews in his first week behind bars, authorities cut Gohl off from the press, realizing that he provided explanations that countered the rumors circulating. Concerned that the union agent might communicate with the outside world, police kept Gohl isolated in the Chehalis County jail until mid-March, when he received a cell mate.[36] Gohl spent his long hours of solitude continuing his legal studies in quarters the press described as a "steel tank."[37] Sheriff Payette worked to keep Gohl from getting in touch with Lauritz Jensen, his fellow unionist and one time boarder at the Gohl residence.[38] In Payette's words, "We were trying all the time to keep Gohl from communicating with Jensen," but Gohl did manage to pass a note to his comrade via a trusty working in the jail kitchen. As Payette contended: "We are on the watch for almost anything to happen while Gohl is in jail here."[39]

Forbidden to speak with members of the press or fellow unionists, Gohl worked to rehabilitate his public image by writing letters to the latter and to friends.[40] One such letter was written on February 7 to the Aberdeen branch of the SUP in a challenge to the widely reported claims that Gohl intended to divulge damaging information about SUP "higher-ups."[41] Gohl wrote, "Comrades . . . this is absolute falsehood since I never at any time have been questioned by any official about my case and nothing of it has been discussed in jail."[42]

Shortly after his segregation ended in mid-March, Gohl stopped a vicious assault on prisoner Frank Sporan by a prisoner named Alexander Dzgeoff (Gohl punched the latter in the face). Dzgeoff swore revenge, saying he would "get" Gohl, before he, Dzgeoff, was transported to the state penitentiary. And he succeeded, sneaking up behind Gohl and beating him over the head with a chair. Only "the sight of the deputy's gun," it was reported, stopped the assault.[43] Apparently unwilling to let the stresses and violence of jail grind him down, Gohl used his intellect and legal skills in aiding one of his fellow inmates in preparing his defense.[44]

While Gohl demonstrated his proclivity for aiding his fellows, the local and regional press displayed little regard for accuracy or objectivity, preferring to work up the blood lust of Pacific Northwest readers. For Gohl's sake it was bad enough that the press called so much attention to what they deemed his obvious guilt for the crime of which he was charged. It was, however, quite another thing for them to lay every possible crime committed during the previous seven years, every rumor circulated, and every drunken whisper uttered about Gohl at his door.

Despite the generally friendly interviews, in the first few days after Gohl's arrest the press reached consensus on his responsibility for an endless string of crimes.[45] The die was cast on the day of his arrest when the *Daily World* reported: "The theory of the police in the Gohl murder mystery rivals the shocking disclosures of the Gunness murder farm," a reference to Belle Gunness, a Norwegian American serial killer in Indiana.[46] The *Herald* followed a few days later, writing: "The atmosphere is filled with rumors of so many crimes attributed to Gohl—ranging from murder to petit larceny—that wonder is expressed that the man should have been permitted to go on in his career for over six years without being overhauled by the authorities."[47] The call for Gohl's blood came loudest from an editorial in the *Washingtonian*. Addressing Gohl directly, the paper said: "Do you imagine that you hear the roar of the mob in pursuit of a human being? A mob swayed by passion! William Gohl, can you hear it? The yelp of the wolf, the horrid laugh of the hyena, the growl of the bear, the howl of the dog, all combining to make the wild cry of the mob, seeking in vengeance the blood of a fellow man?"[48] The *Vidette* was hardly exaggerating when it suggested that Gohl "was being accused of every crime in the decalogue."[49]

In retrospect, it is easy to dismiss the content of these exaggerated, even silly, "yellow press" accounts published in an era known for its sensationalistic news coverage. On the other hand, these newspapers reached a wide audience, with the *Herald*, *Daily World*, and *Daily Washingtonian* all boasting circulations of several thousand subscribers.[50] Potential Chehalis County jurors—property-holding men over the age of twenty-one—were the main audience for these newspapers. Certainly every resident in the county would have read the lurid tales pouring forth from the papers or heard them related secondhand. How an unbiased jury might have been gathered for a trial in this atmosphere is anyone's guess.

A year after Gohl's trial, W. J. Patterson, one of Gohl's main antagonists, would contend that one of the most damning pieces of evidence against Gohl was that he received no support during his case from the SUP or the larger labor movement. Subsequent writers have repeated Patterson's claim. Indeed, unlike the cases of the Haymarket Martyrs, Joe Hill, or the McNamara brothers in the 1910 Los Angeles

Times Building bombing, in Gohl's trial no great class war prisoner defense funds were raised, no mass parades or general strikes were held, and no great network of labor-left support was mobilized.

However, these contentions ignore two facts. First, Gohl's case did not occur during a strike or organizational drive, and thus it made little sense for a union to devote its limited resources for the defense of an alleged murderer. Gohl pointed this out in an interview: "It is a personal matter with me. . . . Had I become involved in trouble during a strike or was in any way connected with the Sailors' Union, they would have helped me but the union has nothing to do with my case. I must fight it alone and as an individual."[51]

Second, despite this, the labor movement *did* fight on Gohl's behalf, although without the heavy funding and mass organization that marked some other celebrated cases. Bessie Gohl visited unions throughout the Pacific Northwest and, along with labor supporters, secured financial assistance. The Pierce County Labor Council in Tacoma sent a letter of support to Gohl, although a motion to send $50 to his defense team was ruled out of order by the body.[52]

On the day of Gohl's arrest, the Aberdeen local of the Sailors' Union had voted a motion of confidence for their agent and begun planning for his defense.[53] The *Coast Seamen's Journal* ran a supportive editorial, condemning the corrupt, antiunion officials of Grays Harbor for their attacks on Gohl and the Sailors' Union. The piece also expressed disbelief that the dead body found belonged to Hadberg and discussed the history of legal frame-ups against Sailors' Union activists. The editorial is important because it shows the union's support for Gohl and provides context for the persecution of union leaders. The *Journal* praised Gohl's work as an agent: "Further, it may be said that there is absolutely nothing in Comrade Gohl's conduct as Agent of the Union to create the slightest suspicion that he is other than a thoroughly honest man. Such is Gohl's record, official and unofficial, so far as the Union is concerned. Upon that record the Union will act, in the hope and belief that, given a fair trial, the innocence of Comrade Gohl will be fully established."[54] The case against Gohl hinged on "suspicion," concluded the union newspaper. "In every instance these charges have failed of proof. The only thing really proved in each of such cases was the existence of a plot to discredit the Union and the employment of desperadoes to carry out the details of the villainy. This knowledge makes us especially cautious in considering the present case."[55]

Rank-and-file seamen took additional steps to aid their union agent. Unlike courtroom maneuvers and argument in legislative assemblies, these methods drew on their rough lives at sea and in Sailortowns. In Grays Harbor, between February and May 1910, the SUP rank-and-file sailors remained adamant in their contention that the dead body did not belong to Hadberg.[56] And some turned to writing anonymous threatening letters to those responsible for Gohl's plight. Historian E. P. Thompson would later write extensively on this form of oppositional politics, calling the anonymous threatening letter "a characteristic form of social protest in any society . . . in which forms of collective organized defence are weak, and in which individuals who can be identified as the organizers of protests are liable to immediate victimization."[57] As Thompson's statement suggests, workers lacking wealth, elite status, or political connections cannot readily access the traditional means for contesting those in power and may face retribution should they step out of line. Anonymous letters allowed those living on society's margins to have their voices heard without fear of reprisal. One such letter appeared at the offices of the *Daily World* shortly after Gohl's arrest:

> I have been taken particular Notice of the Rotten News You have been printing about our Comrad Gohl and if you keep this kind of prociding up an Longer You will wake up some Morning to find your damned Print Shop in Ashes—Our Union is a Strong organization and although we have gotten the worst of It in this Rotten old town We are still organiced and stick up for our Rights Gohl has always treated us fair and pulled us out of Many Holes and dangerous Ones at That and Now since [he] is behind the Baars We Propos to stick to him.—You Yello Yournals write any old thing about a poor Fellow when he is down and out—Why Didn't you com out with Your Cullors When Gohl was a Free man—because You did not dare you

were to Cowardly dats why—But when Frank [Gohl] becomes a free
man he will show you Rascals where your Bred is Buttered.

Your Police Force is Rotten They is a Bad lot they dont work on
Fakts any old theery is good enough—Remember our Warning to
you —Jack.[58]

Three months later, Gohl's successor as union agent, Harry Lund-
berg, carried a gun into the courtroom to intimidate witnesses, and,
after being expelled from the courtroom, he picked a fistfight with an
important state witness.[59]

From the start of the legal process in the case against him, Gohl also
experienced difficulties with his attorneys. When Wilson Buttner,
Gohl's longtime attorney, arrived in Montesano on February 4, he was
noticeably drunk, and Gohl, fearing for his life, fired him.[60] Gohl then
hired attorney A. M. Abel, but on February 7 the *Daily World* ran an
article claiming that Gohl might hire "Counsel for the Damned" Clar-
ence Darrow for the fee of $16,000.[61] Despite rumors that Gohl was in
league with "higher ups" in the union to acquire an attorney of such
national renown, he insisted these rumors were "without foundation"
and that Abel would remain his lawyer.[62] A. M. Abel's brother, W. H.
Abel, occasionally assisted in the defense. Moreover, Gohl, who recently
declared bankruptcy, certainly could not have generated even a frac-
tion of the asking fee for Darrow's services.

Abel did little to serve Gohl in the murder case, and his repeated
insistence on securing a stay of trial harmed the defense case and
even cast serious doubt about his loyalty to his client. Abel worked to
have the trial delayed from its scheduled March 25 start date.[63] Finally
securing a postponement because he had not "perfected his defense
and was without witnesses," Abel's efforts resulted in a May 2 start
date for the trial.[64] Then, with his stay of trial, Abel abandoned the
case.[65] One reason for Abel's departure was that Gohl's meager funds
had dried up. Without an income of any kind, William could simply
not afford Abel's services for more than ten weeks and was thus left
to plead poverty to the court. The *Washingtonian* pointed out the great
expense of hiring defense counsel for a murder trial, writing: "It is

said that Abel demanded $5,000, but that $1,000 was all that Gohl could raise at the time."[66]

It is little wonder why working people faced such difficulties hiring lawyers, a rather obvious example of structural inequality in the American criminal justice system. A member of the SUP averaged only $50 per month in wages, making it difficult to meet attorney costs. Unable to pay for a defense attorney, Gohl pled indigence. The court appointed attorneys J. A. Hutcheson of Montesano and A. E. Cross of Aberdeen to handle the defense.[67] Thus, after nearly three months and numerous legal arrangements, Gohl finally had his trial attorneys. Unfortunately, the new defense team had only slightly over a week to prepare a case against a massively funded prosecution in league with the Aberdeen citizens' committee, the Thiel detective agency, many Grays Harbor employers, and every public law enforcement body available.

The postponement of the trial gave police and Thiel detectives an extra five weeks in the field to hunt for, intimidate, and interrogate witnesses. The Aberdeen citizens' committee used this time to search for the missing links in the case: a sailor named John Klingenberg and the supposedly deceased John Hoffman. State and private parties spared neither time nor money searching the Chehalis River for Hoffman's body. According to the *Washingtonian*, Chehalis County spent $2,000 on the search, while the International Order of Oddfellows offered a $500 reward for the body.[68] Newspapers deluged their readers with daily reports of the fruitless searches for Hoffman's body, and Hoffman was never seen again, dead or alive.[69]

The Aberdeen citizens' committee did get its hands on Klingenberg, a thirty-two-year-old Danish immigrant. After emigrating from Denmark, Klingenberg had worked as a sailor for fourteen years and lived in one of the harbor shacks that Gohl had helped construct. He proved to be the only person who ever provided conclusive evidence linking Gohl to a crime.[70] The stay of court secured by Abel proved vital in this respect but not to Gohl's advantage. Hearing that Klingenberg was working aboard the *A. J. West*, en route to Mexico, Gohl's old enemy, Slade mill superintendent W. B. Mack, wired to Santa

Rosalia, Mexico, requesting that Captain H. H. Smith of the *A. J. West* prevent Klingenberg from going ashore. Obeying, Smith refused Klingenberg the right to quit, drugged and shanghaied the sailor, held him against his will during the long voyage back from Mexico, and forcibly returned him to Grays Harbor.

In his autobiography, Sailors' Union member William "Milo" Coffman described meeting Smith some years after the Gohl trial. Here, in his words, is what Smith told him:

> I left Aberdeen with a load of lumber and had hardly dropped anchor in Santa Rosalia Bay when a telegram came from the chief of police of Aberdeen asking me to hold John Klingenberg, my donkeyman [winch driver], as an accessory to murder.
>
> Maybe John smelled a rat. Anyway, he asked to be paid off right away. I couldn't discharge cargo without a donkeyman, so I refused, but I offered to pay him off when the last stick of lumber went over the side. He agreed.
>
> When the last slingload dropped on the lighter alongside, he packed his dunnage bag and came aft for his money. I had it counted and ready.
>
> "Well, John," said I, "I hate to lose a good donkeyman, but a deal's a deal, so let's have a little farewell drink on it."
>
> John downed a stiff shot of rum and soon keeled over, dead to the world. He never knew what hit him. I had added a few drops of chloral just for good measure. When he woke up we were well down the gulf and headed for Aberdeen
>
> When John got around to asking what happened, I told him he'd better get his heart examined if he couldn't stand a jolt of liquor. When we crossed Grays Harbor bar a couple of weeks later the Aberdeen police were there with the welcome sign.[71]

On reaching land, Klingenberg was taken to the Baldwin Hotel. There, according to the *Aberdeen Herald*, he was forcibly interrogated by a "businessman," who was likely either Gohl's nemesis W. B. Mack or McHugh, the labor spy. The interrogation took place before the noticeably frightened sailor had access to an attorney or translator. The experience must have been terrifying for the Danish immigrant. A slight man, Klingenberg stood only five foot three, weighed 130 pounds, and possessed limited English skills. Based on these facts, and considering Klingenberg's recent experiences as a victim of shanghaiing, it would be difficult to place much stock in the "confession" that followed. After his private questioning of the sailor, Mack or McHugh released the frightened man to the sheriff, to whom he made his confession. The *Grays Harbor Post* described Klingenberg's fearful reaction in vivid ter ms: "Tears streamed down the prisoner's cheeks and he repeatedly exclaimed to the detective nearest him, 'This is Hell. Won't you shoot me and put me out of my misery?'"[72] In October 1910, as Klingenberg faced his own trial for these crimes, he condemned the state's actions against him, declaring that he had been promised immunity in return for cooperating in the prosecution of Gohl, and stating that the murder charges against him were "a put up job."[73]

Klingenberg's affidavit, signed April 4, 1910, and reprinted in each of the major local newspapers, cast a pall over the trial. The confession told of violent events on December 21 and 22, 1909, and laid the blame squarely on Gohl. According to Klingenberg, Gohl had recruited Hoffman and him to help Gohl murder Hadberg. Before the group killed Hadberg, Klingenberg said, Gohl had fired four bullets into Hoffman's back and one into his head. Along with Klingenberg, Gohl had tied Hoffman to an anchor and dropped him in the Chehalis River. That night they had met with Hadberg and slept at his cabin, one of the many cabins that sailors maintained around Grays Harbor. The next morning, in Klingenberg's words:

> I was walking up and down the cabin when Billy Gohl come to me, come from outside. He says to me "You take him. If you don't take him, I take him." I know the meaning by that. He came out in the stream. Charlie Hatberg [*sic*] had a revolver in his pocket. Then Billy Gohl gave me a sign to shoot, and I done so, because I know if I had not done it, Billy Gohl would have shot the pair of us. We tied

the man to an anchor which Billy Gohl and Charlie Hatberg had stolen from the gasoline launch Logger, and throwed him in.

Throughout the remainder of his confession Klingenberg played the complete innocent, in constant fear, saying, "Billy Gohl wanted to try and get me into to a place where he could put lead into me."[74]

Klingenberg delivered a similar confession during the trial in early May. What goes largely ignored, however, is that Klingenberg had a motive for killing Hoffman and Hadberg. Indeed, Klingenberg had feared that Hadberg and Hoffman intended to kill him, and thus he claimed to have killed the two men partly out of self-defense. Thus, unlike Gohl, whose motives were hazy at best, Klingenberg had a good reason to either fight or flee to escape potential harm at the hands of Hoffman and Hadberg, two men he felt had bad intentions. According to Klingenberg, he eventually chose both to fight—killing Hoffman and Hadberg—and to flee, which he did when he sailed to Mexico.

It is difficult to fully understand the intimidation workers must experience as they step into a courtroom. Although Gohl was no stranger to legal proceedings, he couldn't have helped feeling threatened by his surroundings when in a courtroom. Seated at a desk above the courtroom floor was a judge, a man whose wealth and power towered above most of those appearing in court. No one from Gohls' class had a position of power in the Chehalis County Superior Court. Class prejudice, though, ran far beyond the top layer of judges and attorneys, infecting every aspect of the legal system. This is clearly apparent in the makeup of the jury for Gohl's case and the Washington State laws guiding jury selection. On April 14–15, 1910, the Chehalis County Superior Court drew a special venire of three hundred potential jurors for the case. The court drew such a large venire because of the difficulties in securing an impartial jury, especially given all the sensationalistic reporting on the case since Gohl's arrest in early February.[75] Local and regional newspapers did all they could, it seems, to jaundice public opinion of the defendant, asserting Gohl's guilt months before his trial. So many names were drawn that the

Washingtonian revealed on April 26 that "several of the names [were] those of persons who [had] been dead for several years and that at least 10 per cent of the names [were] those of persons incapacitated for duty."[76]

During the questioning of potential jurors, Gohl and attorney Hutcheson laid the groundwork to establish the existence of an anti-union conspiracy against the defendant, one that originated because of Gohl's union activities. The union agent assisted his attorneys in questioning jurors, emphasizing questions pertaining to union activities, strikes, and sailors.[77]

The defense also objected to the selection of the jury. According to Hutcheson, the jury selection process "was in direct violation to section 22 of article 1 of the state constitution, and also in violation of the 14th amendment to the Federal constitution because it deprived the defendant of his life and liberty without due process of law and ... equal protection of the law."[78] State law disallowed jurors who didn't pay property taxes, a handy way to remove itinerant and impoverished workers, those most likely to sympathize with Gohl.[79] Gohl and his attorney rightly saw the law's intent to discriminate against working people. For example, John Carlson, a local longshoreman and sailor, was dismissed from jury duty because he was not a taxpayer.[80] Along with non-taxpayers and women, the latter group also proscribed from Washington State jury duty, the state systematically removed dozens of potential jurors for their opposition to the death penalty.[81] Considering that the structural inequities of the US legal system made workers the most likely group to be killed by the state, removing death penalty opponents was another way to rig the system against working people.

All told, jury selection took three days. The defense, hindered by the prohibition against non-taxpayers, the removal of death penalty opponents, and its limited number of peremptory challenges, knew that the deck was heavily stacked against Gohl. The result made a mockery of the idea that a jury would be composed of one's peers. In a region rightly described by historian Philip J. Dreyfus as "overwhelmingly working class," the selected jury of twelve men contained only

Inside the courtroom during Gohl's murder trial. *Courtesy of Southwest Washington Archives, Olympia, Washington.*

three wage laborers.[82] Equally curious was the selection of six jurors —half of the jury—who made their living as ranchers in a county that counted only a small number of ranches.

Armed with sensational evidence and prepared testimony from many of the region's elites, the state's case was judged by one newspaper to be a "tightening of the coils of the law about William Gohl."[83] Prosecutor William Campbell's opening statement detailed Klingenberg's confession but of course ignored both Klingenberg's motive for killing Hoffman and Hadberg and the kidnapping and shanghaiing of the sailor in Mexico. The statement also introduced a theme that would pervade the remainder of the trial. Whenever possible, the prosecution would mention or would induce witnesses to mention Gohl's alleged shooting of Hoffman, a murder he had not been charged with and whose body had not been found. During his opening statement, Campbell stated: "That a half hour later shots were fired from the launch, some four or five, and the death cries of John Hoffman were heard, when he screamed, 'For god's sake don't kill me, Billy.'" When the defense protested vigorously, claiming that mentioning

Hoffman would bias the jury, Judge Ben Sheeks denied their objection but told the state to refrain from further mentioning Hoffman in the opening statement.[84] Still, the specter of Hoffman would make repeated appearances during the trial.

The state introduced several pieces of physical evidence. First, it introduced a three-by-eight-inch piece of skin tattooed with a dagger driven through a rose, a smaller tattoo of a red heart with a dagger through it, and the initials "H. H." above the smaller tattoo.[85] Hadberg had spent much of his life as a seaman and thus likely acquired tattoos. In the words of the *Grays Harbor Post*: "With consummate skill, the fresh color of the skin had been renewed and the beautiful tattoo marks on the arm brought out in their original colors. This work was done by the use of formaldehyde, arsenic, and a hypodermic syringe."[86]

The state next exhibited three loaded revolvers allegedly found near the body. The revolvers, like the body, had drifted over three hundred yards from the point where Klingenberg claimed the murder occurred to the shores of Indian Creek. Authorities had been puzzled as to how a body held down by a fifty-pound anchor had drifted over three hundred yards.[87] More puzzling still was how three revolvers had drifted along precisely the same route as the body and how, despite their immersion in water were rust-free and appeared "in good condition."[88] This reeked of conspiracy, and Gohl, judging from his reaction, knew that his pistol could not have been found at the scene. Defense attorney J. A. Hutcheson made this clear during his final statement, arguing that Gohl's "powerful enemies" had placed the guns near the body well after the man's death.[89] Had Gohl or his lawyers known that Thiel agents had been in on the case their suspicion would have grown stronger.

While examining the physical evidence, E. E. Boner, an assistant to the prosecution, recited the story of the murder of Hadberg and, according to the *Washingtonian*, "picked up the exhibits and waved them before the jury and Gohl's face."[90] After the state concluded with its examination of the physical evidence, the skin, guns, and anchor were all laid on a table beside Gohl. The *Post* reported that on seeing these "gruesome relics" the union agent's "face blanched and mouth twitched convulsively."[91]

While prosecutors and journalists hammered away at Gohl both inside and outside the courtroom, his defense attorney argued that Gohl was the victim of an antiunion conspiracy. This line of defense became clear during jury selection when Gohl prompted his attorney to question potential jurors about their views on unions and strikes.[92] Defense witnesses also provided an alibi for Gohl on the night of the murder.[93]

Still, the defense's case was surprisingly disappointing to many observers. Since the onset of the case, Gohl's attorneys had promised a quick and successful defense; yet when it came time to actually present their case the defense appeared confused, more content to raise objections to the prosecution's case than score any solid points of their own.[94] On May 3 the defense subpoenaed twelve witnesses, including Gohl's former attorney A. M. Abel, local attorney W. H. Abel, Bessie Gohl, William's sister-in-law Josie and brother-in-law Robert, and at least six men who promised to provide alibis for the defendant.[95] The defense opened its case on May 9 and questioned six witnesses, a process that took only eighty minutes.[96] The lone high point in the otherwise sad spectacle came from W. H. Abel, who attempted to impugn McHugh's credibility. According to Abel, McHugh had offered to leave the county in return for $7,000—a bribe.[97] But McHugh, widely hailed variously as a "strong witness" and "the most important witness," remained at the center of the state's case against Gohl.[98]

After Abel's testimony, the *Washingtonian* did not exaggerate when it wrote: "The bottom fell out of the defense for William Gohl."[99] Only six men came to the stand in Gohl's defense.[100] Although expected to be called as witnesses by the defense, Bessie Gohl and her siblings all failed to testify on William's behalf. No legitimate reason was ever given for this, although the *Herald* suggested that Mrs. Gohl feared giving away more incriminating information during cross-examination by the state.[101] However, it may be more correct to suggest that the presence of thugs from the Thiel agency around town persuaded Mrs. Gohl and her siblings to remain off the stand. During his testimony, Klingenberg claimed that William Gohl told him that Bessie would commit Hadberg's and Hoffman's murders should Klingenberg refuse. The thought that she might be accused in open court of planning a double homicide must have been frightening for Bessie, and it's certainly possible that she wished to avoid antagonizing a prosecution that she believed was engaged in a conspiracy against her husband.[102] Gohl also refused to testify on his own behalf. Gohl and his lawyers never explained why he did not take the stand, although it is possible that, after the stresses of four months in jail and fearing for his life, Gohl's attorneys thought he would make an unsympathetic witness. Considering that the case involved a capital crime and all death penalty opponents had been removed from the jury, an unfortunate misstatement by the defendant could lead to his execution at the hands of the state. Furthermore, Gohl's testimony about a state conspiracy would have angered the judge, a man with the power to have Gohl executed if the jury declared him guilty.

Lingering over the proceedings was the question of Hoffman's body, a constant source of grist for the rumor mill. Speculation about this filled newspaper headlines, legal proceedings, and local public fascination throughout much of 1910. It is important to note again that Hoffman's body never would be recovered, and no one has ever been convicted of his murder. This was not for want of trying. Between February and May, Chehalis County expended no less than $2,000 on efforts trying to recover a corpse.[103] In May 1910, in the waning days of the trial, Grays Harbor newspapers ran stories reporting that O. Peterson, an Aberdeen fisherman, had raised the body of Hoffman to water's surface with his net and that just as he reached for the body it had slipped off his net and sunk. Mere days before Gohl's conviction, Peterson visited the *Grays Harbor Post*, examined a picture of Hoffman, and declared that it matched the body he had raised three days previously. No one mentioned that if the body was Hoffman's it would have been underwater for six months and likely decomposed beyond recognition by the time Peterson found it.[104] News of the findings pushed the county prosecutor to file information against Gohl for the murder of Hoffman, while again reminding the public that they were not dealing with a man but a "ghoul."[105] Rumors circulated throughout the courtroom during the final days of the trial about Peterson's supposed near catch, and according to the *Washingtonian* the news "created considerable excitement."[106]

In what was already an emotionally charged trial, a fever swept over the courtroom during closing arguments. It could hardly have been otherwise. The prosecution opened with attacks on the defendant's character. A member of the prosecution team called Gohl a "cowardly cur."[107] Campbell presented his vision of what had occurred on the night of December 21: "Cannot you picture that scene, when, after Klingenberg had fired only two or three shots, he stood facing Gohl, who also had a revolver in his hand? Can you not understand the feeling within those two men when Gohl said, 'We have no more use for these guns,' and standing with hands raised over the water, holding the weapons, they gave the signal and dropped them at the same time?"[108]

After contesting all the defense alibis, describing how the defendant had used the small launch where Hadberg was killed as a "splendid washtub to obliterate the blood," and referring to Gohl as "one of the finest schemers in Chehalis County," Campbell turned the floor over to the defense at 3:10 p.m. on May 10.[109]

Left with only the friendly testimony of a half-dozen working people, and up against an elite-dominated prosecution, the defense returned to its main line of argument: the conspiracy against Gohl.[110] During his two-hour closing statement the defense attorney returned frequently to some of the themes presented in this book, and while no transcript of the speech was kept, each of the local newspapers noted that he focused his speech on frame-ups, Gohl's powerful enemies, "interests," the persecution of the defendant, and more specific legal improprieties, such as the planting of evidence near the crime site.[111] The state could not ignore the conspiracy charge, likely due to the prosecutors' understanding of just how common conspiracies against union activists were during the early twentieth century. When an opportunity arose, prosecutor Campbell rose to his feet and shouted: "May my God strike me dead if such a condition exists."[112]

Despite the great deal of time and energy expended during the investigation and trial, the state had difficulty convincing the jury of Gohl's guilt. In early balloting, two jurors voted for acquittal. At 11:55 p.m., after the seventh ballot, the jury returned to ask for further instructions because jurors W. J. Nealy and Ned Hackett asked if a second-degree murder conviction was possible. Hackett was one of the sole members of the jury who, like Gohl, was a wage laborer.[113] Sheeks responded curtly, informing the jurors "that the instructions were full," and he directed them to "return to the jury room and read the directions."[114] Forty minutes later the jury returned the verdict:—"guilty of murder in the first degree"—and recommended "as much leniency as possible."[115] Considering that every potential juror with an objection to the death penalty had been systematically removed from the jury pool, the call for leniency was likely more than the defense expected.

Gohl's reaction to the judgment was shock mixed with anger. He had sat patiently through the trial and seen the many condemnations in the press, but the whitewashing never shook his belief in his own innocence or his faith that Grays Harbor employers and politicians had conspired to put him away. When the jury returned its verdict at the late hour of 12:30 a.m. on May 11, a pale-looking Gohl was marched from his cell, a far cry from his usual jovial, defiant self. When jury foreman L. O. Stewart announced the jury's verdict, Gohl collapsed into his chair.[116] Bessie Gohl visited her husband in his cell shortly after the verdict was reached. She declared that she would "work her arms off to her shoulders and her limbs to her knees before she would desert him."[117] Even after being imprisoned at the state penitentiary, Gohl would maintain his innocence, declaring that "personalities" lay at the heart of his conviction.[118]

Considering the hostility he had faced in the courtroom and press, Gohl must have understood that the guilty verdict meant a life behind bars or execution. Following the verdict, the *Grays Harbor*

Washingtonian ran the headline: "Prisoner Sits Unmoved While Hearing Words which Sentence Him to Die by Hanging."[119] Bearing in mind the paper's earlier editorial urging that Gohl be lynched, the headline was perhaps wishful thinking. On May 24, the defense presented motions for acquittal, arrest of the judgment, and a new trial, but Judge Sheeks summarily dismissed all three motions.[120] He then sentenced Gohl to "confinement at hard labor in the state penitentiary for life." The sentence proved a relief to Gohl, especially considering that the press had judged—and even hoped—that he would be executed.[121] Since Klingenberg's return from Mexico, Gohl understood that his fate rested on his fellow sailor either wavering from his original story or admitting that he had been bribed or coerced. Hoping to gain some insight into how Klingenberg's confession matched up so closely to McHugh's story, on April 6 W. H. Abel forced his way into Klingenberg's cell to conduct his own interview.[122] To deter Abel from derailing their case, however, the state had him forcibly removed from Klingenberg's cell, then issued very public threats of disbarment should the attorney pursue the matter further.[123] Gohl and Abel's contentions were validated by Klingenberg, who would later inform the court that he had been promised immunity by the state in exchange for testifying against Gohl.[124] At Klingenberg's murder trial in October 1910, his attorneys argued that their client's April confession was coerced and should be disregarded. Reporting on the trial, the *Aberdeen Herald* wrote that "the defense was working under the theory that the confession made in April by Klingenberg was obtained under such circumstances that the jury should utterly disregard the confession."[125] Indeed, it is difficult to comprehend how, if a legal system was seeking fair trials for Gohl or Klingenberg, its agents would rely on such blatantly tainted evidence.

Bessie Gohl stuck by William throughout the trial, offering comfort to her husband and participating in the defense in a variety of ways. Showing a little direct action of her own, Bessie met an unnamed state witness on the streets of Aberdeen and threatened his life.[126] Sheriff Payette was so distressed over her presence in Montesano that he would write to Warden C. S. Reed at the state penitentiary after the trial, but before Gohl's transport to the prison, telling him that "[Gohl's] wife is not acting just right and may try something desperate when she finds he is going away. She came up from Aberdeen on the train this morning and was making all kinds of talk against all the offices of this County from the police department to the sheriffs office so that I wouldnt be surprised if she was to try something."[127] Throughout the trial proceedings Bessie intently watched every move of the court. On May 8, she jumped from her seat in the audience to challenge a state witness whose name was not on the witness list and who had sat in the courtroom throughout the proceedings, a violation of court protocol.[128] When the jury first retired for deliberations, Bessie rushed to her husband, looking for consolation. William reacted calmly, stating: "Don't worry, no matter what the verdict is. Be cool and calm." Bessie responded: "I will prepare myself for a verdict of guilty. If the verdict is not guilty, I will have a pleasant surprise."[129] That the wife of a condemned man should have been "trouble" for those responsible for his fate should not surprise us, but her devotion to William went above and beyond the call of duty. Bessie visited him in jail frequently, as one of the only people allowed to see William during his many months in city and county jail.

In October 1910, the state tried Klingenberg on a charge of second-degree murder for killing Hadberg. During his trial, Klingenberg called the murder charges "a put up job" and demanded that Gohl be present at his trial.[130] But his confession, whether true, false, or coerced, had done its damage. By October, Gohl was in prison, and Klingenberg's request that he be present was denied.[131] After a rapid trial and three hours of jury deliberations, Klingenberg was found guilty and sentenced to "not less than 10 nor more than 25 years in the state penitentiary at Walla Walla."[132]

9

MAKING THE GHOUL
OF GRAYS HARBOR

IN JUNE 1910, a group of Chehalis County sheriff's deputies transported Gohl in secret from his cell in the Chehalis County Jail to the Washington State Penitentiary in Walla Walla. Sheriff Payette ordered that the 320-mile trip be conducted in secret, ostensibly out of fears that Bessie Gohl or other Gohl allies might raid the transport and help the prisoner escape. Writing in advance to the penitentiary's warden, C. S. Reed, the sheriff warned of this possibility: "I want to keep the day of his departure secret from the public as much as possible as his wife is not acting just right and may try something desperate when she finds he is going away."[1] Whether this was pragmatic concern for officer safety or overblown fear generated by sensational press coverage, the prison transport experienced no difficulties of note, and Gohl began his new life, behind bars in a state penitentiary in eastern Washington, on June 17, 1910.[2]

Few records from Gohl's seventeen years behind bars remain, and we know precious little about his day-to-day existence on the inside. But several prisoners whose terms overlapped with William's recounted their experiences, providing valuable insights on life in the penitentiary. In 1916, an especially detailed account came not from a prisoner but from an enterprising investigative journalist, E. A. Peters, who infiltrated the Washington State Penitentiary by posing as a convicted forger who had been sentenced to the pen. In March that year, Peters showed up at the front gate and told officers he was due to begin his sentence. After a brief meeting with the warden, Peters spent three days as a prisoner in the state penitentiary.[3] He then reported on his experiences in a series of articles published in the *Seattle Star* and *Tacoma Times*. The journalist's major takeaways were the constant reminders of lost freedom. Behind steel bars, armed guards forced inmates to remain silent, march in single-file lines, and perform manual labor in the prison's industrial operations.[4]

The Walla Walla penitentiary was a vast complex composed of housing units, farmland, a dairy, horse barn, and industrial locations. Gohl was one of nearly a thousand inmates confined to the prison during the early 1910s and certainly had at least passing familiarity with some of his fellow inmates. His inmate number was 5779, and inmate number 5778 was John Berglund, who, like Gohl, was a thirty-seven-year-old sailor from Aberdeen. Berglund reached the penitentiary shortly before Gohl. If Gohl and Berglund wished to reminisce with others about their sailing experiences, they had plenty of opportunity. Of the 951 inmates housed at the penitentiary in October 1912, 27—roughly 3 percent—were seamen, indicating that the men who shared Gohl's occupation sometimes found themselves on the wrong side of the law. Immigrant sailors from northern Europe likely gained some comfort from the fact that so many of their fellow inmates spoke their native language and might relate to their immigrant experiences. Gohl joined 38 other German-born inmates in the penitentiary in 1912, while Berglund, a Swede, was one of 29 prisoners from the Scandinavian countries of Sweden, Norway, and Denmark.[5]

In the decade after Gohl's arrival in prison, a rush of labor activists joined him on the inside. Although William hadn't previously showed sympathy toward the left wing of the labor movement, he might have felt differently when he and Wobblies found themselves behind bars together. At the end of the 1910s, the ranks of the Walla Walla penitentiary's political—or class war—prisoners swelled, as dozens of Wobblies, convicted of violating the criminal syndicalism law, faced long prison terms. Their offense: membership in the Industrial Workers of the World. The Washington State legislature's criminal syndicalism bill, which became law in 1919, criminalized involvement with this revolutionary labor organization.[6]

At the state pen, inmates like Gohl labored in a variety of jobs. Most male prisoners worked in the jute mill or kitchen, producing burlap bags or cooking meals for fellow prisoners. Reporter-prisoner Peters described the overseers of the several hundred jute mill workers: "Guards with rifles patrolled a tunnel-like cage of bars that ran the entire length of the building overhead."[7] A few men worked in more skilled positions, such as librarian or physician's assistant. As a metalworker, Gohl fell into this group. Beginning shortly after his life sentence started, Gohl trained to become a tinsmith, a position he would hold until at least 1920, according to the US Census. Unlike the men who worked in the jute mill by the hundreds, only a handful of inmates worked as tinsmiths at the prison.[8] Warden C. S. Reed provided an account of the value of Gohl's shop: "We have manufactured during the past two years [1910–12] 2,250 pieces of sheet metal and tin ware at a cost of about $950.00, saving about $1,500.00 by the use of convict labor."[9]

William's metalwork kept him occupied and apparently provided some satisfaction, to the degree that this was possible for a man condemned to spend his remaining years behind bars. In 1914, Gohl's status made front-page news when a penitentiary guard visited Aberdeen and discussed Gohl's prison life. The *Aberdeen Herald* reported: "Gohl is one of the model prisoners of the pen. He has learned the trade of tinsmith and spends his spare time making curios, at which he is quite expert and which he sells."[10]

One of the sole freedoms allowed prisoners in Walla Walla was the liberty to read whatever one could acquire. The prison library had thousands of books and periodicals, and it was a favorite place for inmates to spend time. Peters reported that ten to twelve trusties worked in the library and that some even slept there. Eugene Barnett, an imprisoned Wobbly, later remembered, "You could get anything you wanted. Anything that was printed, you could get."[11] Facing the prospect of hard times ahead, Gohl tried to remain optimistic about the possibilities for scholarly advancement on the inside. He hoped to devote his time in prison to reading and studying, to further himself intellectually. In an interview with the *Tacoma Daily News*, he stated that he planned to spend his "spare time" "keep[ing] busy enough with his books, which will be forwarded to Walla Walla." The same article reported, "[Gohl] has been studying law through a correspondence school for two years and has another year of work ahead of him, which he says he is going to complete. He also expects to do considerable writing and has asked that his typewriter also be forwarded to the state prison."[12]

Gohl used his freedom to read a trade magazine, the *Sheet Metal Worker*, which related to his work as a tinsmith. We know of his reading habits because Gohl wrote to Edwin A. Scott, New York–based publisher of *Sheet Metal Worker*, and the two struck up an acquaintanceship and exchanged letters for many years, and Scott sent free copies of his magazine. Impressed with Gohl, whom he termed "unusually industrious" and someone who "will prove an industrious worker and a law abiding member of his community if he were released," Scott wrote to the state penitentiary's warden John W. Pace and to Gohl's parole agent to try to secure his release. Scott's 1923 letter to the parole agent heaped praise on Gohl and stated that "if given his freedom he will go straight and become an industrious, conscientious, and honest workman."[13]

Given the sensational rumors spread in the press after Gohl's arrest and throughout his trial, it is not surprising that Grays Harbor residents harbored fears that Gohl might find his way out of prison. Just before shipping Gohl to Walla Walla, Sheriff Payette wrote to Warden Reed of his concerns that the "clever" Gohl "would take a chance [to escape] if he had it."[14] In January 1915, the Grays Harbor area press again stoked fears of "the ghoul," reporting on the mere rumor of his possible escape from the penitentiary. According to the *Aberdeen Herald*, "[A] rumor secured credence in the city yesterday to the effect that William Gohl, the notorious murderer of Aberdeen, has escaped from the penitentiary, where he is serving a life sentence."

The report proved to be unfounded, to the relief of a number whom Gohl had threatened in this city. "Gohl has proved a model prisoner during his incarceration of about four years," the *Herald* reported. "And, being a man of remarkable shrewdness, he has aimed at becoming a 'trusty' in the pen, but it is doubtful if the authorities will give such a criminal that privilege or take any chances upon his escape."[15]

As was his right, Gohl sought legal ways to get out of prison. By the late 1910s, he pursued parole and solicited letters from Scott to assist in this. In 1918, Gohl contacted his onetime lawyer A. M. Abel, seeking assistance in procuring release. The *Grays Harbor Washingtonian*, which, eight years prior had advocated lynching Gohl, reported that the former union agent wanted to help win the war—by being released from prison so he could enlist. The editor's view was clear: "Any effort for a pardon for Gohl will be opposed strenuously."[16]

The *Aberdeen Daily World* further poisoned the well of public opinion: "It may be stated in this connection that word from the state prison recently was to the effect that Gohl was still breathing vengeance against a number of men here who were instrumental in his conviction."[17] Aberdeen banker W. J. Patterson wrote to Governor Ernest Lister, opposing a pardon: "I am promoted to write you, due to the fact that I was personally very familiar with all of Gohl's operations, and sincerely trust that his application will not receive favorable consideration without giving the people of this community an opportunity to protest against it."[18] Given the notoriety of Gohl's case, Lister needed little convincing and wrote back to Patterson: "My recollection of this case is that the evidence indicated that Gohl was not only guilty of one crime, but of many crimes."[19] In 1927, Patterson, who had served at the core of antiunion struggles in the Grays Harbor area, would find himself serving in the Walla Walla penitentiary, four years after Gohl had been removed to the Eastern State Hospital. Long viewed as the wealthiest man in Grays Harbor, Patterson was sentenced to a year in prison after being convicted of a financial crime.[20]

Nearly all the other Grays Harbor elites who opposed Gohl and carried out his removal from the region thrived in the years following his trial. In sharp contrast, the trade union movement, which Gohl helped to build, endured hard times. Removing Gohl from office was an important part of the antiunion campaign waged by the area's employers and their allies. The most immediate effect of Gohl's arrest on murder charges was subsequent condemnation not only of the union agent but also "his gang of murderers," as one newspaper labeled his fellow unionists.[21] By connecting militant unionism—especially membership in the Sailors' Union—to criminality, local newspapers and employers provided a pretext for state actions to the degree that the state itself became a potent union-busting force. Between February and May 1910, police rounded up Gohl's "gang," itinerant sailors living in the many riverside shacks Gohl had helped them build. In mid-February, police dragged Gohl's former roommate, sailor Lauritz Jensen, from his cabin and held him in the Aberdeen jail for eighteen days before charging him with killing a dog. Authorities then kept Jensen in jail until mid-May as they investigated the charge.[22] Concerned that Jensen might aid Gohl's defense, the county's jailers went to great lengths to keep the prisoners separate. After Gohl's conviction, with the SUP rank and file in tatters and its agent serving a life sentence, one local union member stated in 1911, "The Aberdeen local has been most unfortunate. . . . The Gohl case was a heavy blow to our cause and even now the union is suffering from this source. We are trying to run the union 'on the square.'"[23]

After 1910, the SUP, the oldest local labor union, declined. It did not take a lead role in a single labor conflict in the 1910s, and in 1912 several sailors joined the Marine Transport Industrial Workers' Union, a branch of the IWW.[24] Thus, the campaign against Gohl had the effect of weakening the trade union movement, albeit not working-class expressions of solidarity.

Arguably of greater significance, however, was that the men who led the anti-Gohl campaign gained the public's esteem and trust, seen as protectors of "law and order" in the face of a monster who had used his union office to commit unspeakable crimes. Whether or not Gohl committed any murders, by February 1910 the perception of him as a vicious killer became cemented in the public mind. This helped generate support for employers and authorities whose "citizens' committee" took the lead in the "investigation," trial, and press campaign against Gohl. The wealthy businessmen who led the committee gained credibility with the public. Patterson in particular held court at the Aberdeen City Council in August 1911 to discuss how he had altruistically paid labor spies for the Gohl investigation. Patterson had "believed it was his duty and of every citizen's duty who had contributed to this fund to assist in helping the city and the county in bringing this criminal to justice," noted the region's largest daily paper.[25]

The combination of employers, press, and the state into a law-and-order force provided these groups with a great deal of latitude in their actions against unionists, legitimizing antiunion violence. Meanwhile Aberdeen city officials apparently had little interest in actual criminal justice. They made this clear with the selection of Lewis D. Templeman, a spy "loaned" to the City of Aberdeen by the Thiel agency, as police chief in 1911. The timing of Templeman's hire was no coincidence. In 1911, the Industrial Workers of the World began a massive organizational campaign in Aberdeen, which culminated in an IWW free speech fight from November 1911 until January 1912, followed by a massive lumber strike of thousands of immigrant mill workers. At the fore of the antiunion struggle was a coalition forged during the campaign against Gohl, including Chief Templeman and a new and enlarged citizens' committee. During the free speech fight and concomitant strike, Templeman and local employers relied on extensive antilabor violence, shooting, beating, and deporting left-wing street speakers and strikers. Many of these businessmen had earlier belonged to the citizens' committee that had hired labor spies to rid the region of Gohl and his associates.[26]

Long-standing interest in the Wobblies has led to the unearthing of useful historical documentation of antiunion violence on the harbor and throughout the Pacific Northwest. But the record of scores of antiunion beatings and deportations have done nothing to dispel the myth of Gohl and "the Ghoul." No one writing about Gohl has mentioned that those who led the campaign to oust him—united into a citizens' committee—were the same men who a year later formed a new citizens' committee and committed violent acts motivated by their antiradical, antiunion views.

The absence of class analysis related to Gohl's life and early twentieth-century violence in Grays Harbor cannot be attributed to a lack of writings on the topic. Few subjects in Pacific Northwest history have received as much attention as "the Ghoul of Grays Harbor." Not long after Gohl's arrest, locals and historians began to blame him for the much of the region's violent past. By the 1930s, popular history writers were beginning to put a different spin on the facts, casting the region as a coastal version of the rough and gritty Wild West. Said to be a "wide open town," Aberdeen had boasted dozens of saloons and brothels, and accounts of deadly brawls, shoot-outs, and knifings colored the town's early history. Popular historian Stewart Holbrook noted: "The city of Aberdeen, on Washington's west coast, presented a more typical sort of Skidroad than either Spokane or Seattle, or even Portland. Aberdeen was and is a pure sawmill town of classic vintage, nearer to the old Saginaw and older Bangor than anything in the West. Only Aberdeen was tougher, much tougher."[27] With titles such as "The Ghoul of Grays Harbor" and "Plank Streets and Shady Dealings," later writers picked up on the claims made by Holbrook in the 1930s.[28]

The initial campaign to blame Gohl for all of the region's violent past makes sense from a public relations standpoint. As historians Carlos A. Schwantes and James P. Ronda write: "The modern West was in many ways the outcome of a massive sales campaign.... It was in the economic interest of every westerner to brag about the seemingly unlimited resources of his or her newfound home."[29] Boosters in the early twentieth century framed Aberdeen and the wider region as safe and family-friendly, good destinations for tourism, settlement, and investment. With Gohl removed, the harbor region could grow and thrive.

Lumber and shipping bosses, along with detectives from the Thiel agency, had played prominent roles in spreading rumors that Gohl was an arsonist. One was Ralph Peasley, one of the bosses for the strikebreaking Grays Harbor Stevedore Company and owner of the

Zelasko Building in Aberdeen. On June 11, 1909, the Zelasko Building burned, and authorities claimed that the fire resulted from arson. Police arrested Charles Bealey, a local African American man, for the crime. Bealey was arrested and charged with the crime but was acquitted in trial. But Peasley later testified at Gohl's trial that he suspected that Gohl was responsible for the fire.[30] In 1912, Bealey sued several Aberdeen city officials for $15,000, claiming false imprisonment because he had not committed the arson and asserting that Gohl was responsible for the criminal act.[31] Unfortunately, the legal system did not provide much in the way of justice for Bealey. According to an Olympia newspaper, two years after Bealey sued Aberdeen's public officials for damages he had received no compensation. Dogged by creditors, Bealey left the city, hoping to avoid his debts.[32]

George Dean, the Aberdeen chief of police, gained renown for a time for his involvement in bringing down "the Ghoul of Grays Harbor." But soon after Gohl's trial, Dean's life took significant turns. In December 1910, the Aberdeen City Council removed him as chief following allegations, later substantiated, that his officers were brutalizing suspects—for example, that they had assaulted a logger named Harry Cardigan who had been arrested for drunkenness.[33] This was nothing new in Aberdeen and the harbor region more widely, as police used excessive force in making arrests, even for those suspected of minor crimes, and tortured prisoners in the region's jails.[34] In August 1911, new charges came from the city council that Dean had misused public funds, and in November he resigned from the police department and joined his brother in purchasing the Fan, a cigar store and billiard room on Heron Street. For two years he took a lower profile in Aberdeen.[35]

Dean would become Aberdeen's police chief again later in the decade, as the City of Aberdeen joined employers and vigilantes to assault, round up, and jail IWWs. And two decades later Dean would play a shameful role in December 1939, when his officers allowed vigilantes to raid and destroy the massive and ornate Finnish Socialist Hall, which had stood as the center of left-wing political activity on the harbor for nearly four decades. Three weeks later, Laura Law, the

Finnish-American wife of labor activist Richard Law, was blud-
geoned to death in her home, and Dean's police force never arrested
anyone—the case went unsolved. Battling lingering illness, Dean
retired in July 1941 and died at home in Aberdeen during August 1943.
In an obituary, the myth of "Gohl the Ghoul" was perpetuated—with
sheer falsehoods: "Some time after his conviction, [Gohl] confessed
to the murder of Hedburg [*sic*] and his companion, John Hoffman.
He also admitted responsibility in the death of many of the other victims of the 'floater fleet,' which was estimated up to 40 victims."[36]

Dean had contributed to the myth to boost his own fame. Following
Gohl's removal from the harbor, Dean as police chief gave occasional
interviews in which he claimed to have played a leading role in ending
Gohl's "reign of terror." Dean's great niece Pamela Aho, who penned
articles about Gohl, was clear enough about this: "George Dean was
known to cultivate his image as the man who caught Billy Gohl."[37]

While Dean basked in celebrity, Gohl did his best to survive in
prison. The year 1912 brought an end to two of his longest relationships: with his union and with his wife, Bessie. At an October 28, 1912,
meeting at the Sailors' Union headquarters in San Francisco, Gohl
was expelled from the union, as was a second Aberdeen SUP agent,
William Vortman, who had stolen the Aberdeen union treasury,
absconding with it to parts unknown. One can imagine why the union
expelled Gohl, but it is difficult to determine why the expulsion hadn't
come sooner.[38]

After Gohl's trial, Bessie moved first to nearby Montesano and
later 320 miles east to Walla Walla, where her husband was condemned to spend the remainder of his days. In his final newspaper
interview, conducted in June 1910 by the *Tacoma Daily News*, Gohl
praised his loving and devoted wife. He stated: "It has been a great
encouragement to me to have her near. I don't know that I would have
been able to stand up under the strain of false accusations had it not
been for her encouragement. . . . I know that many efforts were made
during the trial to turn her against me, but none of them was successful."[39] Still, after almost two years in Walla Walla, Bessie, still in her
early thirties at the time, knew that her husband stood little chance of

release and sought to restart her life on her own. In February 1912, she filed for divorce from the man she loved and had stuck by through thick and thin.[40]

Bessie would live the remainder of her years in Walla Walla, only a short distance from the penitentiary and Gohl's cell. While she eventually remarried a farmer named Leonard Naught, Bessie continued to sometimes use the surname "Gohl" until her death. In her new life, Bessie worked alongside her husband on a family farm. Although details about her later years are sparse, it is likely that her experience as a small proprietor in Aberdeen aided her in the business aspects of running a farm. Bessie died in September 1945 at the age of sixty-six.[41]

William Gohl's health declined during the late 1910s and early 1920s, and this may have been exacerbated by the eventual realization that he would never be released from prison. Conditions there are known to have been harsh. Journalist E. A. Peters, who had himself experienced the prison firsthand, reported in 1916 of the experiences of one John Hildebrandt, who had lately been released from Walla Walla: "He spoke of the horrible tortures of former administrations. Of the dungeon sentences, and the torture of the stream of cold water turned upon the convicts' naked bodies, and the whippings that were a regular course of prison discipline." Peters commented: "Records show that tortures caused many to commit suicide."[42]

On September 22, 1923, the physician for the Washington State Penitentiary certified that Gohl suffered from a "Paranoiac State" due to dementia paralytica, resulting from syphilis. The doctor wrote that in his opinion, "the welfare of the person above named requires that he be removed to a hospital for the insane for treatment." As a result, authorities transferred Gohl from the penitentiary to the Eastern State Hospital at Medical Lake "for treatment and confinement until such time as the Superintendent of said hospital shall deem it advisable to return him to the Penitentiary."[43] Gohl never returned to the prison, dying in Medical Lake in March 1927.[44]

Now more than a century has passed since Gohl's removal from public life in 1910, and what remains are interpretations of his life

LET NOTHING INTERFERE WITH YOUR PLANS

To attend the annual banquet of the Hoquiam Commercial Club at the Hotel Gray-port, Friday evening, February 11. Wives and sweethearts are expected to be present.

Grays Harbor Daily Washingtonian

OLDEST AND BEST—ONLY PAPER IN HOQUIAM RECEIVING TELEGRAPHIC DISPATCHES OF ANY KIND

Tides Today
High Water

Low Water

Weather Forecast
Rain.

TWENTIETH YEAR. NO. 258. HOQUIAM, WASH., SUNDAY MORNING, FEBRUARY 6, 1910. PRICE, FIVE CENTS

RED RECORD OF CRIME ON GRAYS HARBOR CHARGED TO WILLIAM GOHL

"Forty men are known to have been murdered on the Harbor in recent years. I believe that William Gohl was the prime mover in many times forty murders, many of which have never come to light. Just at present I cannot say upon what I base this statement."—Chief of Police Dean, of Aberdeen

Article from the February 6, 1910, issue of the *Daily Washingtonian*. The headline provides an example of the way much of the press covered Gohl's arrest and rumors of his criminal activities.

that amount to myth, crafted by writers with diverse interests but chiefly motivated by profit. Gohl stories have long been popular among true crime authors and popular historians looking to sell Wild West books, and they have been written too by Grays Harbor boosters to foster tourism in an area hit hard by recession due to the declining timber industry. These stories and the overall myth have far overshadowed the actual substance of Gohl's life and times.

After the removal of Gohl from Aberdeen in 1910, some began to imagine that the region had become a model of safety and stability. Local newspapers ran articles claiming that Aberdeen ranked as one of the country's healthiest cities. As one booster claimed in 1911: "The city is well policed and healthful. It is but a short journey by Steamboat and train to the seashore, where the broad expanse of the Pacific stretches away from the sandy beaches and comfortable hotels offer every modern convenience for the tourist and sightseers."[45] In 1912, the *Grays Harbor Post* ran a front-page article boasting of Aberdeen's "remarkable" child death rate, noting that with seventeen hundred students in the city schools, "[only] one death occurred during the school year."[46] In early 1917, an *Aberdeen Daily World* headline declared, "Aberdeen Still Healthiest City."[47] The same newspaper ran a long article in January 1924, attesting to Aberdeen's record as a safe city and noting growth: "Births outstrip deaths for 1923."[48] Leaders of a growing industrial city saw that it was important to position the harbor as safe for investment, settlement, and tourism. And the press agreed, with headlines like "Quiet Reigns Now in Old Redlight Region. No Revelry This New Year in Old District Once Bright with Lights and Reeking with Evil."[49]

Such reportage went back to the time of Gohl's murder trial. The *Seattle Star* had then contended that Gohl was a product of "a frontier town" but that Aberdeen had changed, going "from a picturesque town of tough saloons, tougher dance halls, and countless sudden deaths to a modern city of paved streets and respect for law." The union agent and alleged serial killer was thus both a product of the frontier and the cause of the region's epic violence. The law and order of "a modern city," so the argument went, had brought Gohl to justice.[50] The *Aberdeen Daily World* celebrated, "Aberdeen breathes freer today, and feels that that page of savagery and medievalism represented by William Gohl has been torn out of the book, with only a bad memory remaining."[51] In this way, the chapter of "Wild West" history in Grays Harbor had ended, as the region became sanitized and safe.

Showing how completely fused the notions of violence and disorder had become with Gohl, in November 1911 the *Aberdeen Daily World* editorialized: "This is not a backwoods camp, but a modern, civilized city. The days of the Gohls have gone by, and those who would attempt to revive them will learn to their cost."[52] Written amid a massive outbreak of antilabor vigilantism against members and supporters of the IWW, instigated in part by newspapers such as the *World*, the editorial's message was clear. Gohl symbolized the "old Aberdeen," an uncivilized place where violent workmen stood in the way of progress. The editorial threatened punishment for those who stepped out of line, punishment such as Gohl had received a year earlier. While calling out Gohl for violence, ostensibly a thing of the past, the *World* incited violent vigilantism against members of the IWW.[53]

The reality was more complex than the myth peddled after Gohl's removal. Long after Gohl was behind bars, dead bodies continued to show up. As Gohl had long pointed out, accidental and violent deaths were inevitable in a port town like Aberdeen with dozens of saloons, an unguarded and unlit waterfront, and hundreds of itinerant workers. Records of Aberdeen's Whiteside Funeral Home provide a detailed look at the harbor's deaths. The funeral home prepared dozens of death certificates for people who drowned during the 1910s. More specifically, the Whiteside buried more than a dozen drowning victims in the first year of Gohl's confinement at the penitentiary.[54] To explain the continued appearance of "floaters," journalists and local officials for a year or two continued to sometimes blame the deaths on Gohl. Over time, though, these claims became increasingly untenable. In March 1912, with Gohl behind bars for more than two years, the *Aberdeen Herald* ran a front-page article reporting the recent discovery of a human skull and saying it might represent a victim of Gohl.[55]

More tellingly, Aberdeen continued to experience extremely high violent death rates, far higher than other Northwest cities. Following the 1910 US Census, which showed that Aberdeen's population had reached 13,660, the Census Bureau conducted detailed examinations of the city's mortality statistics. The bureau found that 121 Aberdeen residents died during 1910 and that, of that number, 22 persons, or 18 percent, had died "violent deaths excluding suicide," a category that includes accidents and murders. The 18 percent was far higher than that of Washington's other cities with populations of ten thousand or more, which ranged from 5.6 percent in Bellingham to 12 percent in Everett, both lumber towns. Even in Seattle, with its rough and rowdy reputation, violent deaths comprised only 9 percent of fatalities, roughly half the rate of Aberdeen. A year after Gohl's imprisonment, the pattern continued: Aberdeen's violent death rate remained higher than similar Pacific Coast port towns including Bellingham, Everett, Seattle, Tacoma, Portland, and San Francisco.[56]

The year 1911 marked an important point in the effort to increase industrial safety, as Washington State adopted a workers' compensation law that required employers to pay into a state accident fund administered by an independent commission. Workplaces—especially in the lumber industry—remained (and remain) dangerous, but the law provided for compensation to injured workers and the families of those who died in workplace accidents, thus encouraging employers to adopt workplace safety measures.[57] And by the end of 1914, the saloons—according to Gohl one of the sources of Aberdeen's drowning deaths—had been removed. That year all of Washington State went dry, as voters approved a statewide prohibition initiative.[58]

Still, people continued to die in the harbor's waterways, much as they did in other port towns. Between 1915 and 1918, at least sixteen Finnish immigrants—seven adults and nine children—drowned in Grays Harbor.[59] This unfortunate group included Victor Anderson, a seaman who had made his home in Hoquiam. Anderson perished in October 1914 after a night of bar-hopping ended with him accidentally plunging into the Hoquiam River. He drowned shortly before "a would-be rescuer" arrived in a boat, according to the *Aberdeen Herald*.[60] In the 1920s, as Gohl's health declined in a prison hundreds of miles from Aberdeen bodies continued turning up in the harbor's waterways, and police and journalists persisted in using the term "floaters" for these. In April 1926, no fewer than three men died in the Wishkah and Chehalis Rivers; another drowned in late May, followed by two more in July.[61]

Seamen continued to live harsh and unpredictable lives, made worse by police intent on criminalizing their lifestyles. In November 1913, Sailors' Union member Albert Fors hanged himself in his jail cell while being held on charges of insanity. Local authorities routinely jailed those experiencing mental illness, a condition criminalized in the early twentieth century.[62] The next year, French sailor Louis Lois leaped from the steamer *Saginaw* into the waters just off the entry to Grays Harbor. Observing that Lois had been acting "queerly" before his death, authorities ruled it a suicide, the result of "insanity."[63] In September 1914, the bodies of sailors John Johnson and Henry F. Otto, who had been killed in the wreck of the steamer *F. H. Leggett*, washed ashore on one of the harbor's beaches.[64] In May 1915, Alfred Malm, who, after years of work as a sailor, was described by the *Aberdeen Herald* as "aged and crippled," fell into the Hoquiam River while climbing out of a boat and drowned.[65]

Using Grays Harbor as a site of historical violence, with Gohl playing a leading role, boosters in the late twentieth century tried to turn the region into a tourist destination. In a single-industry region facing at a bleak future of industrial decline and long-term recession, Grays Harborites needed other sources of income. Grays Harbor is a short distance from Washington's beaches, the only rainforests in the continental United States, and the majestic Olympic Mountains. But Aberdeen and Hoquiam are not beach towns. They have long been industrial cities in decline, and, though tourists might stop to buy gas while passing through, few want to stay. To capture tourist dollars, locals hoped to capitalize on the area's gritty past.[66]

As part of a local historical commission report in 1969, local historian Anne Cotton wrote that Gohl was Aberdeen's "only first-rate tourist attraction." Hoping to capitalize on the image of Aberdeen as a site of violence and vice, Cotton advised the city to develop the neighborhood that formerly housed the Sailors' Union hall into an "entertainment and apartment house district" as had been done "in other American cities with colorful history."[67] Examples of such tourist destinations stretch across the West, including Deadwood, South Dakota, and Tombstone, Arizona. And so the Gohl myth continues. A travel guide titled *Weird Washington* hyperbolically places him at the center of Aberdeen's violent past: "Gohl was most uncooperative in accounting for all the men he murdered, but if the accepted body count of 124 is accurate (to say nothing of suspicions that many more bodies remained underwater or were washed out to sea), he was likely the most prolific serial killer in American history."[68]

Interest in Gohl extends beyond Grays Harbor. The Southwest Regional Branch of the Washington State Archives in Olympia holds several collections with material related to Gohl, and archivists there have made use of Gohl in much the same way that Grays Harbor boosters have done. In 2012, the state archives hosted a "Law & Order in the Archives" month, advertised by posters and a website that included Gohl's mug shot. The website stated that Gohl "was suspected of killing more than 40 men between 1905 and 1910." As part of its "Law & Order" month, the institution provided "haunted

archives tours," featuring staff and volunteers dressing as prominent criminals from Washington State history. A 2018 version of the
haunted tour at the archives featured a "Billy Gohl" character standing behind bars and describing his life in subdued tones. In 2011,
Vanity Fair magazine ran a short, playful piece titled "Serial Killers
vs. American Icons: A Users' Guide to Ensure a Gaffe-Free Conversation," that placed Gohl alongside notorious criminals like Ted Bundy
and the Hillside Strangler within the serial killer category, not to be
confused with Billy Joel, Al Bundy, and prefab folk group the Hillside Singers.[69]

Most writings about Gohl fall into the nonfiction category,
although, as this book has argued, they lack veracity. Gohl stories have
long bridged fact and fiction. It is thus unsurprising that novelists
have found inspiration in Gohl's life and crimes. Best-selling writer
Garth Stein weaves a story about Gohl into his novel *A Sudden Light*.
In the book, a father tells his son about the life and times of their
ancestor, a timber baron turned conservationist, stories of the wild
and woolly Pacific Northwest of yesteryear. After discussing the
terrible conditions loggers faced and the "brothels, which were full of
STDs," the father speaks of "the Ghoul of Grays Harbor," a man who
"murdered hundreds of men in his bar." Although Gohl only makes
a brief appearance in *A Sudden Light*, Stein likely chose "the Ghoul"
to capture the violence and horrid conditions of the frontier Pacific
Northwest. Indeed, few other men in the region's history are so
emblematic of its troubled past.[70]

Gohl was far from being the first real or alleged murderer whose
life has been monetized by entrepreneurs looking to drum up tourism. In the early twenty-first century, true-crime-oriented products
and tourist destinations have become big business, with "murdera-
bilia" (as artifacts from serial killers have been called) generating
a bonanza for sellers.[71] The 2018 Netflix documentary series *Dark
Tourist* popularizes the idea of visiting locations associated with
death and tragedy, just the latest in a long and deep connection
between consumers and sites of perceived historical violence.[72] Seattle's Underground Tour focuses on the city's early history of crime,

sex, and violence. Thousands of visitors take the tour annually, making the Seattle Underground an important destination, one focused
on the gritty past of a city now identified with the tech industry,
grunge music, and its proximity to rainforests, mountains, islands,
and the ocean.[73]

Dozens of podcasts and documentary films rehash questionable
and downright wrongful convictions, while still others focus on police
corruption, inadequate defense counsel, and the deeply biased American criminal justice system. In Gohl's day and in the present, this
system appears to be designed to oppress blacks, immigrants, and
members of the working class, and to protect those at the top.

More than a century after Gohl's imprisonment, writings describing the union agent's alleged nefarious activities continue to be published, comprising a veritable cottage industry. They all tell slight
variations of the same story, one first crafted in local newspapers and
rarely, if ever, publicly challenged. Like Billy the Kid and Jesse James,
"Gohl the Ghoul" has reached mythic status. But William Gohl was
convicted of a single murder, that of Charles Hadberg, and another
man, John Klingenberg, admitted to shooting Hadberg. Moreover, the
entire case was determined mostly by testimony from a labor spy
(Paddy McHugh) and Klingenberg, a sailor shanghaied in a foreign
port, forcibly transported more than two thousand miles, and subjected to interrogation by a private citizen who also happened to be
one of Gohl's greatest enemies. It is possible that Gohl had a hand in
the death of Hadberg and even perhaps others, but to accept the version of history peddled by the union activist's enemies and uncritically repeated in self-published books is shortsighted. The myth of
"Gohl the Ghoul" was founded on the destruction of the life and reputation of an activist labor leader and on turning him into a monster.
To accept and repeat the myth is to ignore and erase the reality of
class struggle.

NOTES

INTRODUCTION

1. See, for example, Pamela Dean Aho, "The Ghoul of Grays Harbor," in *On the Harbor: From Black Friday to Nirvana*, edited by John C. Hughes and Ryan Teague Beckwith (Aberdeen, WA: Daily World, 2001), 18–31; C. J. Lind, "The Port of Missing Men," *Tacoma News-Tribune*, February 23, 1969; Frank J. Zoretich, "Plank Streets and Shady Dealings," *Pacific Slope*, February 1978, 12–13; William J. Betts, "Launched 100 Murders," *Golden West* 6, no. 2 (January 1970): 19–21, 56–58; Richard J. Goodrich, "The Madman of Aberdeen," *Harborquest* 3 (August 1992): 8–9, 23; Jan Holden, "Billy Gohl: The Ghoul of Grays Harbor," *Old West* (Fall 1995): 26–30; Hollis B. Fultz, "The Constable of Cosmopolis," in *Famous Northwest Manhunts* (Elma, WA: Fulco Publishing, 1955), 27–52; Anne Cotton, "History of Aberdeen: 1775–1982," in *Aberdeen Comprehensive Development Plan, Phase I, Profile of Aberdeen* (Aberdeen, WA: Grays Harbor Regional Planning Commission, 1969), 1–66; Dennis Pence, *The Ghoul of Grays Harbor* (Aberdeen, WA: Authorhouse, 2004); Stewart H. Holbrook, *Holy Old Mackinaw: The Natural History of the American Lumberjack* (New York: Ballantine Books, 1971), 193–94.

2. Jeff Davis and Al Eufrasio, *Weird Washington: Your Travel Guide to Washington's Local Legends and Best Kept Secrets* (New York: Sterling

Publishing, 2008), 111–12. See also Marques Vickers, *Murder in Wash-ington: The Topography of Evil: Notorious Washington State Murder Sites* (Larkspur, CA: Marquis Publishing, 2016), 29–31; C. J. March, *The Ghoul of Grays Harbor: Murder and Mayhem in the Pacific North-west* (Minneapolis: Slingshot Books, 2019).

3. Cotton, "History of Aberdeen," 40.

4. Aho, "Ghoul of Grays Harbor," 18; Cotton, "History of Aberdeen," 40.

5. *Grays Harbor Washingtonian*, May 6, 1910. Sources use variant spell-ings of "Hadberg." "Hadberg" is the most common, so I have used it throughout the text.

6. "State Penitentiary at Walla Walla, Description of Convict William Gohl," March 3, 1927, Billy Gohl Documentation, Southwest Regional Branch, Washington State Archives, Olympia; *Grays Harbor Post* (Aberdeen, WA), December 29, 1923; Aho, "Ghoul of Grays Harbor," 31.

7. *Aberdeen Daily World*, February 3, 1910.

8. *Oakland Tribune*, February 4, April 5, 6, 1910; *Los Angeles Herald*, Febru-ary 4, 5, 6, 7, 1910; *San Francisco Call*, February 4, 1910 ("Gunness Farm" alluded to murders committed by Belle Gunness in LaPorte, Indiana).

9. United States Commission on Industrial Relations, *Industrial Relations: Final Report and Testimony submitted to Congress by the Commission on Industrial Relations, created by the Act of August 23, 1912* (Washing-ton, DC: Government Printing Office, 1916), 5394.

10. Hugh Davis Graham and Ted Robert Gurr, *Violence in America: Histori-cal and Comparative Perspectives*, vol. 1 (Washington, DC: US Govern-ment Printing Office, 1969), 241.

11. *Grays Harbor Washingtonian*, February 8, 1910.

12. On the lives of migratory workers in early twentieth-century North America, see Gunther Peck, *Reinventing Free Labor: Padrones and Immigrant Workers in the North American West, 1880–1930* (Cam-bridge: Cambridge University Press, 2000); Greg Hall, *Harvest Wob-blies: The Industrial Workers of the World and Agricultural Laborers in the American West, 1905–1930* (Corvallis: Oregon State University Press, 2001); Frank Tobias Higbie, *Indispensable Outcasts: Hobo Workers and Community in the American Midwest* (Urbana: University of Illi-

nois Press, 2004); Gabriel Thompson, *Chasing the Harvest: Migrant Workers in California Agriculture* (London: Verso Books, 2017).

13. Mark Leier, *Rebel Life: The Life and Times of Robert Gosden, Revolutionary, Mystic, Labour Spy*, 2nd ed. (Vancouver: New Star Books, 2013), 9.

14. The quotation appeared in the *Grays Harbor Washingtonian* (Hoquiam, WA). Cited in John Hughes and Ryan Teague Beckwith, eds., *On the Harbor: From Black Friday to Nirvana* (Aberdeen, WA: Daily World, 2001), 72; Fred Lockley, "Grays Harbor: The Largest Lumber-Shipping Port in the World," *Pacific Monthly*, June 1907, 721.

15. Charles Yale Harrison, *Generals Die in Bed: A Story from the Trenches* (New York: W. Morrow, 1930).

16. Stephen Schwartz, *Brotherhood of the Sea: A History of the Sailors' Union of the Pacific, 1885–1985* (San Francisco: Sailors' Union of the Pacific, 1986), 20–27; Hyman Weintraub, *Andrew Furuseth: Emancipator of the Seamen* (Berkeley: University of California Press, 1959), 36–39; Bruce Nelson, *Workers on the Waterfront: Seamen, Longshoremen, and Unionism in the 1930s* (Urbana: University of Illinois Press, 1990), 11–14.

17. Nelson, *Workers on the Waterfront*, 11–38; Weintraub, *Andrew Furuseth*, 3–10.

18. "Log Book for *Dauntless*," October 10, 1907, United States Customs, Puget Sound Collection District, Series 31 Log Books, National Archives, Seattle; Nelson, *Workers on the Waterfront*, 14–15, 35; *Aberdeen Daily Bulletin*, June 9, 1906; Paul S. Taylor, "The Sailors' Union of the Pacific" (PhD dissertation, University of California, 1922), 24.

19. Gill, Peter, "The Sailors' Union of the Pacific," manuscript, 1942, 1, University of Washington, Digital Archives, http://digitalcollections.lib.washington.edu/cdm/ref/collection/pnwhm/id/1068.

20. Nelson, *Workers on the Waterfront*, 12; Schwartz, *Brotherhood of the Sea*, 4–5.

21. Weintraub, *Andrew Furuseth*, 3–4.

22. *Coast Seamen's Journal*, January 26, 1898.

23. Weintraub, *Andrew Furuseth*, 37–38; Nelson, *Workers on the Waterfront*, 13.

24. Susan Armitage, "Through Women's Eyes: A New View of the West," in *The Women's West*, edited by Susan Armitage and Elizabeth Jameson (Norman: University of Oklahoma Press, 1987), 17.

25. Elizabeth Fox-Genovese and Eugene D. Genovese, "The Political Crisis of Social History," *Journal of Social History* 10, no. 2 (Winter 1976): 219.

26. William G. Robbins, *Colony and Empire: The Capitalist Transformation of the American West* (Lawrence: University Press of Kansas, 1994), 20.

27. Rosemary Feurer and Chad Pearson, eds., *Against Labor: How U.S. Employers Organized to Defeat Union Activism* (Urbana: University of Illinois Press, 2017), 1.

28. Lawrence Richards, *Union-Free America: Workers and Antiunion Culture* (Urbana: University of Illinois Press, 2008), 15. On the long history of anti-unionism in the United States, see Feurer and Pearson, *Against Labor*. For a classic study on the intense struggles between labor and capital, see Sidney Lens, *Labor Wars: From the Molly Maguires to the Sit Downs* (Garden City, NY: Doubleday, 1973).

29. United States Commission on Industrial Relations, *Industrial Relations, Final Report*, 4278.

30. *Grays Harbor Post*, January 7, 1905.

31. *Aberdeen Daily World*, August 10, 14, 1911.

32. *Aberdeen Herald*, April 7, 1910.

33. Murray Morgan, *The Last Wilderness* (Seattle: University of Washington Press, 1955), 122–52.

34. Ed Van Syckle, *They Tried to Cut It All: Grays Harbor, Turbulent Years of Greed and Greatness* (Seattle: Pacific Search Press, 1980), 241.

35. Morgan, *The Last Wilderness*, 124.

36. Mark Leier, *Where the Fraser River Flows: The Industrial Workers of the World in British Columbia* (Vancouver: New Star Books, 1990), ii.

37. Holbrook, *Holy Old Mackinaw*, 269.

38. *Aberdeen World*, February 7, 14, 1909.

39. Aho, "Ghoul of Grays Harbor," 21; Cotton, "History of Aberdeen," 43.

40. *Grays Harbor Post*, May 15, 1909.

CHAPTER ONE: BILLY GOHL'S WORLD

1. *Grays Harbor Post*, September 3, 1904; *Aberdeen Daily Bulletin*, October 30, November 3, 1906; letter from W. von Loehneysen, consul for Germany, Seattle, Washington, to the superintendent of the state penitentiary, Walla Walla, Billy Gohl Documentation, Washington State Penitentiary, Southwest Regional Branch, Washington State Archives, Olympia; Correspondence, "Washington State Penitentiary, Biographical Statement of Convict No. 5779," June 18, 1910, Billy Gohl Documentation, Washington State Penitentiary, Southwest Regional Branch, Washington State Archives, Olympia. Gohl's biography in the *Grays Harbor Post* states that he was born in 1872.

2. Karl Marx, *Capital*, vol. I. Translated by Ben Fowkes (London: Penguin Books, 1990).

   On the history of nineteenth-century Germany, see Gordon A. Craig, *Germany, 1866–1945* (Oxford: Oxford University Press, 1978); John Breuilly, ed., *Nineteenth-Century Germany: Politics, Culture and Society, 1780–1918* (London: Bloomsbury, 2003); David Blackbourn, *The Long Nineteenth Century: A History of Germany, 1780–1918* (Oxford: Oxford University Press, 1997).

3. *Aberdeen Daily Bulletin*, June 9, 1906.

4. Greg Gordon, *When Money Grew on Trees: A. B. Hammond and the Age of the Timber Barons* (Norman: University of Oklahoma Press, 2014).

5. *Proceedings of the Fourth Annual Convention of the Washington State Federation of Labor* (Aberdeen, WA: Washington State Federation of Labor, 1906), 42.

6. *Grays Harbor Post*, September 3, 1904.

7. *Chehalis County Vidette*, February 11, 1910. In 1904, 21.5 percent of SUP members were German immigrants, making Germans the fourth-largest ethnic group in the union. *Coast Seamen's Journal*, August 17, 1904.

8. *Aberdeen Daily Bulletin*, June 9, 1906.

9. *Grays Harbor Post*, September 3, 1904.

10. Stephen Schwartz, *Brotherhood of the Sea: A History of the Sailors' Union of the Pacific, 1885–1985* (San Francisco: Sailors' Union of the Pacific, 1986), 11; Hyman Weintraub, *Andrew Furuseth: Emancipator of the Seamen* (Berkeley: University of California Press, 1959), 77; Michael Kazin, *Barons of Labor: The San Francisco Building Trades and Union Power in the Progressive Era* (Urbana: University of Illinois Press, 1987), 29; "Wm. Gohl's Friends," Billy Gohl Documentation, Chehalis County Sheriff's Correspondence, Southwest Regional Branch, Washington State Archives, Olympia.

11. Bruce Nelson, *Workers on the Waterfront: Seamen, Longshoremen, and Unionism in the 1930s* (Urbana: University of Illinois Press, 1990), 11–38.

12. "Log Book for *Dauntless*," October 10, 1907, United States Customs, Puget Sound Collection District, Series 31 Log Books, National Archives, Seattle.

13. Nelson, *Workers on the Waterfront*, 42.

14. Paul S. Taylor, "The Sailors' Union of the Pacific" (PhD dissertation, University of California, 1922), chap. 1; *Cargo Handling and Longshore Labor Conditions*, Labor Statistics Bureau Bulletin 550 (Washington, DC: US Bureau of Labor Statistics, 1932), 48.

15. See Jake Alimahomed-Wilson and Immanuel Ness, eds., *Choke Points: Logistics Workers Disrupting the Global Supply Chain* (London: Pluto Press, 2018); Peter Cole, *Dockworker Power in Durban and the San Francisco Bay Area* (Urbana: University of Illinois Press, 2018).

16. Nelson, *Workers on the Waterfront*, 14–15, 35; *Aberdeen Daily Bulletin*, June 9, 1906; Taylor, "Sailors' Union of the Pacific," 24.

17. Cited in Taylor, "Sailors' Union of the Pacific," chap. 2.

18. *Aberdeen Herald*, December 30, 1909.

19. *Aberdeen World*, February 14, 1909.

20. Nelson, *Workers on the Waterfront*, 12; S. Schwartz, *Brotherhood of the Sea*, 4–5; Taylor, "Sailors' Union of the Pacific," chap. 1.

21. Nelson, *Workers on the Waterfront*, 14.

22. Jack London, *The Sea-Wolf* (London: William Heinemann, 1917), chap. 6.

23. *Coast Seamen's Journal*, March 19, 1902; *Coast Seamen's Journal*, April 16, 1902.

24. *Coast Seamen's Journal*, April 16, 1902.

25. Leon Fink, *Sweatshops at Sea: Merchant Seamen in the World's First Globalized Industry, from 1812 to the Present* (Chapel Hill: University of North Carolina Press, 2011).

26. *Aberdeen World*, February 14, 1909.

27. Lance S. Davidson, "Shanghaied! The Systematic Kidnapping of Sailors in Early San Francisco," *California History* 64, no. 1 (1985): 13.

28. Davidson, "Shanghaied!," 17.

29. *Evening Statesmen* (Walla Walla, WA), October 17, 1904.

30. *Evening Statesmen*, June 12, 1906.

31. *Aberdeen Daily Bulletin*, June 13, 14, 1906.

32. *Coast Seamen's Journal*, March 3, 1915.

33. Nelson, *Workers on the Waterfront*, 12–18; Weintraub, *Andrew Furuseth*, 34.

34. Taylor, "Sailors' Union of the Pacific," chap. 1.

35. Furuseth quote in Ottilie Markholt, "Against the Current: A Social Memoir," unpublished manuscript, 7, University of Washington, Digital Archives, http://digitalcollections.lib.washington.edu/cdm/ref/collection/pnwhm/id/837.

36. *Coast Seamen's Journal*, January 16, 1907.

37. *Coast Seamen's Journal*, vol. 17 index, September 1903–September 1904.

38. *Coast Seamen's Journal*, April 5, 1905.

39. Rob Nixon, *Slow Violence and the Environmentalism of the Poor* (Cambridge: Harvard University Press, 2011), 2; Nelson, *Workers on the Waterfront*, 15.

40. *Aberdeen Herald*, March 8, 1900.

41. *Grays Harbor Post*, September 3, 1904.

42. *Aberdeen Daily Bulletin*, March 19, 1906.

43. Taylor, "Sailors' Union of the Pacific," chapter 4.

44. *San Francisco Call*, March 9, 10, 1900.

45. United States Bureau of the Census, *Twelfth Census of the United States Taken in the Year 1900*.

46. See, for instance, Pamela Dean Aho, "The Ghoul of Grays Harbor," in *On the Harbor: From Black Friday to Nirvana*, edited by John C. Hughes and Ryan Teague Beckwith (Aberdeen, WA: Daily World, 2001), 20; "Application for Membership, Fraternal Order of Eagles, Aerie No. 24," 1908, Billy Gohl Collection, Aberdeen Historical Museum, Aberdeen, Washington.

47. B. R. Burg, "Sailors and Tattoos in the Early American Steam Navy: Evidence from the Diary of Philip C. Van Buskirk, 1884–1889," *International Journal of Maritime History* 60, no. 1 (June 1994): 161–74.

48. "Physician's Certificate," September 22, 1923, Washington State Penitentiary Records, Billy Gohl Documentation, Southwest Regional Branch, Washington State Archives, Olympia.

49. *Tacoma Daily Ledger*, February 8, 1910; *Aberdeen Daily World*, February 8, 1910.

50. *Grays Harbor Post*, September 3, 1904; application for Membership, Fraternal Order of Eagles, Aerie No. 24," 1908, Billy Gohl Collection, Aberdeen Historical Museum, Aberdeen, Washington.

51. See the *Coast Seamen's Journal* between 1900 and 1903.

52. John C. Hughes and Ryan Teague Beckwith, eds., *On the Harbor: From Black Friday to Nirvana* (Aberdeen, WA: Daily World, 2001), 4–13.

53. *Seattle Daily Times*, April 4, 1909.

54. *Seattle Daily Times*, April 4, 1909.

55. United States Bureau of the Census, *Twelfth Census of the United States Taken in the Year 1900*, San Francisco, State of California.

56. Nelson, *Workers on the Waterfront*, 43; S. Schwartz, *Brotherhood of the Sea*, chap. 1.

57. On Gill, see Markholt, "Against the Current," 6.

58. Taylor, "Sailors' Union of the Pacific," chap. 4.

59. For background on the Knights of Labor, see Leon Fink, *Workingmen's Democracy: The Knights of Labor and American Politics* (Urbana: University of Illinois Press, 1983).

60. Nelson, *Workers on the Waterfront*, 40–42.

61. Paul Avrich, *The Haymarket Tragedy* (Princeton: Princeton University Press, 1984); James Green, *Death in the Haymarket: The Story of Chicago, the First Labor Movement, and the Bombing that Divided Gilded Age America* (New York: Random House, 2006).

62. Melvyn Dubofsky, *We Shall Be All: A History of the Industrial Workers of the World* (Chicago: Quadrangle Books, 1973), 36.

63. David R. Berman, *Radicalism in the Mountain West, 1890–1920* (Boulder: University of Colorado Press, 2007), 120–23.

64. Philip S. Foner, "Communications, James McParlan and the Molly Maguires," *Science and Society* 31, no. 1 (Winter 1967): 77.

65. The Steunenberg murder case has been the subject of numerous works. See Joseph R. Conlin, *Big Bill Haywood and the Radical Union Movement* (Syracuse: Syracuse University Press, 1969), 52–68; J. Anthony Lukas, *Big Trouble: A Murder in a Small Western Town Sets off a Struggle for the Soul of America* (New York: Simon and Schuster, 1997); Philip S. Foner, *History of the Labor Movement*, vol. 4, *The Industrial Workers of the World, 1905–1917* (New York: International Publishers, 1965), 40–59; Melvyn Dubofsky, *"Big Bill" Haywood* (Manchester: Manchester University Press, 1987); Berman, *Radicalism in the Mountain West*, 154–59.

66. Taylor, "Sailors' Union of the Pacific," chap. 4.

67. *Aberdeen Herald*, December 15, 1892.

68. *Aberdeen Herald*, February 16, 1893. "Enticing" nonunion seamen to leave ship was a frequent tactic used by unionists in Aberdeen before Gohl became agent. See also *Aberdeen Herald*, March 2, 1893.

69. Weintraub, *Andrew Furuseth*, 57.

70. State of Washington, *Seventh Biennial Report of the Bureau of Labor Statistics and Factory Inspection*, 1909–1910 (Olympia: C. W. Gorham, Public Printer, 1908); US Department of Labor, Bureau of Labor Statistics, *Union Scale of Wages and Hours of Labor* (Washington, DC: Government Printing Office, 1913).

71. Nelson, *Workers on the Waterfront*, 42; State of California, *Eleventh Biennial Report of the Bureau of Labor Statistics for the State of California (1903–1904)* (Sacramento: W. W. Shannon, Superintendent State Printing, 1904), 50–64.

72. Taylor, "Sailors' Union of the Pacific," chap. 3.

73. John Elrick, "Social Conflict and the Politics of Reform: Mayor James D. Phelan and the San Francisco Waterfront Strike of 1901," *California History* 88, no. 2 (2011): 8; Thomas Walker Page, "The San Francisco

Labor Movement in 1901," *Political Science Quarterly* 17, no. 4 (December 1902): 664–67.

74. Cited in Robert Edward Lee Knight, *Industrial Relations in the San Francisco Bay Area, 1900–1918* (Berkeley: University of California Press, 1960), 85.

75. Elrick, "Social Conflict and the Politics of Reform," 8.

76. Elrick, "Social Conflict and the Politics of Reform," 14–15.

CHAPTER TWO: BILLY GOHL'S GRAYS HARBOR

1. *Aberdeen Daily Bulletin,* April 6, 1906.

2. Robert Weinstein, *Grays Harbor, 1885–1913* (New York: Penguin Books, 1978), 154.

3. Fred Lockley, "Grays Harbor: The Largest Lumber-Shipping Port in the World," *Pacific Monthly,* June 1907, 724.

4. *Aberdeen Herald,* September 27, 1906.

5. R. L. Polk and Company's *Grays Harbor Cities Directory,* 1910, 26.

6. Holbrook, *Little Annie Oakley and Other Rugged People* (New York: Macmillan, 1948), 45–46.

7. Adam Woog, *Haunted Washington: Uncanny Tales and Spooky Spots from the Upper Left-Hand Corner of the United States* (Guilford, CT: Morris, 2013), 119.

8. Ava Baron, ed., *Work Engendered: Toward a New History of American Labor* (Ithaca, NY: Cornell University Press, 1991), 19–20.

9. Stephen Meyer, *Manhood on the Line: Working-Class Masculinities in the American Heartland* (Urbana: University of Illinois Press, 2016), 2.

10. *Aberdeen Herald,* January 19, 1903.

11. Anne Cotton, "History of Aberdeen: 1775–1982," in *Aberdeen Comprehensive Development Plan, Phase I, Profile of Aberdeen* (Aberdeen, WA: Grays Harbor Regional Planning Commission, 1969), 41; Ed Van Syckle, *They Tried to Cut It All: Grays Harbor, Turbulent Years of Greed and Greatness* (Seattle: Pacific Search Press, 1980), 173; Murray Morgan, *The Last Wilderness* (Seattle: University of Washington Press, 1955), 138–39.

12. Morgan, *The Last Wilderness,* 138–41.

13. Merle A. Reinikka, "Death Certificates of Finns in Chehalis County, Washington, 1907–1947," Genealogical Society of Finland, https://www.genealogia.fi/emi/emi3d20v2e.htm.

14. *Aberdeen Daily Bulletin*, May 15, 22, 1905.

15. Carlos Arnaldo Schwantes, *Hard Traveling: A Portrait of Work Life in the New Northwest* (Lincoln: University of Nebraska Press, 1994), 19.

16. "Washington State, Chehalis County, City of Aberdeen," in United States Bureau of the Census, *Thirteenth Census of the United States Taken in the Year 1910* (Washington, DC: Government Printing Office, 1913), 997, 989; United States Bureau of the Census, *Abstract of the Fourteenth Census of the United States Taken in the Year 1920* (Washington, DC: Government Printing Office, 1923), 62; United States Bureau of the Census, *Twelfth Census of the United States Taken in the Year 1900* (Washington, DC: Government Printing Office, 1902), 526.

17. Elizabeth Jameson, *All that Glitters: Class, Conflict, and Community in Cripple Creek* (Urbana: University of Illinois Press, 1998), 128.

18. Mary Murphy, *Mining Cultures: Men, Women, and Leisure in Butte, 1914–1941* (Urbana: University of Illinois Press, 1997), 77.

19. *Aberdeen Herald*, April 30, 1908.

20. "Washington State, Chehalis County, Cities of Aberdeen and Hoquiam," in United States Bureau of the Census, *Twelfth Census of the United States*.

21. City of Hoquiam, Police Record, 1905–1915, Southwest Regional Branch, Washington State Archives, Olympia.

22. Van Syckle, *They Tried to Cut It All*, 177.

23. *R. L. Polk and Company's Grays Harbor Cities Directory, 1908*, 65, 125.

24. Mrs. Gohl is most commonly referred to as "Bessie," although Chehalis County Superior Court records document that her name was actually Edith, "Bessie" being her nickname. Pamela Dean Aho, "The Ghoul of Grays Harbor," in *On the Harbor: From Black Friday to Nirvana*, ed. John C. Hughes and Ryan Teague Beckwith (Aberdeen, WA: Daily World, 2001), 19; *Chehalis County Vidette* (Montesano, WA), May 19, 1905; "Service on Witnesses," May 4, 1910, *State of Washington v. William Gohl*, No. 8658, Superior Court of the State of Washington, for Chehalis

County (1910), Billy Gohl Documentation, Southwest Regional Branch, Washington State Archives, Olympia.

25. United States Census Office, *Tenth Census of the United States*, 1880, Sunfield, Eaton, Michigan; Hazel Hill, Johnson, Missouri.

26. William Gohl and Bessie Hager, Application for License to Wed, May 16, 1905, Grays Harbor County Auditor, Marriage Records, 1871–Present, Washington State Archives, Digital Archives, http://digital archives.wa.gov.

27. Cited in Aho, "Ghoul of Grays Harbor," 19.

28. Patricia Nelson Limerick, *The Legacy of Conquest: The Unbroken Past of the American West* (New York: W. W. Norton, 1987), 48–50.

29. *Chehalis County Vidette*, May 19, 1905.

30. *Grays Harbor Post*, August 4, 1907.

31. *Grays Harbor Post*, February 15, 1908.

32. *Tacoma Daily Ledger*, February 6, 1910.

33. *Constitution and By-Laws of the Sailors' Union of the Pacific* (San Francisco: James H. Barry, 1907), 14–15.

34. *Aberdeen Daily Bulletin*, September 6, 1906.

35. *Aberdeen Daily Bulletin*, January 5, 1906.

36. *Aberdeen Daily Bulletin*, August 16, 1904.

37. *Aberdeen Daily Bulletin*, March 12, 1906.

38. *Aberdeen Daily Bulletin*, April 13, 1906.

39. *Aberdeen Daily Bulletin*, April 11, 1906.

40. City of Hoquiam, Police Record, 1905–1915, Southwest Regional Branch, Washington State Archives, Olympia.

41. Eric Loomis, *Empire of Timber: Labor Unions and the Pacific Northwest Forests* (Cambridge: Cambridge University Press, 2016), 28.

42. *Aberdeen Daily Bulletin*, March 12, 1906.

43. *Aberdeen Herald*, May 18, 1907.

44. Andrew Mason Prouty, *"More Deadly Than War!" Pacific Coast Logging, 1827–1981* (Seattle: University of Washington Press, 1985), xvii–xix, 143, 190–95; Charlotte Todes, *Labor and Lumber* (New York: International Publishers, 1931), 137.

45. *Aberdeen Daily World*, December 19, 1904.

46. *Aberdeen Daily World,* February 6, 1909.

47. Todes, *Labor and Lumber,* 135.

48. *Aberdeen Herald,* October 25, 1900.

49. *Grays Harbor Post,* July 30, 1904.

50. *Aberdeen Herald,* July 6, 1905; May 25, December 24, 1908.

51. *Tacoma Daily Ledger,* February 10, 1905.

CHAPTER THREE: UNION

1. Harvey Schwartz, *The March Inland: Origins of the ILWU Warehouse Division, 1934–1938* (Los Angeles: Institute of Labor Relations, University of California, 1978); Bruce Nelson, *Workers on the Waterfront: Seamen, Longshoremen, and Unionism in the 1930s* (Urbana: University of Illinois Press, 1990), 219–21.

   Howard Kimeldorf elucidates the left-wing political aims of the ILWU in his *Reds or Rackets? The Making of Radical and Conservative Unions on the Waterfront* (Berkeley: University of California Press, 1988), 4–5. On the history of waterfront unions in the United States, see Peter Cole's *Wobblies on the Waterfront: Interracial Unionism in Progressive-Era Philadelphia* (Urbana: University of Illinois Press, 2007) and *Dockworker Power: Race and Activism in Durban and the San Francisco Bay Area* (Urbana: University of Illinois Press, 2018).

2. *Coast Seamen's Journal,* April 27, 1898; *Proceedings of the Fourth Annual Convention of the Washington State Federation of Labor* (Aberdeen, WA: Washington State Federation of Labor, 1906), 11–12.

3. *Proceedings of the Third Annual Convention of the Washington State Federation of Labor* (Everett: Washington State Federation of Labor, 1905), 27; *Coast Seamen's Journal,* August 17, 1898.

4. *Coast Seamen's Journal,* April 27, 1898; *Proceedings of the Fourth Annual Convention of the Washington State Federation of Labor,* 11–12.

5. *Proceedings of the Third Annual Convention of the Washington State Federation of Labor,* 27; *Seattle Union Record,* January 25, 1902; *Aberdeen Herald,* January 16, 1902.

6. For the early history of the Washington State Federation of Labor, see Carlos A. Schwantes, *Radical Heritage: Labor, Socialism, and Reform in Washington and British Columbia, 1885–1917* (Seattle: University of Washington Press, 1979).

7. *Aberdeen Herald*, April 17, Aug. 7, 1902; *Coast Seamen's Journal*, April 30, 1902.

8. *Aberdeen Herald*, May 12, 1902.

9. *Aberdeen Herald*, September 1, 1902.

10. *Proceedings of the Third Annual Convention of the Washington State Federation of Labor*, 27.

11. *Proceedings of the Third Annual Convention of the Washington State Federation of Labor*, 12.

12. Charles Pierce LeWarne, "The Aberdeen, Washington, Free Speech Fight of 1911–1912," *Pacific Northwest Quarterly* 66 (January 1975): 8.

13. *Aberdeen Herald*, October 11, 1894, March 7, June 6, 1895.

14. *Aberdeen Daily Bulletin*, May 9, 1906; *Grays Harbor Post*, December 2, 1905; *Grays Harbor Washingtonian*, July 4, 1906.

15. Ralph Kendall Forsyth, "The Wage Scale Agreements of Maritime Unions," *Annals of the American Academy of Political and Social Science* 36, no. 2 (September 1910): 103–4.

16. Paul S. Taylor, "The Sailors' Union of the Pacific" (PhD dissertation, University of California, 1922), 67–68.

17. Quoted in *Aberdeen Herald*, February 9, 1899.

18. *Aberdeen Herald*, November 30, December 7, 1899.

19. *Aberdeen Daily Bulletin*, June 6, 1906.

20. *Aberdeen Herald*, April 17, 1902.

21. State of California, *Eleventh Biennial Report of the Bureau of Labor Statistics for the State of California (1903–1904)* (Sacramento: W. W. Shannon, Superintendent State Printing, 1904), 50–65.

22. *Grays Harbor Post*, October 24, 1908; *R. L. Polk and Company's Grays Harbor Cities and Chehalis County Directory*, 1908, 116. Gronow's saloon is listed at 315 South F Street. This would put it less than a block away from the SUP office.

23. *Constitution and By-Laws of the Sailors' Union of the Pacific* (San Francisco: James H. Barry, 1905), 14–15; *C. F. Drake and H. Van Tassel,*

Partners, doing business as Grays Harbor Stevedoring Company vs. Aberdeen Branch Sailors Union of the Pacific, and Wm. Gohl, Agent, and each and all of the members of the said union, also, Longshoremen's Union Local No. 2, Charles Larsen, President thereof; A. Jonas, Recording Secretary; M. Inglebreitsen, Walking Delegate, and Andrew Nelsen, Pete Wilson, Emil Anderson, H. L. Green, members of said union, also all other members of said Longshoremen's Union Local No. 2, whose names are unknown to plaintiffs, No. 6431, Superior Court of the State of Washington, for Chehalis County (1906), Southwest Regional Branch, Washington State Archives, Olympia.

24. *Coast Seamen's Journal,* May 15, September 18, October 30, 1901, January 15, 1902, April 5, 12, 19, 26, May 3, 10, 17, 24, 31, June 7, 14, 21, 28, July 5, 1905.

25. *Coast Seamen's Journal,* May 15, September 18, October 30, 1901; January 15, 1902; April 5, 12, 19, 26, May 3, 10, 17, 24, 31, June 7, 14, 21, 28, July 5, 1905.

26. *Grays Harbor Post,* June 4, 1904.

27. *Coast Seamen's Journal,* July 8, 1903.

28. *Coast Seamen's Journal,* June 30, July 9, 15, 1902, January 7, 14, 1903. The agent position passed from Gronow to R. Wilson, who turned affairs over to B. L. Hamilton, with A. Jonas, later an official with the local longshoremen's union, serving temporarily in January 1903. Some of the dates when Gohl was temporarily replaced as local agent: January 4, 1904, when C. Langbehn filled in while Gohl attended the WSFL convention in Spokane; December 5, 1904, when George Oftinger served while Gohl attended the International Seamen's Union convention in San Francisco; and July 1, 1907, while Gohl was out with a "case of bad blood poisoning" and Charles F. Hammarin served in his place. *Coast Seamen's Journal,* December 14, 1904, July 11, 18, November 28, 1906, January 14, 21, July 10, 1907; *Grays Harbor Post,* August 3, 1907.

29. *Proceedings of the Third Annual Convention of the Washington State Federation of Labor,* 27.

30. These figures are based on population estimates printed in *R. L. Polk and Company's Grays Harbor Cities and Chehalis County Directory,* 1900 and 1907.

31. *Aberdeen Daily Bulletin*, March 19, 1904; *Proceedings of the Third Annual Convention of the Washington State Federation of Labor*, 27.

32. *Trades Council Gazette* (Aberdeen), June 23, 1906.

33. John C. Hughes and Ryan Teague Beckwith, eds., *On the Harbor: From Black Friday to Nirvana* (Aberdeen, WA: Daily World, 2001), 2–3.

34. *Grays Harbor Post*, February 8, 1908.

35. *Grays Harbor Post*, April 2, 1904.

36. *Grays Harbor Post*, April 16, 1904.

37. *Coast Seamen's Journal*, August 17, 1904.

38. *Constitution and By-Laws of the Sailors' Union of the Pacific* (San Francisco: James H. Barry, 1907), 8–9.

39. David T. Beito, *From Mutual Aid to Welfare State: Fraternal Societies and Social Services, 1890–1967* (Chapel Hill: University of North Carolina Press, 2000), 13.

40. *Aberdeen Daily Bulletin*, March 10, 1906; Beito, *From Mutual Aid to Welfare State*, 12, 218.

41. *Aberdeen Herald*, July 18, November 7, 1904, July 10, December 18, 1905, January 15, 1906; *Aberdeen Daily Bulletin*, March 10, 1906; *R. L. Polk and Company's Grays Harbor Cities and Chehalis County Directory*, 1903, 29; *R. L. Polk and Company's Grays Harbor Cities and Chehalis County Directory*, 1907, 43.

42. *R. L. Polk and Company's Grays Harbor Cities and Chehalis County Directory*, 29; *Seattle Times*, June 19, 1904.

43. *Proceedings of the Third Annual Convention of the Washington State Federation of Labor*, 27; *Aberdeen Daily Bulletin*, July 9, 16, 1904.

44. *Grays Harbor Post*, September 3, 1904; *Daily Washingtonian*, September 8, 1904; *Aberdeen Daily Bulletin*, July 16, 1904.

45. *Daily Washingtonian*, September 8, 1904.

46. *Grays Harbor Post*, September 7, 1907.

47. *Aberdeen Herald*, June 12, 1905; *Grays Harbor Post*, July 1, 1905.

48. *Aberdeen Herald*, July 5, 1905.

49. *Grays Harbor Post*, April 23, 1904.

50. *Shingle Weaver*, March 1906.

51. *Grays Harbor Post*, February 3, 17, 1906; *Shingle Weaver*, March 1906; *Hoquiam Washingtonian*, February 1, 1906.

52. *Aberdeen Daily Bulletin*, July 16, 1904; *Grays Harbor Post*, August 12, 1905; September 5, 1908.

53. *Grays Harbor Post*, September 1, 1906, November 14, 1908, July 17, 1909. For a general survey of the Women's Union Card and Label League, see K. J. Oberdeck, "'Not Pink Teas': The Seattle Working-Class Women's Movement, 1905–1918," *Labor History* 32, no. 2 (Spring 1991): 205; and Maurine Weiner Greenwald, "Working-Class Feminism and the Family Wage Ideal: The Seattle Debate on Married Women's Right to Work, 1914–1920," in *Women in Pacific Northwest History*, edited by Karen Blair, revised edition (Seattle: University of Washington Press, 2001), 105–7.

54. *Grays Harbor Post*, January 20, 1906.

55. *Grays Harbor Post*, October 7, 1905.

56. Jan Holden, "Billy Gohl: The Ghoul of Grays Harbor," *Old West*, Fall 1995, 26; *Grays Harbor Washingtonian*, May 4, 7, 8, 1910.

57. *Aberdeen Daily Bulletin*, March 9, 1906.

58. Another 212 local unions composed of an unknown number of members were not affiliated with the federation. State of Washington, *Ninth Biennial Report of the Bureau of Labor Statistics, 1913–1914* (Olympia: Public Printer, 1914), 100.

59. *Grays Harbor Post*, January 15, 1910; *Grays Harbor Post*, December 2, 1905. For further evidence of leading Grays Harbor area unionists' racist views, see *Grays Harbor Post*, July 17, 1909. On the ethnicity and race of SUP members, see *Coast Seamen's Journal*, August 17, 1904; and Nelson, *Workers on the Waterfront*, 48–50.

60. Nelson, *Workers on the Waterfront*, 50.

61. *Proceedings of the Fourth Annual Convention of the Washington State Federation of Labor*, 42–43.

62. *Aberdeen Daily Bulletin*, June 14, 1906.

63. *Constitution and By-Laws of the Sailors' Union of the Pacific*, 17.

64. Mark Leier, *Red Flags and Red Tape: The Making of a Labor Bureaucracy* (Toronto: University of Toronto Press, 1995), 132–33.

65. Denis Kearney and H. L. Knight, "Appeal from California: The Chinese Invasion: Workingmen's Address," *Indianapolis Times*, February 28, 1878; Alexander Saxton, *The Indispensable Enemy: Labor and the*

Anti-Chinese Movement in California (Berkeley: University of California Press, 1971). See also Tomás Almaguer, *Racial Fault Lines: The Historical Origins of White Supremacy in California* (Berkeley: University of California Press, 1994); Neil Foley, *White Scourge: Mexicans, Blacks, and Poor Whites in Texas Cotton Culture* (Berkeley: University of California Press, 1997); Chris Friday, *Organizing Asian-American Labor: The Pacific Coast Canned-Salmon Industry, 1870–1942* (Philadelphia: Temple University Press, 1994); David Roediger, *Working toward Whiteness: How America's Immigrants Became White, the Strange Journey from Ellis Island to the Suburbs* (New York: Basic Books, 2005).

66. Art Chin, *Golden Tassels: A History of the Chinese in Washington State, 1857–1977* (Seattle: Chin, 1977), 58.

67. Nelson, *Workers on the Waterfront*, 49.

68. Taylor, "Sailors' Union of the Pacific," 156.

69. *Coast Seamen's Journal*, August 17, 1904; Nelson, *Workers on the Waterfront*, 48–50.

70. *Grays Harbor Post*, September 3, 1904.

71. *Grays Harbor Post*, July 30, 1910. See also *Grays Harbor Post*, January 23, 1909.

72. *Grays Harbor Post*, February 15, 1908.

73. Quoted in the antilabor *Aberdeen Daily Bulletin*, June 26, 1906, under this line: "The following paragraph appears in the Trades Council Gazette, the free edition of the Weekly Post."

74. *Grays Harbor Post*, February 15, 1908.

75. *Shingle Weaver*, December 1907.

76. *Aberdeen Herald*, September 1, 1902.

77. Alice Kessler-Harris, *Out to Work: A History of Wage-Earning Women in the United States* (Oxford: Oxford University Press, 1982), 153.

78. Ben K. Weatherwax, "Hometown Scrapbook," October 29, 1953, Aberdeen: Before 1920 Collections, Aberdeen Timberland Library, Aberdeen, Washington; *Morning Olympian*, October 11, 1905.

79. See *Grays Harbor Post*, May 3, 1905; January 20, 25, March 21, August 22, 1908.

80. *Grays Harbor Post*, May 20, June 10, December 2, 1905. In the May 3, 1905, *Grays Harbor Post*, labor declared a "special fight" "against the Chinese laundries in the city."

81. *Grays Harbor Post*, May 13, 1905, August 23, 1913; *Seattle Union Record*, May 12, 1906.

82. David Montgomery, *Workers' Control in America: Studies in the History of Work, Technology, and Labor Struggles* (Cambridge: Cambridge University Press, 1979), 13.

83. *Grays Harbor Post*, January 20, 1906.

84. *Grays Harbor Post*, January 20, 1906.

85. *Shingle Weaver*, August 1907.

86. *Grays Harbor Post*, August 20, 1904.

87. *Trades Council Gazette* (Aberdeen, WA), June 23, 1906.

88. William Gohl, letter to editor, *Grays Harbor Post*, January 7, 1904.

89. For local examples of violence against scabs, see *Aberdeen Herald*, October 1901; "In the Justice's Court City of Aberdeen Precinct, Aug. 30, 1906," *State of Washington v. William Gohl*, No. 6499, Southwest Regional Branch, Washington State Archives, Olympia; *Aberdeen Daily Bulletin*, July 12, August 25, 1906.

90. *Aberdeen Herald*, October 31, 1901; *Aberdeen Daily Bulletin*, August 22, September 18, 19, 1906.

91. *Shingle Weaver*, August 1906; *Shingle Weaver*, September 1906; *Shingle Weaver*, September 21, November 9, 1912.

92. *Aberdeen Daily Bulletin*, September 18, 19, 1906.

93. Taylor, "Sailors' Union of the Pacific," 154.

94. *Constitution and By-Laws of the Sailors' Union of the Pacific*, 14-16, 27-29.

95. *Grays Harbor Post*, May 4, August 31, 1907. The *Grays Harbor Post* carried several articles mentioning that Gohl planned union members' funerals.

96. Michael K. Rosenow, *Death and Dying in the Working Class, 1865–1920* (Urbana: University of Illinois Press, 2015), 86.

97. *Grays Harbor Post*, May 4, 1907.

98. *Morning Oregonian* (Portland), Feb. 9, 1910; *Aberdeen Daily Bulletin*, July 5, August 22, 1905; *Aberdeen World*, August 25, 1908; February 4, 14,

1909; *Grays Harbor Post,* June 8, August 7, 10, 24, 31, December 21, 1907, May 15, 1909.

99. Charles Richmond Henderson, "Industrial Insurance. III. Benefit Features of the Trade-Unions," *American Journal of Sociology* 12, no. 6 (1907): 756–78.

100. *Grays Harbor Post,* May 4, 1907.

101. Taylor, "Sailors' Union of the Pacific," appendix 4.

102. *Aberdeen Daily Bulletin,* July 3, 1906; *Grays Harbor Post,* February 17, 1906.

103. *Grays Harbor Post,* October 29, 1910.

104. *Grays Harbor Post,* March 10, 1906.

CHAPTER FOUR: BILLY GOHL AND THE 1906 MARITIME STRIKE

1. *Grays Harbor Post,* June 16, 1906; *Aberdeen Daily Bulletin,* June 13, 1906.

2. *Aberdeen Daily Bulletin,* June 13, 1906.

3. *Aberdeen Daily Bulletin,* June 13, 1906.

4. *Grays Harbor Post,* June 16, 1906; *Aberdeen Daily Bulletin,* June 13, 1906.

5. *Aberdeen Daily Bulletin,* June 13, 14, 1906.

6. *Grays Harbor Post,* June 16, 1906; *Aberdeen Daily Bulletin,* June 13, 1906.

7. *Grays Harbor Post,* June 16, 1906; *Aberdeen Daily Bulletin,* June 13, 15, 1906.

8. *Aberdeen Daily Bulletin,* June 13, 1906.

9. *Coast Seamen's Journal,* April, 27, August 17, 1898; *Proceedings of the Third Annual Convention of the Washington State Federation of Labor* (Everett: Washington State Federation of Labor, 1906), 27; *Proceedings of the Fourth Annual Convention of the Washington State Federation of Labor* (Aberdeen: Washington State Federation of Labor, 1906), 11–12.

10. *Pacific Lumber Trade Journal* (Seattle), May 1906.

11. *Coast Seamen's Journal,* May 2, 1906; *Aberdeen Daily Bulletin,* April 21, 1906.

12. *Aberdeen Daily Bulletin,* April 25, 1906.

13. *Grays Harbor Post,* June 9, 1906; *Aberdeen Daily Bulletin,* June 9, 1906.

14. *Grays Harbor Post,* June 9, 16, 1906.

15. *Coast Seamen's Journal*, June 13, 1906.

16. Hyman Weintraub, *Andrew Furuseth: Emancipator of the Seamen* (Berkeley: University of California Press, 1959), 75; *Coast Seaman's Journal*, March 15, 1906.

17. *San Francisco Call*, June 14, 1906.

18. *Aberdeen Herald*, January 3, November 7, 1895.

19. *Grays Harbor Post*, February 27, 1904; Franklin Harper, ed. *Who's Who on the Pacific Coast: A Biographical Compilation of Notable Living Contemporaries West of the Rocky Mountains* (Los Angeles: Harper Publishing, 1913), 375; Thomas William Herringshaw, *American Blue-Book of Biography: Prominent Americans of 1912—an Accurate Biographical Record of Prominent Citizens of All Walks of Life* (Chicago: American Publishers' Association, 1913), 423; *Aberdeen Daily World*, June 10, 1933.

20. *Aberdeen Herald*, October 11, 1894; *Grays Harbor Post*, March 12, 1903, March 4, 1905, February 27, 1909, February 11, 1911.

21. Herringshaw, *American Blue-Book of Biography*, 423.

22. *Grays Harbor Post*, May 25, 1912; *Aberdeen Daily Bulletin*, July 19, 1905; *Aberdeen Daily World*, June 6, 1909, May 18, 1910.

23. *Aberdeen Herald*, July 20, 24, 1905, May 15, 1910; *Grays Harbor Post*, May 29, July 3, 1909; *Aberdeen Daily World*, May 18, 1910.

24. *Grays Harbor Post*, February 5, 1910.

25. *Aberdeen Herald*, July 24, 1905; *Aberdeen Daily Bulletin*, July 18, 24, 1905, June 13, 15, 1906; *Grays Harbor Post*, June 16, 1906.

26. *Aberdeen Daily Bulletin*, August 18, 1905; *Grays Harbor Post*, July 4, 1906, February 5, 1910; State of Washington, *Fourth Biennial Report of the Bureau of Labor Statistics and Factory Inspection, 1903–1904* (Olympia: Blankenship Satterlee, 1904), 213; Fred Lockley, "Grays Harbor: The Largest Lumber-Shipping Port in the World," *Pacific Monthly*, June 1907, 720–29.

27. Ronald E. Magden, *The Working Longshoreman* (Tacoma, WA: R-4 Typographers, 1991), 43; Paul S. Taylor, "The Sailors' Union of the Pacific" (PhD dissertation, University of California, 1922), 104–6.

28. Bruce Nelson, *Workers on the Waterfront: Seamen, Longshoremen, and Unionism in the 1930s* (Urbana: University of Illinois Press, 1990),

11–38; Howard Kimeldorf, *Reds or Rackets? The Making of Radical and Conservative Unions on the Waterfront* (Berkeley: University of California Press, 1988), 20–25.

29. Stephen Schwartz, *Brotherhood of the Sea: A History of the Sailors' Union of the Pacific, 1885–1985* (San Francisco: Sailors' Union of the Pacific, 1986), 6.

30. *Los Angeles Herald*, June 9, 1906.

31. *Aberdeen Daily Bulletin*, June 14, 1906.

32. Nelson, *Workers on the Waterfront*, 12.

33. *Aberdeen Daily Bulletin*, July 12, 1906.

34. Affidavit of Charles R. Sauers, July 14, 1906, Chehalis County Superior Court, Case No. 6431; *R. L. Polk and Company's Grays Harbor Cities Directory for 1907*, 133.

35. Affidavit of R. F. Cox, July 14, 1906, Chehalis County Superior Court, Case No. 6431.

36. *C. F. Drake and H. Van Tassel, Partners, Doing Business as Grays Harbor Stevedoring Company v. Aberdeen Branch Sailors Union of the Pacific, and Wm. Gohl, et al.*, (1906), No. 6431, Southwest Regional Branch, Washington State Archives, Olympia.

37. Affidavit of James Beckey, July 14, 1906, Chehalis County Superior Court, Case No. 6431.

38. *Aberdeen Daily Bulletin*, June 9, 1906; "Information for Unlawfully Organizing, Maintaining, and Employing an Armed Body of Men," September 17, 1906, *State of Washington v. William Gohl*, No. 6499, Superior Court of the State of Washington, for Chehalis County (1906), Southwest Regional Branch, Washington State Archives, Olympia.

39. Nelson, *Workers on the Waterfront*, 59; "Affidavit of Wm. Gohl," November 5, 1906, *State of Washington v. William Gohl*, No. 6499, Superior Court of the State of Washington, for Chehalis County (1906), Southwest Regional Branch, Washington State Archives, Olympia.

40. *Aberdeen Daily Bulletin*, June 5, 6, August 22, 1906.

41. "Affidavit of Wm. Gohl"; *Aberdeen Daily Bulletin*, June 9, 1906.

42. *Aberdeen Daily Bulletin*, June 6, 9, 1906; *Aberdeen Herald*, August 20, 1906.

43. *Aberdeen Daily Bulletin*, August 18, 22, 1906.

44. "In the Justice's Court, City of Aberdeen Precinct," August 30, 1906, *State of Washington v. William Gohl*, No. 6499, Southwest Regional Branch, Washington State Archives, Olympia; *Aberdeen Daily Bulletin*, August 25, 1906.

45. *Trades Council Gazette*, June 23, 1906.

46. *Aberdeen Daily Bulletin*, August 22, October 10, 1906.

47. *Aberdeen Herald*, August 27, 1906.

48. *Aberdeen Daily Bulletin*, August 22, 1906; *Aberdeen Herald*, August 27, 1906.

49. *Aberdeen Daily Bulletin*, June 26, October 9, 10, 11, 1906; "Verdict," October 10, 1906, *State of Washington v. William Gohl*, No. 6499, Superior Court of the State of Washington, for Chehalis County (1906), Southwest Regional Branch, Washington State Archives, Olympia.

50. Robert F. Utter and Hugh D. Spitzer, *The Washington State Constitution*, 2nd ed. (Oxford: Oxford University Press, 2013), 52.

51. *Washington v. Gohl*, 46 Wash. 408, 90 P. 259 (WA Sup. Ct. 1907).

52. *Aberdeen Daily Bulletin*, June 18, 1906.

53. *Trades Council Gazette*, n.d.

54. *Trades Council Gazette*, June 23, 1906.

55. *Aberdeen Daily Bulletin*, June 13, 16, 1906.

56. *Aberdeen Daily Bulletin*, June 21, 1906.

57. *Aberdeen Herald*, May 27, 31, 1909.

58. Elizabeth Jameson, *All that Glitters: Class, Conflict, and Community in Cripple Creek* (Urbana: University of Illinois Press, 1998), 217–20; Philip S. Foner, *History of the Labor Movement in the United States*, vol. 3, *The Policies and Practices of the American Federation of Labor, 1900–1909* (New York: International Publishers, 1964), 36–37; David R. Berman, *Radicalism in the Mountain West, 1890–1920* (Boulder: University of Colorado Press, 2007), 125–27.

59. *Grays Harbor Post*, June 23, 1906.

60. "Resolution of the SUP and Longshoremen's Union," June 16, 1906, *C. F. Drake and H. Van Tassel, Partners, doing business as Grays Harbor Stevedoring Company v. Aberdeen Branch Sailors Union of the Pacific, and Wm. Gohl, et al.*, No. 6431, Southwest Regional Branch, Washington State Archives, Olympia.

61. *Grays Harbor Post*, February 21, 1906.

62. *Grays Harbor Post*, June 23, 1906.

63. *Grays Harbor Post*, July 28, 1906.

64. Stephen H. Norwood, *Strikebreaking and Intimidation: Mercenaries and Masculinity in Twentieth Century America* (Chapel Hill: University of North Carolina Press, 2002), 4.

65. *Trades Council Gazette*, n.d.

66. *Grays Harbor Post*, September 8, 1906, February 23, 1907; *Aberdeen Herald*, September 3, 1906; Weintraub, *Andrew Furuseth*, 77.

67. *Grays Harbor Post*, February 23, 1907.

68. *Aberdeen Daily Bulletin*, June 25, 1906.

69. *Aberdeen Daily Bulletin*, June 7, 9, 1906.

70. *Aberdeen Daily Bulletin*, June 16, 21, 1906.

71. *Trades Council Gazette*, n.d.

72. *Trades Council Gazette*, June 23, 1906; *Aberdeen Daily Bulletin*, June 25, 1906.

73. Motion for Temporary Restraining Order, Case No. 6431, July 12, 1906, Chehalis County Superior Court, Southwest Regional Branch, Washington State Archives, Olympia.

74. Affidavit of R. F. Cox, Case No. 6431, Chehalis County Superior Court, Southwest Regional Branch, Washington State Archives, Olympia.

75. Opinion of the Court, Case No. 6431, July 26, 1906, Chehalis County Superior Court, Southwest Regional Branch, Washington State Archives, Olympia.

76. Opinion of the Court, Case No. 6431, July 26, 1906, Chehalis County Superior Court, Southwest Regional Branch, Washington State Archives, Olympia.

77. *Aberdeen Daily Bulletin*, July 27, 1906.

78. Cited in Weintraub, *Andrew Furuseth*, 77, and referenced on page 214 as "Ellison to Gohl, Feb. 7, 1907."

79. *Aberdeen Daily Bulletin*, September 1, 1906.

80. *Aberdeen Herald*, November 8, 1906; Robert Edward Lee Knight, *Industrial Relations in the San Francisco Bay Area, 1900–1918* (Berkeley: University of California Press, 1960), 171–72.

81. *Pacific Lumber Trade Journal*, October 1906.

82. *Pacific Lumber Trade Journal*, November 1906.

83. *Shingle Weaver*, October 1906, February 1907; *Grays Harbor Post*, September 15, 1906; *Chehalis County Vidette*, November 3, 1906.

84. *Shingle Weaver*, October 1906.

CHAPTER FIVE: STRUGGLING FOR RESPECTABILITY

1. *R. L. Polk and Company's Grays Harbor Cities Directory*, 1908, 43–44; "Application for Membership, Fraternal Order of Eagles, Aerie No. 24," 1908, Billy Gohl Collection, Aberdeen Historical Museum; *Grays Harbor Post*, February 8, 15, 1908.

2. Union and fraternal organization meeting days appeared in *R. L. Polk and Company's Grays Harbor Cities Directory*, 1908.

3. *Grays Harbor Post*, May 14, 1904.

4. *R. L. Polk and Company's Grays Harbor Cities Directory*, 1908, 113.

5. *Grays Harbor Post*, March 10, 1906.

6. *Grays Harbor Post*, July 28, 1906.

7. Stephen Meyer, *Manhood on the Line: Working-Class Masculinities in the American Heartland* (Urbana: University of Illinois Press, 2016), 3; Heather Mayer, *Beyond the Rebel Girl: Women and the Industrial Workers of the World in the Pacific Northwest, 1905–1924* (Corvallis: Oregon State University Press, 2018), 7–8.

8. *R. L. Polk and Company's Grays Harbor Cities Directory*, 1908, 509.

9. *Grays Harbor Post*, May 18, 1905.

10. *R. L. Polk and Company's Grays Harbor Cities and Chehalis County Directory*, 1907, 82, 133; Anne Cotton, "History of Aberdeen: 1775–1982," in *Aberdeen Comprehensive Development Plan, Phase I, Profile of Aberdeen* (Aberdeen, WA: Grays Harbor Regional Planning Commission, 1969), 46–47.

11. *R. L. Polk and Company's Grays Harbor Cities Directory*, 1908, 509; *Grays Harbor Post*, December 26, 1908.

12. *Aberdeen Daily World*, February 3, 1910.

13. *R. L. Polk Company's Grays Harbor Cities Directory*, 1910, 110; *Chehalis County Vidette*, February 11, 1910.

14. Cited in Cotton, "History of Aberdeen," 41.

15. United States Bureau of the Census, *Thirteenth Census of the United States Taken in the Year 1910*, Aberdeen, Chehalis, Washington State.

16. *Aberdeen Herald*, November 29, 1906, April 4, 1907.

17. Barbara Wertheimer, *We Were There: The Story of Working Women in America* (New York: Pantheon Books, 1977), 201.

18. *R. L. Polk Company's Grays Harbor Cities Directory*, 1907, 274.

19. *Aberdeen Daily Bulletin*, March 10, 1906.

20. *Aberdeen Daily Bulletin*, November 10, 1902.

21. *R. L. Polk Company's Grays Harbor Cities Directory*, 1907, 101, 274; *Aberdeen Herald*, January 10, 1907.

22. *Grays Harbor Post*, September 15, 1906.

23. *Grays Harbor Post*, September 15, 1906.

24. Proceedings of the Fifth Annual Convention of the Washington State Federation of Labor, January 1907, 5.

25. *Grays Harbor Post*, January 25, 1907; *Grays Harbor Post*, March 30, 1907.

26. *Aberdeen World*, February 11, 1909.

27. *Grays Harbor Post*, January 8, 15, 1910.

28. *Tacoma Daily-Ledger*, February 6, 1910; *Proceedings of the Fourth Annual Convention of the Washington State Federation of Labor* (Aberdeen, WA, 1906), 43.

29. *Tacoma Daily Ledger*, January 11, 1908.

30. *Coast Seamen's Journal*, April 3, 1907.

31. *Hoquiam Washingtonian*, June 14, 1906; *Aberdeen Daily Bulletin*, July 16, 1904, June 15, July 15, 1906.

32. *Hoquiam Washingtonian*, June 14, 1906.

33. *Aberdeen Daily World*, March 2, 1909

34. *Aberdeen Daily World*, April 7, 1909.

35. Leon Fink, *Sweatshops of the Sea: Merchant Seamen in the World's First Globalized Industry, from 1812 to the Present* (Chapel Hill: University of North Carolina Press, 2011). See also Bruce Nelson, *Workers on the Waterfront: Seamen, Longshoremen, and Unionism in the 1930s* (Urbana: University of Illinois Press, 1990), 12–18.

36. In addition to the four men who named their occupation as "sailor" or "seaman," the voting rolls included two maritime engineers, three

captains, and four voters listed as "boat man" or working at "steam-boating." Aberdeen Voting Registers, Grays Harbor County Auditor, Voter Registers, Aberdeen, 1909, Wards 1–4, Southwest Regional Branch, Washington State Archives, Olympia.

37. *Aberdeen Daily Bulletin*, June 14, 1906.

38. *Aberdeen Daily Bulletin*, September 5, 1906.

39. *Aberdeen Herald*, September 6, 10, 1907; *Aberdeen Daily Bulletin*, September 6, 1906.

40. *Aberdeen Daily Bulletin*, December 6, 1906.

41. *R. L. Polk Company's Grays Harbor Cities Directory*, 1907, 39; *R. L. Polk Company's Grays Harbor Cities Directory*, 1908, 35–36; *Aberdeen Herald*, December 3, 1906, April 6, 1911; *Grays Harbor Post*, May 11, 1907.

42. Robert Martin, *Carnegie Denied: Communities Rejecting Carnegie Library Construction Grants, 1898–1925* (Westport, CT: Greenwood Press, 1993).

43. *Aberdeen Daily Bulletin*, July 26, 1906; *Grays Harbor Washingtonian*, July 26, 1906. The *Trades Council Gazette* and *Grays Harbor Post* ran frequent articles and editorials attacking Christensen.

44. *Grays Harbor Post*, July 28, 1906.

45. Quoted in Martin, *Carnegie Denied*, 15.

46. Martin, *Carnegie Denied*, 26–28.

47. *Aberdeen Daily Bulletin*, April 15, 1903.

48. *Aberdeen Herald*, December 13, 1906.

49. *Grays Harbor Post*, December 22, 1906; *Aberdeen Herald*, January 3, 1907. On the Homestead strike, see Arthur G. Burgoyne, *The Homestead Strike of 1892* (Pittsburgh: University of Pittsburgh Press, 1979).

50. *Aberdeen Herald*, January 31, 1907.

51. *Aberdeen Herald*, December 19, 1907.

52. *Aberdeen Herald*, January 16, 1908; *Grays Harbor Post*, January 18, 1908.

53. *Aberdeen Daily Bulletin*, September 13, 1905, November 5, 1906.

54. *Aberdeen Daily Bulletin*, October 18, 29, 1906.

55. *Aberdeen Daily Bulletin*, September 18, 1906, November 1, 1906.

56. *Aberdeen Herald*, September 20, 1906.

57. *Chehalis County Vidette*, February 11, 1910.

58. *Aberdeen Daily Bulletin*, April 3, 1906; *Aberdeen Daily World*, January 10, 1934.

59. *Aberdeen Daily World*, January 10, 1934; *Grays Harbor Post*, July 4, 1908; Ed Van Syckle, *They Tried to Cut It All: Grays Harbor, Turbulent Years of Greed and Greatness* (Seattle: Pacific Search Press, 1980), 172.

60. *Grays Harbor Post*, December 22, 1906.

61. *Chehalis County Vidette*, October 26, 1906.

62. *Chehalis County Vidette*, October 26, 1906.

63. *Aberdeen Daily Bulletin*, October 30, November 3, 1906.

64. *Grays Harbor Post*, November 3, 1906; *Aberdeen Daily Bulletin*, November 3, 1906.

65. *Grays Harbor Post*, November 3, 1906.

66. *Aberdeen Daily Bulletin*, November 7, 1906.

67. *Aberdeen World*, April 4, 1909.

68. Richard Maxwell Brown, "Lumber and Labor: Violence in the Pacific Northwest," 5, unpublished paper presented at the Pacific Northwest Labor History Association Conference, 1986, box 2, folder 11, Pacific Northwest Labor History Association Records, 1947–2015, Accession No. 4552-001, Special Collections, University of Washington Libraries, Seattle; *Grays Harbor Post*, July 18, 1909.

69. *Aberdeen Herald*, April 28, 1902; *Aberdeen Daily Bulletin*, September 13, 1905, September 18, October 26, 1906.

70. *Grays Harbor Post*, June 13, 1908.

71. *Grays Harbor Post*, June 25, 1908.

72. "Articles of Incorporation of Grays Harbor Labor Temple Association," Articles of Incorporation, Chehalis County, State of Washington, July 3, 1908, Southwest Regional Branch, Washington State Archives, Olympia; *Aberdeen World*, April 3, 1909.

73. *Aberdeen Herald*, March 13, 1911.

74. *Aberdeen Herald*, September 20, 1906.

75. *Aberdeen Herald*, August 27, 1906.

76. *Aberdeen Herald*, November 26, 1906. Sailors' Union members occasionally filled in as Aberdeen union agent during Gohl's seven-year term. Dates when Gohl was temporarily replaced as local agent included January 4, 1904, when C. Langbehn filled in while Gohl attended the

WSFL Convention in Spokane; December 5, 1904, when George Oftinger served while Gohl attended the International Seamen's Union convention in San Francisco; and July 1, 1907, when Charles Hammarin served in his place while Gohl was out with blood poisoning. *Coast Seamen's Journal*, December 14, 1904, July 11, 18, 1906, November 28, 1906, January 14, 21, 1907, July 10, 1907; *Grays Harbor Post*, August 3, 1907.

77. *Aberdeen Daily Bulletin*, October 30, November 3, 1906.

78. *Coast Seamen's Journal*, July 10, 1907.

79. *Grays Harbor Post*, August 3, 1907.

80. Elmer E. Shields to Mr. Samuel D. Bridges, Clerk of the United States Court, March 28, 1908, William Gohl Bankruptcy Record, Bankruptcy Records of the United States District Court, Western District of Washington, Western Division, National Archives, Seattle; In the Matter of the Estate of William Gohl, a Bankrupt, Petition No. 653, Bankruptcy Records of the United States District Court, Western District of Washington, Western Division, National Archives, Seattle.

81. Schedule A.3., In the Matter of the Estate of William Gohl, a Bankrupt, Petition No. 653, Bankruptcy Records of the United States District Court, Western District of Washington, Western Division, National Archives, Seattle.

82. Warren A. Worden, March 30, 1908, In the Matter of William Gohl, Bankrupt, In Bankruptcy, No. 653, Bankruptcy Records of the United States District Court, Western District of Washington, Western Division, National Archives, Seattle.

83. L. G. Humbargar, April 14, 1908, Affidavit of Publication of Bankruptcy Notice for William Gohl, Bankruptcy Records United States District Court, Western District of Washington, Western Division, National Archives, Seattle.

84. *Sam Jacobson v. William Gohl and Mrs. William Gohl*, No. 7397, Superior Court of the State of Washington, for Chehalis County (1908), Billy Gohl Documentation, Southwest Regional Branch, Washington State Archives, Olympia.

85. *Grays Harbor Post*, May 2, 1908; *Aberdeen Herald*, April 30, 1908.

86. *Sam Jacobson v. William Gohl and Mrs. William Gohl*, Petition, A. E. Cross, Attorney for Petitioner, Chehalis/Grays Harbor Superior Court,

Civil Court Docket, 1908, box 106, Southwest Regional Branch, Washington State Archives, Olympia.

87. *Sam Jacobson v. William Gohl and Mrs. William Gohl*, Petition, A.E. Cross, Attorney for Petitioner, Chehalis/Grays Harbor Superior Court, Civil Court Docket, 1908, box 106, Southwest Regional Branch, Washington State Archives, Olympia.

88. *Grays Harbor Post*, September 7, 1907.

89. *Aberdeen Herald*, October 3, 10, 1907; *Grays Harbor Post*, September 28, 1907.

90. *Aberdeen Herald*, December 9, 1907.

91. *Aberdeen Herald*, March 26, 1908.

92. *Aberdeen Herald*, January 10, 1910.

93. *Aberdeen Daily Bulletin*, October 30, 1906.

CHAPTER SIX: THE FLOATER FLEET

1. *Grays Harbor Post*, May 11, 1907; Coroner's Inquest into Connie Lockett, May 6, 1907, Chehalis County Coroner's Record, Southwest Regional Branch, Washington State Archives, Olympia.

2. *Grays Harbor Post*, May 11, 25, June 1, 1907.

3. *Aberdeen Herald*, February 10, 1910.

4. *Grays Harbor Post*, May 11, 1907.

5. Ed Van Syckle, *They Tried to Cut It All: Grays Harbor, Turbulent Years of Greed and Greatness* (Seattle: Pacific Search Press, 1980), 12.

6. *Aberdeen Daily Bulletin*, May 15, 22, 1905.

7. *Aberdeen World*, September 21, 1908. The case was dismissed from the Aberdeen Police Court due to insufficient evidence. See *Aberdeen Herald*, September 24, 1908.

8. *Aberdeen World*, September 16, 1908, February 15, 1909.

9. *Aberdeen Herald*, September 2, 1907.

10. *Grays Harbor Post*, November 7, 1908.

11. *Grays Harbor Post*, January 25, 1908.

12. *Aberdeen World*, February 4, 1909.

13. *Aberdeen World*, August 25, 1908; *Grays Harbor Post*, August 29, 1908.

14. *Aberdeen Herald*, November 12, 1908.

15. *Aberdeen Herald*, June 6, 1907.

16. Matthew Morse Booker, *Down by the Bay: San Francisco's History between the Tides* (Berkeley: University of California Press, 2013), 51.

17. *Aberdeen Daily Bulletin*, January 22, 1904.

18. Anne Cotton, "History of Aberdeen: 1775–1982," in *Aberdeen Comprehensive Development Plan, Phase I, Profile of Aberdeen* (Aberdeen, WA: Grays Harbor Regional Planning Commission, 1969), 40.

19. *Aberdeen Daily Bulletin*, June 12, 1906.

20. *Grays Harbor Post*, August 10, 1907.

21. *Morning Oregonian* (Portland), February 9, 1910; *Grays Harbor Post*, June 8, 1907.

22. *Grays Harbor Post*, February 9, 1907.

23. *Grays Harbor Post*, May 11, 1907.

24. Record of Deaths, City of Aberdeen, 1890–1907, City of Aberdeen Records, Southwest Regional Branch, Washington State Archives, Olympia.

25. C. J. March, *The Ghoul of Grays Harbor: Murder and Mayhem in the Pacific Northwest* (Minneapolis: Slingshot Books, 2019), 21–22.

26. This section is based on my analysis of the Chehalis County Coroner's Record, Southwest Regional Branch, Washington State Archives, Olympia.

27. Chehalis County coroner's record for Edward Jacobbsen, June 1907, Southwest Regional Branch, Washington State Archives, Olympia.

28. The Chehalis County coroner's office called coroner's juries to investigate the deaths of Rudolph Alterman (gunshot), Gabrielle Auested (drowning), Filippe Dios (gunshot), Rizoni Goreri (crushed), and Michael Madden (hit by streetcar).

29. Chehalis County Coroner's Record for Gabrielle Auested, June 1907, Southwest Regional Branch, Washington State Archives, Olympia.

30. Coroner's Record, Chehalis County, Southwest Regional Branch, Washington State Archives, Olympia.

31. *Aberdeen Herald*, June 3, 1907.

32. *Aberdeen Daily Bulletin*, April 13, 1906.

33. *Aberdeen Daily Bulletin*, January 23, 1906.

34. Norman H. Clark, *The Dry Years: Prohibition and Social Change in Washington*, rev. ed. (Seattle: University of Washington Press, 1988), 108–29, 134.

35. *Grays Harbor Post*, April 17, 1909.

36. Clark, *Dry Years*, 82.

37. Clark, *Dry Years*, 82–107.

38. "Aberdeen Saloon Men Arrested," *American Issue* (Anti-Saloon League), Washington ed., March 1908, 8.

39. *Grays Harbor Post*, April 4, 1908; *Aberdeen World*, June 18, September 17, 1908.

40. *Aberdeen World*, February 7, 1909; *Grays Harbor Post*, February 29, 1908.

41. *Aberdeen World*, March 28, 1909.

42. *Grays Harbor Post*, June 8, 1907.

43. *Grays Harbor Post*, May 15, 1909.

44. In the *Grays Harbor Washingtonian*, February 8, 1910, Gohl recalled the great deal of assistance he had lent local officials during his time in Aberdeen. He told a reporter, "I was the first man to go to the police and county officials to tell them of crimes committed and the possible doing away of some person."

45. Letter from William Gohl, *Aberdeen World*, February 14, 1909.

46. *Aberdeen World*, February 15, 1909.

47. Letter from William Gohl, *Aberdeen World*, February 14, 1909.

48. Letter from William Gohl, *Aberdeen World*, February 7, 1909.

49. Letter from William Gohl, *Aberdeen World*, February 14, 1909.

50. Letter from William Gohl, *Aberdeen World*, February 7, 1909.

51. Anna Sloan Walker, "History of the Liquor Laws of the State of Washington," *Washington Historical Quarterly* 5 (April 1914): 118.

52. Letter from William Gohl, *Aberdeen World*, February 7, 1909.

53. Quoted in Philip S. Foner, *History of the Labor Movement in the United States*, vol. 5, *The AFL in the Progressive Era, 1910–1915* (New York: International Publishers, 1980), 59.

54. Foner, *History of the Labor Movement in the United States*, vol. 5, 59.

55. Application for Membership, Fraternal Order of Eagles, Aerie No. 24, 1908, Billy Gohl Collection, Aberdeen Historical Museum.

56. *Grays Harbor Washingtonian*, February 8, 1910.

57. Letter from William Gohl, *Aberdeen World*, February 14, 1909.

58. Aberdeen voting registers, Grays Harbor County Auditor, Voter Registers, Aberdeen, 1909, Wards 1–4, Southwest Regional Branch, Washington State Archives, Olympia.

59. *R. L. Polk Company's Grays Harbor Cities Directory*, 1908, 65, 125.

60. State of Washington v. William Gohl, Undertaking, in the Justice Court of the City of Aberdeen Precinct, Chehalis County, Washington, E. H. Fox, Justice of the Peace, August 25, 1906, *State of Washington v. William Gohl*, No. 6499, Southwest Regional Branch, Washington State Archives, Olympia.

61. *Grays Harbor Post*, October 24, 1908; *R. L. Polk Company's Grays Harbor Cities Directory*, 1908, 116.

62. Application for Membership, Fraternal Order of Eagles, Aerie No. 24, 1908, Billy Gohl Collection, Aberdeen Historical Museum.

63. Letter from A. Kninitzer, H. Sivertsen, E. F. Swedstrup, H. R. E. Christensen, Geo. Gram, and Fred E. Olsen, *Aberdeen World*, February 15, 1909.

64. *Aberdeen World*, February 7, 1909; *R. L. Polk Company's Grays Harbor Cities Directory*, 1910, 608.

65. Letter from William Gohl, *Aberdeen World*, February 7, 1909.

66. *Grays Harbor Washingtonian*, February 8, 1910; *Tacoma Daily-Ledger*, February 8, 1910; *Morning Oregonian* (Portland), February 8, 1910.

67. Clippings from the *Aberdeen Daily World*, no date, Billy Gohl Records, Aberdeen Historical Museum.

68. *Aberdeen Herald*, August 23, 1909.

69. *Tacoma Daily Ledger*, February 8, 1910.

70. *Aberdeen Daily Bulletin*, April 27, 1906.

71. *Aberdeen Herald*, April 22, 1907; *Grays Harbor Post*, June 20, 1908.

72. *Aberdeen Herald*, March 26, 1908; *Grays Harbor Post*, March 14, 1908.

73. *Aberdeen Herald*, March 9, 26, 30, 1908.

74. *Aberdeen Daily Bulletin*, April 3, 14, 1906; *Aberdeen Herald*, April 16, 19, 1906.

75. *Aberdeen Daily Bulletin*, April 21, 25, 1906.

76. *Aberdeen Herald*, April 15, 1909; *Aberdeen Daily World*, April 10, 1909.

77. Hugh M. Delanty, *Along the Waterfront: Covering a Period of Fifty Years on Grays Harbor and the Pacific Northwest* (Aberdeen, WA: Quick Print, 1943), 37.

78. *Aberdeen Herald*, November 4, 1909.

79. *Aberdeen Herald*, January 25, 1909.

80. *Aberdeen Herald*, January 31, 1909.

81. *Grays Harbor Post*, August 13, 1904.

82. Van Syckle, *They Tried to Cut It All*, 174.

83. *Grays Harbor Washingtonian*, May 13, 1910.

CHAPTER SEVEN: SOLIDARITY REPRISE

1. *Aberdeen Daily Bulletin*, September 24, 1904; *Aberdeen Herald*, September 26, 1904.

2. "Temple Dedicated to Fidelity, Justice, Brotherly Love and Charity," *Fireside Chatter*, November 1982, Hoquiam Elks Archives, Hoquiam, Washington; *Fireside Chatter: Centennial Edition, 1907–2007*, Hoquiam Elks Records, Hoquiam, Washington; *Aberdeen Daily Bulletin*, September 24, 1904.

3. *Aberdeen Daily Bulletin*, September 24, 1904.

4. *Aberdeen Herald*, September 26, 1904.

5. *Aberdeen Herald*, July 20, 1905; *Aberdeen Daily Bulletin*, July 24, 1905.

6. *Grays Harbor Post*, May 29, 1909; August 29, 1908.

7. *Aberdeen Daily World*, November 24, 1911.

8. *Aberdeen Herald*, January 11, 1912; *Grays Harbor Post*, January 20, 1912.

9. *Aberdeen Daily World*, November 25, 1911.

10. *Aberdeen Daily World*, November 24, 1911.

11. *Grays Harbor Post*, September 8, 1906.

12. *Grays Harbor Post*, May 2, June 6, 1908.

13. *Aberdeen Herald*, September 24, 1908; *Grays Harbor Post*, September 26, 1908.

14. *Aberdeen Daily Bulletin*, July 27, 1906.

15. *Aberdeen Herald*, August 5, 1907.

16. Delanty had persistent conflict with the harbor's maritime unions, largely because of his enforcement of the open shop, which weakened

labor power. Hugh M.Delanty, *Along the Waterfront: Covering a Period of Fifty Years on Grays Harbor and the Pacific Northwest* (Aberdeen, WA: Quick Print, 1943), 37–38; *Proceedings of the Sixth Annual Convention of the Pacific District of the International Longshoremen's Association*, 1913, 37–38.

17. *Aberdeen Herald*, June 24, 1909.

18. *Aberdeen Daily World*, February 4, 1910.

19. On the power exerted by lumbermen in the Washington state legislature, see *Aberdeen Daily Bulletin*, November 14, 1904; Robert E. Ficken, *Lumber and Politics: The Career of Mark E. Reed* (Seattle: University of Washington Press, 1980). See also Herbert Hunt and F. C. Kaylor, *Washington, West of the Cascades: Historical and Descriptive: The Explorers, the Indians, the Pioneers, the Modern* (Seattle: S. J. Clarke, 1917), 130–31, 393–95, 476.

20. Ronald E. Magden, *A History of Seattle Waterfront Workers, 1884–1934* (Seattle: Trade Printery, 1991), 59–61.

21. Articles of Incorporation of the Grays Harbor Stevedore Company, Chehalis County, State of Washington, September 18, 1908, Articles of Incorporation, Grays Harbor County Government Records, Southwest Regional Branch, Washington State Archives, Olympia.

22. *Grays Harbor Washingtonian*, April 10, 1910; United States Bureau of the Census, *Thirteenth Census of the United States Taken in the Year 1910*, Washington State, Chehalis County, City of Aberdeen.

23. *Aberdeen Herald*, October 8, 15, 1908.

24. *Aberdeen Herald*, May 27, 1912.

25. *Grays Harbor Post*, January 22, 1910.

26. *Aberdeen World*, January 1, 14, February 14, 1909, 1, 14 January 1909; *Aberdeen Daily World*, August 10, 1911.

27. In the *Grays Harbor Post*, July 28, 1906, Mack was described as "part of a powerful combination" trying to destroy the SUP.

28. *Aberdeen Daily World*, August 10, 1911; Pamela Dean Aho, "The Ghoul of Grays Harbor," in *On the Harbor: From Black Friday to Nirvana*, edited by John C. Hughes and Ryan Teague Beckwith (Aberdeen, WA: Daily World, 2001), 22.

29. *Aberdeen World*, February 7, 1909.

30. *Aberdeen Daily World*, January 14, 1911; *R. L. Polk and Company's Grays Harbor Cities Directory*, 1908, 69.

31. *Aberdeen Daily World*, January 14, February 2, 14, 1911.

32. *Aberdeen Daily World*, February 2, 14, 1909.

33. *Aberdeen Daily World*, March 9, 10, 1910.

34. *Aberdeen Daily World*, March 9, 1909.

35. *Session Laws of the State of Washington, 1903* (Tacoma, WA: Allen & Lamborn, 1903), 52–53.

36. F. Dowell, *History of Criminal-Syndicalist Legislation in the United States* (Baltimore: Johns Hopkins University Press, 1939); Aaron Goings, Brian Barnes, and Roger Snider, *The Red Coast: Radicalism and Anti-Radicalism in Southwest Washington* (Corvallis: Oregon State University Press, 2019), 87–100.

37. Hollis B. Fultz, *Famous Northwest Manhunts* (Elma, WA: Fulco Publishing, 1955), 32.

38. *Aberdeen Daily World*, March 19, April 7, 1909; Fultz, *Famous Northwest Manhunts*, 27.

39. *Aberdeen World*, September 17, 1908.

40. *Aberdeen Herald*, May 13, 1909.

41. Lowell Stillwell Hawley and Ralph Bushnell Potts, *Counsel for the Damned: A Biography of George Francis Vanderveer* (Philadelphia: J. B. Lippincott, 1953); J. F. Rhodes and W. H. Margason to George F. Vanderveer, November 15, 1917, box 99, file 1, *United States v. Haywood, et al.*, Industrial Workers of the World Collection, box 110, folder 3, 5713, Walter P. Reuther Library, Wayne State University, Detroit.

42. Richard O. Boyer and Herbert M. Morais, *Labor's Untold Story: The Adventure Story of the Battles, Betrayals, and Victories of American Working Men and Women* (New York: Cameron Associates, 1955), 151–57.

43. There exists a sizeable literature on the history of labor spies. See Frank Morn, *"The Eye that Never Sleeps": A History of the Pinkerton National Detective Agency* (Bloomington: Indiana University Press, 1982); Robert P. Weiss, "Private Detective Agencies and Labour Discipline in the United States, 1855–1946," *Historical Journal* 29,

no. 1 (1986): 87–107; Leo Huberman, *The Labor Spy Racket* (New York: Modern Age Books, 1937); Robert M. Smith, *From Blackjacks to Briefcases: A History of Commercialized Strikebreaking and Union-busting in the United States* (Athens: Ohio University Press, 2003); Stephen H. Norwood, *Strikebreaking and Intimidation: Mercenaries and Masculinity in Twentieth-Century America* (Chapel Hill: University of North Carolina Press, 2001); Rhodri Jeffreys-Jones, *Violence and Reform in American History* (New York: New Viewpoints, 1978), 100–114.

44. J. Anthony Lukas, *Big Trouble: A Murder in a Small Western Town Sets off a Struggle for the Soul of America* (New York: Simon and Schuster, 1997), 84–85; Smith, *From Blackjacks to Briefcases*, 21.

45. Boyer and Morais, *Labor's Untold Story*, 151–57; Morn, "*The Eye that Never Sleeps*," 103; Vernon H. Jensen, *Heritage of Conflict: Labor Relations in the Nonferrous Metals Industry up to 1930* (Ithaca, NY: Cornell University Press, 1950), 202.

46. *R. L. Polk Company's Seattle City Directory*, 1900, 1158; *R. L. Polk and Company's Seattle City Directory*, 1901, 1309–10; *R. L. Polk and Company's Seattle City Directory*, 1905, 1449; *R. L. Polk and Company's Grays Harbor Cities Directory*, 1908, 19, 553; Philip J. Dreyfus, "Timber Workers, Unionism and Syndicalism in the Pacific Northwest, 1900–1917" (PhD dissertation, Graduate School of the City University of New York, 1993), 159–60; *Aberdeen World*, February 11, 1909.

47. *Aberdeen Daily World*, March 3, 1909.

48. Emily M. Wilson, *From Boats to Board Feet: The Wilson Family of the Pacific Coast* (Seattle: Wilson Brothers Family Foundation, 2007), 146.

49. John D. Fairbairn, "Fairbairn's Guide to History of Logging in Chehalis-Grays Harbor County since 1882," 145, Aberdeen: Before 1920 Collection, Special Collections, Aberdeen Timberland Library, Aberdeen; *Aberdeen Daily Bulletin*, June 16, 1904; *R. L. Polk and Company's Grays Harbor City Directory*, 1902, 43.

50. *Aberdeen Daily Bulletin*, June 16, 1904.

51. *R. L. Polk Company's Grays Harbor Cities Directory*, 1907, 110; *Aberdeen Daily Bulletin*, June 16, 1904.

52. *Hoquiam Sawyer*, August 10, 1907; *Aberdeen Herald*, August 10, 1907.

53. *Grays Harbor Post*, April 9, 1910; Van Syckle, *They Tried to Cut It All: Grays Harbor, Turbulent Years of Greed and Greatness* (Seattle: Pacific Search Press, 1980), 244; Aho, "Ghoul of Grays Harbor," 23–24.

54. *Aberdeen Daily World*, August 10, 1911.

55. *Grays Harbor Post*, May 29, 1909.

56. *Grays Harbor Washingtonian*, May 8, 1910.

57. "Wm. Gohl's Friends," Billy Gohl Documentation, Chehalis County Sheriff's Correspondence, Southwest Regional Branch, Washington State Archives, Olympia.

58. *Grays Harbor Washingtonian*, May 8, 1910; *Aberdeen Daily World*, August 10, 1911; Aho, "Ghoul of Grays Harbor," 23.

59. *Aberdeen Herald*, May 9, 1910.

60. Aho, "Ghoul of Grays Harbor," 23; *Morning Oregonian* (Portland), February 8, 1910.

61. *Grays Harbor Washingtonian*, May 14, 1910.

62. *R. L. Polk and Company's Grays Harbor Cities Directory*, 1907, 225; *Aberdeen Herald*, July 12, 1909.

63. *Aberdeen Herald*, July 12, 29, 1909.

64. *Aberdeen Herald*, July 29, 1909.

65. *Tacoma Daily Ledger*, July 11, 1909.

66. *Bellingham Herald*, July 29, 1909.

67. *Aberdeen Daily World*, December 30, 1909. In a story about Gohl, the *Tacoma Daily Ledger*, October 4, 1928, reminded its readers of Gohl's efforts to call a general strike, writing: "He was bitterly opposed to non-union workmen and at the time of his arrest was holding out a threat of a general strike here."

CHAPTER EIGHT: GOHL ON TRIAL

1. *Grays Harbor Post*, October 15, 1910; *Aberdeen Daily World*, February 3, 1910.

2. *Aberdeen Herald*, May 16, 1910.

3. *Grays Harbor Washingtonian*, February 8, 1910; *Aberdeen World*, September 10, 17, 1908. No letters or notes between Chief Dean and Sheriff Payette exist in Chehalis County sheriff's correspondence in the 1910

Gohl trial file (Billy Gohl Documentation. Southwest Regional Branch, Washington State Archives, Olympia).

4. *R. L. Polk Company's Grays Harbor Cities Directory*, 1910, 30.

5. *Grays Harbor Washingtonian*, February 4, 1910.

6. *Morning Oregonian* (Portland), February 4, 1910; *Aberdeen Daily World*, February 3, 1910.

7. *Aberdeen Daily World*, February 4, 1910.

8. *Grays Harbor Washingtonian*, February 12, 1910.

9. *Aberdeen Daily World*, February 3, 1910.

10. *Grays Harbor Washingtonian*, February 6, 1910.

11. *Grays Harbor Washingtonian*, February 5, 1910; *Chehalis County Vidette*, February 11, 1910; *Aberdeen Daily World*, February 4, 1910; *Grays Harbor Washingtonian*, February 6, 1910.

12. *Grays Harbor Washingtonian*, February 5, 1910.

13. *Grays Harbor Post*, May 14, 1910.

14. *Aberdeen Daily World*, February 4, 1910.

15. "Coroner's Record for Chas. Hadburg [*sic*], Chehalis County, State of Washington," February 2, 1910, Southwest Regional Branch, Washington State Archives, Olympia; *Grays Harbor Washingtonian*, February 5, 6, 1910; *Morning Oregonian*, February 8, 1910.

16. *Grays Harbor Washingtonian*, February 6, 1910.

17. *Aberdeen Daily World*, February 3, 1910.

18. "Coroner's Record for Chas. Hadburg, Chehalis County, State of Washington," February 2, 1910, Grays Harbor County Government Documentation, Southwest Regional Branch, Washington State Archives, Olympia; *Grays Harbor Washingtonian*, February 5, 6, 8, 1910; *Morning Oregonian*, February 8, 1910; *Aberdeen Daily World*, February 3, 8, 1910.

19. *Grays Harbor Washingtonian*, February 6, 8, 1910; *Aberdeen Daily World*, February 3, 8, 1910; *Morning Oregonian*, February 8, 1910.

20. *Aberdeen Daily World*, May 6, 1910.

21. *Grays Harbor Washingtonian*, May 8, 1910.

22. *Morning Oregonian*, February 8, 1910.

23. *Morning Oregonian*, February 8, 1910.

24. *Morning Oregonian*, February 8, 1910; *Grays Harbor Washingtonian*, March 20, 1910.

25. *Grays Harbor Washingtonian,* February 8, 1910.

26. *Morning Oregonian,* February 5, 1910.

27. *Grays Harbor Washingtonian,* February 8, 1910; *Morning Oregonian,* February 6, 1910.

28. *Aberdeen Herald,* April 19, 25, 1910; *Grays Harbor Washingtonian,* February 9, May 13, 1910.

29. *Aberdeen Daily World,* February 3, 1910; *Chehalis County Vidette,* February 11, 1910; *Grays Harbor Washingtonian,* February 8, 1910; *Tacoma Daily Ledger,* February 8, 1910.

30. *Chehalis County Vidette,* February 11, 1910.

31. *Aberdeen Daily World,* February 8, 1910.

32. *Grays Harbor Washingtonian,* February 8, 9, 1910; *Aberdeen Daily World,* February 8, 1910.

33. *Aberdeen Daily World,* February 8, 1910.

34. *Grays Harbor Washingtonian,* February 8, 1910.

35. *Grays Harbor Washingtonian,* February 8, 1910.

36. Pamela Dean Aho, "The Ghoul of Grays Harbor," in *On the Harbor: From Black Friday to Nirvana,* ed. John C. Hughes and Ryan Teague Beckwith (Aberdeen, WA: Daily World, 2001), 29.

37. *Aberdeen Daily World,* February 14, 1910; *Grays Harbor Washingtonian,* May 1, 1910.

38. *Aberdeen Herald,* March 30, 1910.

39. Sheriff Ed Payette to Sheriff Max Happel, May 17, 1910, Chehalis County Sheriff's Correspondence, Billy Gohl Documentation, Southwest Regional Branch, Washington State Archives, Olympia.

40. *Grays Harbor Washingtonian,* February 8, 1910.

41. *Morning Oregonian,* February 6, 1910.

42. Letter from William Gohl to the Aberdeen Branch of the Sailors Union of the Pacific, February 7, 1910, Chehalis County Sheriff's Correspondence, Billy Gohl Documentation, Southwest Washington Archives, Olympia, Washington.

43. *Aberdeen Daily World,* March 16, 1910; *Grays Harbor Washingtonian,* March 17, 1910; *Aberdeen Herald,* March 17, 1910.

44. *Grays Harbor Washingtonian,* March 20, 1910.

45. *Aberdeen Daily World*, February 3, 4, 5, 7, 8, 9, 11, 1910; *Aberdeen Herald*, February 3, 7, 10, 1910.

46. *Aberdeen Daily World*, February 3, 1910.

47. *Aberdeen Herald*, February 7, 1910.

48. *Grays Harbor Washingtonian*, February 2, 1910.

49. *Chehalis County Vidette*, February 11, 1910.

50. *N. W. Ayer and Son's American Newspaper Annual and Directory: A Catalogue of American Newspapers* (Philadelphia: N. W. Ayer & Son, 1917), 999–1005.

51. *Centralia Daily Chronicle*, May 2, 1910.

52. Minutes, Pierce County Central Labor Council, February 9, 16, 1910; Acc. no 2882-01, Folder Title: "Minutes, Aug. 4, 1909–May 3, 1911," Central Labor Council, Pierce County Collection, Special Collections, University of Washington Libraries, Seattle, WA.

53. *Aberdeen Daily World*, February 4, 1910.

54. *Coast Seamen's Journal*, February 9, 1910.

55. *Aberdeen Daily World*, February 4, 1910; *Coast Seamen's Journal*, February 9, 1910.

56. *Grays Harbor Washingtonian*, February 6, 1910.

57. E. P. Thompson, "The Crime of Anonymity," in *Albion's Fatal Tree: Crime and Society in Eighteenth-Century England*, ed. Douglas Hay and others (New York: Pantheon Books, 1975), 255.

58. *Aberdeen Daily World*, February 7, 1910. The original reads: "You Yello Yournals write any old thing about a poor Fellow when he is down and ont." I revised it for the sake of clarity.

59. *Grays Harbor Washingtonian*, May 10, 1910.

60. *Grays Harbor Washingtonian*, February 8, 1910; *Aberdeen Daily World*, February 4, 5, 1910,

61. *Aberdeen Daily World*, February 7, 1910.

62. *Chehalis County Vidette*, February 11, 1910.

63. *Aberdeen Daily World*, February 9, 11, 1910; *Grays Harbor Post*, February 19, 1910.

64. *Grays Harbor Washingtonian*, March 20, 1910.

65. *Aberdeen Herald*, April 25, 1910.

66. *Grays Harbor Washingtonian,* April 24, 1910.

67. *Grays Harbor Washingtonian,* April 24, 1910.

68. *Grays Harbor Washingtonian,* May 12, 1910.

69. *Aberdeen Daily World,* February 4, 1910; *Grays Harbor Washingtonian,* February 5, 1910.

70. *Grays Harbor Washingtonian,* May 7, 1910.

71. W. M. Coffman, *American in the Rough: The Autobiography of W. M. (Bill) Coffman* (New York: Simon and Schuster, 1955), 191.

72. *Grays Harbor Post,* April 9, 1910; *Grays Harbor Washingtonian,* April 9, 1910; *Aberdeen Herald,* April 7, 11, 1910; *Tacoma Daily Ledger,* April 6, 1910,

73. *Grays Harbor Post,* October 15, 22, 1910; *Aberdeen Herald,* October 13, 1910.

74. *Grays Harbor Washingtonian,* April 6, 1910.

75. A list of the three hundred prospective jurors was listed in the *Grays Harbor Washingtonian,* April 15, 1910.

76. *Grays Harbor Washingtonian,* April 26, 1910.

77. *Grays Harbor Washingtonian,* May 3, 4, 1910.

78. *Grays Harbor Washingtonian,* May 3, 4, 1910.

79. *Aberdeen Herald,* May 23, 1910.

80. *Aberdeen Daily World,* May 4, 1910.

81. *Grays Harbor Washingtonian,* May 3, 4, 1910.

82. Philip J. Dreyfus, "Timber Workers: Unionism and Syndicalism in the Pacific Northwest, 1900–1917" (PhD dissertation, Graduate School of the City University of New York, 1993), 40.

83. *Aberdeen Herald,* May 9, 12, 1910.

84. *Grays Harbor Washingtonian,* May 6, 1910, 1. Prosecutor Campbell's opening statement appeared in full in this issue of the *Washingtonian.*

85. *Grays Harbor Post,* May 7, 1910; *Aberdeen Herald,* May 9, 1910.

86. *Grays Harbor Post,* May 7, 1910.

87. *Aberdeen Daily World,* February 4, 1910.

88. *Aberdeen Daily World,* May 11, 1910.

89. *Grays Harbor Post,* May 7, 1910; *Grays Harbor Post,* May 14, 1910.

90. *Grays Harbor Washingtonian,* May 11, 1910.

91. *Grays Harbor Post,* May 7, 1910.

92. *Grays Harbor Washingtonian*, May 3, 1910.

93. Chehalis County Superior Court, Case no. 8505, "Order for Subpoena Issue," May 3, 1910, Southwest Regional Branch, Washington State Archives, Olympia; *Grays Harbor Washingtonian*, May 10, 1910; *Aberdeen Herald*, May 12, 1910.

94. *Grays Harbor Washingtonian*, February 8, 1910.

95. Chehalis County Superior Court, Case No. 8505, "Order for Subpoena Issue," May 3, 1910, Southwest Regional Branch, Washington State Archives, Olympia; *Grays Harbor Washingtonian*, May 10, 1910; *Aberdeen Herald*, May 12, 1910.

96. *Aberdeen Herald*, May 12, 1910; Minutes, Superior Court, Chehalis County, Washington, Minute Book, vol. 1, Dept. 2, Chehalis County, Southwest Regional Branch, Washington State Archives, Olympia.

97. *Grays Harbor Washingtonian*, May 10, 1910. According to Abel, in return for the bribe McHugh promised that both he and "Billie Montana" would leave the county. Of that amount, McHugh was to receive $4,000 and Montana $3,000.

98. *Grays Harbor Washingtonian*, May 8, 1910; *Aberdeen Herald*, May 9, 1910.

99. *Grays Harbor Washingtonian*, May 10, 1910.

100. Minutes, Superior Court, Chehalis County, Washington, May 9, 1910, Case No. 8505, Chehalis County, Southwest Regional Branch, Washington State Archives, Olympia; *Grays Harbor Washingtonian*, May 10, 1910.

101. *Aberdeen Herald*, May 12, 1910; Service on Witnesses, Superior Court, Chehalis County, Washington, May 5, 1910, Case No. 8505, Chehalis County, Southwest Regional Branch, Washington State Archives, Olympia.

102. *Grays Harbor Washingtonian*, May 7, 9, 1910.

103. *Grays Harbor Washingtonian*, May 12, 1910.

104. *Grays Harbor Post*, May 14, 1910; *Aberdeen Daily World*, May 9, 1910.

105. *Aberdeen Daily World*, May 10, 1910.

106. *Grays Harbor Washingtonian*, May 10, 1910.

107. *Grays Harbor Washingtonian*, May 12, 1910.

108. *Grays Harbor Post*, May 14, 1910.

109. *Grays Harbor Post,* May 14, 1910.

110. Minutes, May 11, 1910, *State of Washington v. William Gohl,* No. 8505, Superior Court of the State of Washington, for Chehalis County (1910), Billy Gohl Documentation, Southwest Regional Branch, Washington State Archives, Olympia.

111. *Grays Harbor Post,* May 14, 1910; *Aberdeen Herald,* May 12, 1910, *Grays Harbor Washingtonian,* May 10, 1910; *Aberdeen Daily World,* May 11, 1910.

112. *Grays Harbor Post,* May 14, 1910.

113. US Bureau of the Census, *Thirteenth Census of the United States Taken in the Year 1910,* Washington State, Chehalis County, City of Elma; *Grays Harbor Washingtonian,* May 14, 1910.

114. Minutes, Chehalis County Superior Court, May 11, 1910, Southwest Regional Branch, Washington State Archives, Olympia; *Grays Harbor Washingtonian,* May 13, 1910.

115. Chehalis County Superior Court, Case No. 8505, Verdict, Southwest Regional Branch, Washington State Archives, Olympia.

116. *Grays Harbor Washingtonian,* May 12, 1910.

117. *Aberdeen Daily World,* May 12, 1910. The *Grays Harbor Washingtonian* of May 13, 1910, recorded Bessie's words differently: "I still love you and I will work my fingers off to see that you get justice. We have been happy dear during the five years we were married and by God's grace we will be happy again."

118. Washington State Penitentiary, Biographical Statement of Convict No. 5779, June 18, 1910, Washington State Penitentiary Records, Billy Gohl Documentation, Southwest Regional Branch, Washington State Archives, Olympia.

119. *Grays Harbor Washingtonian,* May 12, 1910.

120. "Motion for Arrest of Judgment," "Motion for New Trial," "Motion for Judgment of Acquittal non obstante verdicto," all in *State of Washington v. William Gohl,* No. 8505, Superior Court of the State of Washington, for Chehalis County (1910), Billy Gohl Documentation, Southwest Regional Branch, Washington State Archives, Olympia; *Aberdeen Herald,* May 26, 1910.

121. *Grays Harbor Post,* May 28, 1910; *Aberdeen Herald,* May 19, 1910.

122. *Aberdeen Herald*, April 11, 1910.

123. *Grays Harbor Washingtonian*, April 9, 1910.

124. *Grays Harbor Post*, October 15, 1910.

125. *Aberdeen Herald*, October 17, 1910.

126. *Grays Harbor Washingtonian*, May 4, 1910.

127. Letter from Sheriff Ed Payette to C. S. Reed, June 1, 1910, Chehalis County Sheriff's Correspondence, Billy Gohl Documentation, Southwest Regional Branch, Washington State Archives, Olympia.

128. *Grays Harbor Washingtonian*, May 8, 1910. Bessie Gohl's assistance prompted the defense to object to this witness's testimony. Judge Sheeks overruled the objection.

129. *Grays Harbor Post*, May 14, 1910.

130. *Grays Harbor Post*, Oct. 22, 1910.

131. *Aberdeen Daily World*, Oct. 12, 1910.

132. *Grays Harbor Post*, Oct. 29, 1910.

CHAPTER NINE: MAKING THE
GHOUL OF GRAYS HARBOR

1. Sheriff Ed Payette to C. S. Reed, Warden, June 1, 1910, Billy Gohl Documentation, Southwest Regional Branch, Washington State Archives, Olympia.

2. State Penitentiary at Walla Walla, Washington, description of convict William Gohl, Billy Gohl Documentation, Southwest Regional Branch, Washington State Archives, Olympia.

3. *Seattle Star*, March 27, 1916.

4. *Seattle Star*, April 6, 1916.

5. State of Washington, *Sixth Biennial Report of the State Board of Control for the Term Beginning October 1, 1910, and Ending September 30, 1912* (Olympia: Public Printer, 1912), 15, 192–95; Department of Instittions, State Penitentiary—Walla Walla, Commitment Record, 5772-6269 (1910–1911), Acc. No. 72-5-418, box 12, p. 76, Washington State Archives, Olympia.

6. On the criminal convictions that landed dozens of Washington State IWWs in the penitentiary, see Aaron Goings, Brian Barnes, and Roger

Snider, *The Red Coast: Radicalism and Anti-Radicalism in Southwest Washington* (Corvallis: Oregon State University Press, 2019); Tom Copeland, *The Centralia Tragedy of 1919: Elmer Smith and the Wobblies* (Seattle: University of Washington Press, 1993).

7. *Seattle Star*, April 6, 1916.

8. United States Bureau of the Census, *Fourteenth Census of the United States Taken in the Year 1920*, Washington State, Walla Walla County.

9. State of Washington, *Sixth Biennial Report of the State Board of Control*, 185.

10. *Aberdeen Herald*, April 14, 1914.

11. Eugene Barnett interview (conducted by Archie Green), June 5, 1961, tape 2, University of Washington Digital Archives, https://digital-collections.lib.washington.edu/digital/collection/ohc/id/222; State of Washington, *Sixth Biennial Report of the State Board of Control*, 214.

12. *Tacoma Daily News*, June 14, 1910.

13. Edwin A. Scott to Mr. Pace, Warden, December 5, 1922, Inmate #5779, and Edwin A. Scott to Mr. Shattuck, Parole Agent, March 8, 1923, Inmate #5779, both in Billy Gohl Documentation, Southwest Regional Branch, Washington State Archives, Olympia.

14. Letter from Sheriff Ed Payette to C. S. Reed, June 1, 1910, Chehalis County Sheriff's Correspondence, Billy Gohl Documentation, Southwest Regional Branch, Washington State Archives, Olympia.

15. *Aberdeen Herald*, January 15, 1915

16. *Daily Washingtonian*, October 18, 1918.

17. *Aberdeen Daily World*, October 17, 1918.

18. W. J. Patterson to Governor Ernest Lister, October 21, 1918, Billy Gohl Documentation, Southwest Regional Branch, Washington State Archives, Olympia.

19. Governor Ernest Lister to W. J. Patterson, October 23, 1918, Billy Gohl Documentation, Southwest Regional Branch, Washington State Archives, Olympia.

20. John C. Hughes and Ryan Teague Beckwith, eds., *On the Harbor: From Black Friday to Nirvana* (Aberdeen, WA: Daily World, 2001), 79.

21. *Aberdeen Herald*, April 7, 1910.

22. *Grays Harbor Post,* March 30, 1910, May 9, 14, 1910; *Aberdeen Herald,*
     May 19, 1910; *Grays Harbor Washingtonian,* May 12, 1910.

23. *Aberdeen Daily World,* August 14, 1911.

24. *Industrial Worker* (Spokane), February 29, 1912.

25. *Aberdeen Daily World,* August 10, 1911.

26. The account of the Aberdeen Free Speech Fight and Grays Harbor
     Lumber Strike is based on my earlier writings. See especially Goings,
     "Red Harbor: Class, Violence, and Community in Grays Harbor, Wash-
     ington" (PhD dissertation, Simon Fraser University, 2011); and Goings,
     Barnes, and Snider, *Red Coast.*

27. Stewart H. Holbrook, *Holy Old Mackinaw: The Natural History of the
     American Lumberjack* (New York: Ballantine Books, 1971), 192.

28. C. J. March, *The Ghoul of Grays Harbor: Murder and Mayhem in the
     Pacific Northwest* (Minneapolis: Slingshot Books, 2019); Frank J. Zore-
     tich, "Plank Streets and Shady Dealings," *Pacific Slope,* February 1978,
     12–13.

29. Carlos A. Schwantes and James P. Ronda, *The West the Railroads
     Made* (Seattle: University of Washington Press, 2008), 123.

30. Pamel Dean Aho, "The Ghoul of Grays Harbor," in *On the Harbor: From
     Black Friday to Nirvana,* ed. John C. Hughes and Ryan Teague Beck-
     with (Aberdeen, WA: Daily World, 2001), 21; *Aberdeen Herald,* Febru-
     ary 1, 1912.

31. *Aberdeen Herald,* February 1, 1912.

32. *Olympia Daily Recorder,* January 5, 1914.

33. *Seattle Star,* December 29, 1910.

34. For examples of this brutal police behavior, see Goings, Barnes, and
     Snider, *Red Coast.*

35. *Aberdeen Herald,* November 2, 1911; November 4, 1913.

36. Goings, Barnes, and Snider, *Red Coast,* 149–52; *Aberdeen Daily World,*
     August 14, 1943.

37. Aho, "Ghoul of Grays Harbor," 23.

38. *Coast Seamen's Journal,* October 30, 1912.

39. *Tacoma Daily News,* June 14, 1910.

40. *Aberdeen Daily World,* February 19, 1912; *Tacoma Times,* February 19,
     1912.

41. United States Bureau of the Census, *Fourteenth Census of the United States Taken in the Year 1920*, Washington State, Walla Walla County. Bessie Gohl's obituary appeared in the *Walla Walla Union Bulletin*, September 4, 1945.

42. *Tacoma Times*, September 25, 1916.

43. "Physician's Certificate," September 22, 1923, Washington State Penitentiary Records, Billy Gohl Documentation, Southwest Regional Branch, Washington State Archives, Olympia; Aho, "Ghoul of Grays Harbor," 30.

44. "Description of Convict, William Gohl," Washington State Penitentiary Records, Billy Gohl Documentation, Southwest Regional Branch, Washington State Archives, Olympia.

45. *Grays Harbor Post*, September 2, 1911.

46. *Grays Harbor Post*, June 22, 1912.

47. *Aberdeen Herald*, December 11, 1911; *Aberdeen Daily World*, January 12, 1917.

48. *Aberdeen Daily World*, January 11, 1924; January 12, 1917.

49. *Aberdeen Daily World*, January 17, 1917.

50. *Seattle Star*, February 7, 1910.

51. *Aberdeen Daily World*, May 12, 1910.

52. *Aberdeen Daily World*, November 25, 1911.

53. See the *Aberdeen Daily World* front pages and editorial pages between November 1911 and April 1912.

54. Whiteside Funeral Home Records—Death Certificates, Washington State Library, Olympia, Washington. The Whiteside records provide a detailed analysis of the scores of drowning deaths in Grays Harbor during the 1910s, after Gohl's imprisonment.

55. *Aberdeen Herald*, March 7, 1912; *Grays Harbor Post*, August 20, 1910; June 24, 1911; *Aberdeen Daily World*, August 11, 1911.

56. United States Bureau of the Census, *Mortality Statistics 1910, Eleventh Annual Report* (Washington, DC: Government Printing Office, 1913), 274–75. Violent death rates in 1910 were as follows: 18 percent in Aberdeen, 5.6 percent in Bellingham, 12 percent in Everett, 9.3 percent in North Yakima, 9 percent in Seattle, 8.6 percent in Spokane, 8.2 percent in Tacoma, 6.8 percent in Walla Walla. In 1911, Aberdeen's violent death

rate (excluding suicide) of 110 per 100,000 was substantially higher than other cities listed; the city with the closest violent death rate was San Francisco, with a 95 per 100,000 violent death rate. See Bureau of the Census, *Mortality Statistics 1911, Twelfth Annual Report* (Washington, DC: Government Printing Office, 1913), 66–67, 82–87.

57. Joseph F. Tripp, "An Instance of Labor and Business Cooperation: Workmen's Compensation in Washington State (1911)," *Labor History* 17 (Fall 1976): 530–50.

58. Norman H. Clark, *The Dry Years: Prohibition and Social Change in Washington,* rev. ed. (Seattle: University of Washington Press, 1988); Brad Holden, *Seattle Prohibition: Bootleggers Rumrunners, and Graft in the Queen City* (Charleston, SC: History Press, 2019).

59. Merle A. Reinikka, "Death Certificates of Finns in Chehalis [Grays Harbor] County, 1907–1947," Aberdeen History Collection, Aberdeen Historical Museum.

60. *Aberdeen Herald,* October 30, 1914.

61. Police Notes, 1913–1939, Aberdeen History Collection, Aberdeen Historical Museum.

62. *Grays Harbor Washingtonian,* November 5, 1913; *Aberdeen Herald,* November 4, 1913. See also *Aberdeen Herald,* September 21, 1908; February 17, 1914.

63. *Aberdeen Herald,* June 9, 1914.

64. *Aberdeen Herald,* September 29, 1914; Certificate of Death for John Johnsson, September 27, 1914, Whiteside Funeral Home Records—Death Certificates, Washington State Library, Olympia, Washington. The spelling of the surname varies: "Johnson" in the *Herald* and "Johnsson" in the death certificate.

65. *Aberdeen Herald,* May 14, 1915.

66. See Steven Lewis Yaffee, *The Wisdom of the Spotted Owl: Policy Lessons for a New Century* (Washington, DC: Island Press, 1994), 160; "10,000 Are Expected to Lose Jobs to Spotted Owl," *New York Times,* April 28, 1990.

67. Anne Cotton, "History of Aberdeen: 1775–1982," in *Aberdeen Comprehensive Development Plan, Phase I, Profile of Aberdeen* (Aberdeen, WA: Grays Harbor Regional Planning Commission, 1969), 40.

68. Jeff Davis and Al Eufrasio, *Weird Washington: Your Travel Guide to Washington's Local Legends and Best Kept Secrets* (New York: Sterling Publishing, 2008), 111–12. See also Marques Vickers, *Murder in Washington: Notorious Crime Sites: The Topography of Evil: Notorious Washington State Murder Sites* (Larkspur, CA: Marquis Publishing, 2016), 29–31.

69. "Serial Killers vs. American Icons: A Users' Guide to Ensure a Gaffe-Free Conversation," *Vanity Fair*, June 28, 2011, https://www.vanity fair.com/.

70. Garth Stein, *A Sudden Light* (London: Simon and Schuster, 2014), 103; Dennis Pence, *The Ghoul of Grays Harbor* (Aberdeen, WA: AuthorHouse, 2004).

71. David Schmid, *Natural Born Celebrities: Serial Killers in American Culture* (Chicago: University of Chicago Press, 2005), 1–3.

72. Sophie Gilbert, "The Disaster Zone of Netflix's *Dark Tourist*," *Atlantic*, July 26, 2018, https://www.theatlantic.com/.

73. "A Little History," Bill Speidel's Underground Tour, http://www.under groundtour.com/about/history.html; Jeff Dwyer, *Ghost Hunter's Guide to Seattle and Puget Sound* (Gretna, LA: Pelican Publishing, 2008), 206–7; *Bellingham Herald*, May 5, 1987; Jamie Hayes, "The Buried City: The Story of Seattle's Underground," https://www.factinate.com/edito rial/seattle-underground.

BIBLIOGRAPHY

MANUSCRIPT COLLECTIONS

Aberdeen: Before 1920 Collection. Special Collections. Aberdeen Timberland Library, Aberdeen, Washington.

Aberdeen History Collection. Aberdeen Historical Museum, Aberdeen, Washington.

Aberdeen Municipal Government Records. Southwest Regional Branch, Washington State Archives, Olympia.

Articles of Incorporation. Grays Harbor County Government Records. Southwest Regional Branch, Washington State Archives, Olympia.

Bankruptcy Records of the United States District Court, Western District of Washington. National Archives, Seattle.

Billy Gohl Clippings. Vertical Files. Special Collections. University of Washington Libraries, Seattle.

Billy Gohl Collection. Aberdeen Historical Museum, Aberdeen, Washington.

Billy Gohl Documentation. Southwest Regional Branch, Washington State Archives, Olympia.

Chehalis County Coroner's Record. Chehalis County Government Records. Southwest Regional Branch, Washington State Archives, Olympia.

Chehalis (Grays Harbor) County Government Papers. Southwest Regional Branch, Washington State Archives, Olympia.

City of Aberdeen voting registers. Southwest Regional Branch, Washington State Archives, Olympia.

City of Cosmopolis Papers. Special Collections. Aberdeen Timberland Library, Aberdeen, Washington.

City of Hoquiam Papers. Special Collections. Aberdeen Timberland Library, Aberdeen, Washington.

Department of Institutions, State Penitentiary—Walla Walla, Commitment Record, 5772-6269 (1910–11), Acc. No. 72-5-418. Washington State Archives, Olympia.

Edwin Gardner Ames Papers, accession number 3820, box 120, folder 15. Special Collections. University of Washington Libraries, Seattle.

Elerding Mortuary Company Records. Grays Harbor Genealogical Society. Aberdeen, Washington.

Grays Harbor County Auditor, Marriage Records, 1871–Present. Washington State Archives, Digital Archives.

Grays Harbor County Papers. Special Collections. Aberdeen Timberland Library, Aberdeen, Washington.

Governors, State. Ernest Lister Administration. Industrial Workers of the World–Judiciary, box 2H-2-112, 1917–19. Washington State Archives, Olympia.

———. State Secret Service Correspondence Files, 1917–1921, AR2-H-5. Washington State Archives, Olympia.

Governors, State. Marion E. Hay Administration. Judiciary, 1911–Labor Conflicts/I. W. W., box 2G-2-19. Washington State Archives, Olympia.

Governors, State. Roland Hartley Administration. General Correspondence Files and Visiting Card, box 2K-1-28. Washington State Archives, Olympia.

Hoquiam Elks Records. Hoquiam Elks Lodge #1082, Hoquiam, Washington.

Hoquiam History Collection. Hoquiam Timberland Library, Hoquiam, Washington.

Hoquiam Municipal Government Records. Southwest Regional Branch, Washington State Archives, Olympia.

Industrial Workers of the World Collection. Special Collections. University of Washington Libraries, Seattle.

International Longshoremen's and Warehouse Union Local 24 Archives, Aberdeen, Washington.

Merrill and Ring Lumber Company Records. Special Collections. University of Washington Libraries, Seattle.

Ottilie Markholt Papers. Special Collections. University of Washington Libraries, Seattle.

Pacific Northwest History Collection. Special Collections. Aberdeen Timberland Library, Aberdeen, Washington.

Pacific Northwest History Collection. Special Collections. Hoquiam Timberland Library, Hoquiam, Washington.

Pacific Northwest Labor History Association Records, 1947–2015. Special Collections. University of Washington Libraries, Seattle.

United States Customs, Puget Sound Collection District, Series 31 Log Books. National Archives, Seattle.

Whiteside Funeral Home Records—Death Certificates. Washington State Library, Olympia.

PUBLICATIONS

"Aberdeen Saloon Men Arrested." *American Issue* (Anti-Saloon League), Washington ed., March 1908, 8.

Aho, Pamela Dean. "Billy Was the Ghoul of Grays Harbor." *Daily World*, June 29, 1989, 1–7.

———. "The Ghoul of Grays Harbor." In *On the Harbor: From Black Friday to Nirvana*, edited by John C. Hughes and Ryan Teague Beckwith, 18–31. Aberdeen, WA: Daily World, 2001.

Alimahomed-Wilson, Jake, and Immanuel Ness, eds. *Choke Points: Logistics Workers Disrupting the Global Supply Chain*. London: Pluto Press, 2018.

Almaguer, Tomás. *Racial Fault Lines: The Historical Origins of White Supremacy in California*. Berkeley: University of California Press, 1994.

Andrews, Thomas G. *Killing for Coal: America's Deadliest Labor War*. Cambridge: Harvard University Press, 2008.

Armitage, Susan. "Through Women's Eyes: A New View of the West." In *The Woman's West*, edited by Susan Armitage and Elizabeth Jameson, 9–18. Norman: University of Oklahoma Press, 1987.

Avrich, Paul. *The Haymarket Tragedy*. Princeton: Princeton University Press, 1984.

Baron, Ava, ed. *Work Engendered: Toward a New History of American Labor.* Ithaca, NY: Cornell University Press, 1991.

Beito, David T. *From Mutual Aid to Welfare State: Fraternal Societies and Social Services, 1890–1967.* Chapel Hill: University of North Carolina Press, 2000.

Berman, David R. *Radicalism in the Mountain West, 1890–1920.* Boulder: University of Colorado Press, 2007.

Betts, William J. "Launched 100 Murders." *Golden West* 6, no. 2 (January 1970): 19–21, 56–58.

Blackbourn, David. *The Long Nineteenth Century: A History of Germany, 1780–1918.* Oxford: Oxford University Press, 1997.

Bodnar, John. *Workers' World: Kinship, Community, and Protest in an Industrialized Society.* Baltimore: Johns Hopkins University Press, 1983.

Booker, Matthew Morse. *Down by the Bay: San Francisco's History between the Tides.* Berkeley: University of California Press, 2013.

Booth, Brian, ed. *Wildmen, Wobblies, and Whistle Punks: Stewart Holbrook's Lowbrow Northwest.* Corvallis: Oregon State University Press, 1992.

Boyer, Richard O., and Herbert M. Morais. *Labor's Untold Story: The Adventure Story of the Battles, Betrayals, and Victories of American Working Men and Women.* New York: Cameron Associates, 1955.

Breuilly, John, ed. *Nineteeth-Century Germany: Politics, Culture and Society, 1780–1918.* London: Bloomsbury, 2003.

Brissenden, Paul. *The IWW: A Study in Syndicalism.* 2nd ed. New York: Russell and Russell, 1957. First published 1920 by Columbia University (New York).

Bruere, Robert Walter. *Following the Trail of the IWW: A First-Hand Investigation into Labor Troubles in the West—A Trip into the Copper and the Lumber Camps of the Inland Empire with the Views of the Men on the Job.* New York: New York Evening Post, 1918.

Burg, B. R. "Sailors and Tattoos in the Early American Steam Navy: Evidence from the Diary of Philip C. Van Buskirk, 1884–1889." *International Journal of Maritime History* 6, no. 1 (June 1994): 161–74.

Burgoyne, Arthur G. *The Homestead Strike of 1892.* Pittsburgh: University of Pittsburgh Press, 1979.

Cargo Handling and Longshore Labor Conditions. Labor Statistics Bureau Bulletin 550. Washington, DC: US Bureau of Labor Statistics, 1932.

Chin, Art. *Golden Tassels: A History of the Chinese in Washington, 1857–1977.* Seattle: Chin, 1977.

Clark, Norman H. *The Dry Years: Prohibition and Social Change in Washington.* Rev. ed. Seattle: University of Washington Press, 1988.

Clawson, Mary Ann. *Constructing Brotherhood: Class, Gender, and Fraternalism.* Princeton: Princeton University Press, 1989.

Coffman, W. M. *American in the Rough: The Autobiography of W. M. (Bill) Coffman.* New York: Simon and Schuster, 1955.

Cole, Peter. *Dockworker Power: Race and Activism in Durban and the San Francisco Bay Area.* Urbana: University of Illinois Press, 2018.

———. *Wobblies on the Waterfront: Interracial Unionism in Progressive-Era Philadelphia.* Urbana: University of Illinois Press, 2007.

Conlin, Joseph R. *Big Bill Haywood and the Radical Union Movement.* Syracuse: Syracuse University Press, 1969.

Constitution and By-Laws of the Sailors' Union of the Pacific. San Francisco: James H. Barry, 1907.

Copeland, Tom. *The Centralia Tragedy of 1919: Elmer Smith and the Wobblies.* Seattle: University of Washington Press, 1993.

Cotton, Anne. "History of Aberdeen: 1775–1982." In *Aberdeen Comprehensive Development Plan, Phase I, Profile of Aberdeen,* 1–66. Aberdeen, WA: Grays Harbor Regional Planning Commission, 1969.

Cox, John H. "Trade Associations in the Lumber Industry of the Pacific Northwest." *Pacific Northwest Quarterly* 41, no. 4 (October 1950): 285–311.

Cox, Thomas R. *Mills and Markets: A History of the Pacific Coast Lumber Industry to 1900.* Seattle: University of Washington Press, 1974.

Craig, Gordon A. *Germany, 1866–1945.* Oxford: Oxford University Press, 1978.

Davidson, Lance S. "Shanghaied! The Systematic Kidnapping of Sailors in Early San Francisco." *California History* 64, no. 1 (1985): 1–17.

Davis, Jeff, and Al Eufrasio. *Weird Washington: Your Travel Guide to Washington's Local Legends and Best Kept Secrets.* New York: Sterling Publishing, 2008.

Delanty, Hugh M. *Along the Waterfront: Covering a Period of Fifty Years on Grays Harbor and the Pacific Northwest.* Aberdeen, WA: Quick Print, 1943.

Dowell, E. F. *A History of Criminal-Syndicalist Legislation in the United States*. Baltimore: Johns Hopkins University Press, 1939.

Dray, Philip. *There Is Power in a Union: The Epic Story of Labor in America*. New York: Anchor Books, 2010.

Dreyfus, Philip J. "Timber Workers, Unionism and Syndicalism in the Pacific Northwest, 1900–1917." PhD dissertation, Graduate School of the City University of New York, 1993.

Dubofsky, Melvyn. *"Big Bill" Haywood*. Manchester: Manchester University Press, 1987.

———. *We Shall Be All: A History of the Industrial Workers of the World*. Chicago: Quadrangle Books, 1969.

Dwyer, Jeff. *Ghost Hunter's Guide to Seattle and Puget Sound*. Gretna, LA: Pelican Publishing, 2008.

Elrick, John. "Social Conflict and the Politics of Reform: Mayor James D. Phelan and the San Francisco Waterfront Strike of 1901." *California History* 88, no. 2 (2011): 4–23, 54–56.

Emerson, George. "Lumbering on Grays Harbor." *Grays Harbor Post*, October 5, 1907.

Feurer, Rosemary, and Chad Pearson, eds. *Against Labor: How U.S. Employers Organized to Defeat Union Activism*. Urbana: University of Illinois Press, 2017.

Ficken, Robert E. *Lumber and Politics: The Career of Mark E. Reed*. Seattle: University of Washington Press, 1980.

Fink, Leon. *Sweatshops at Sea: Merchant Seamen in the World's First Globalized Industry, from 1812 to the Present*. Chapel Hill: University of North Carolina Press, 2011.

———. *Workingmen's Democracy: The Knights of Labor and American Politics*. Urbana: University of Illinois Press, 1983.

Foley, Neil. *White Scourge: Mexicans, Blacks, and Poor Whites in Texas Cotton Culture*. Berkeley: University of California Press, 1997.

Foner, Philip S. "Communications, James McParlan and the Molly Maguires." *Science and Society* 31, no. 1 (Winter 1967): 77.

———, ed. *Fellow Workers and Friends: IWW Free Speech Fights as Told by Participants*. Westport, CT: Greenwood Press, 1981.

———. *History of the Labor Movement in the United States*, vol. 3, *The Policies and Practices of the American Federation of Labor, 1900–1909*. New York: International Publishers, 1964.

———. *History of the Labor Movement in the United States*, vol. 4, *The Industrial Workers of the World, 1905–1917*. New York: International Publishers, 1965.

———. *History of the Labor Movement in the United States*, vol. 5, *The AFL in the Progressive Era, 1910–1915*. New York: International Publishers, 1980.

Forsyth, Ralph Kendall. "The Wage Scale Agreements of Maritime Unions." *Annals of the American Academy of Political and Social Science* 36, no. 2 (September 1910): 95–111.

Friday, Chris. *Organizing Asian-American Labor: The Pacific Coast Canned-Salmon Industry, 1870–1942*. Philadelphia: Temple University Press, 1994.

Fultz, Hollis B. *Famous Northwest Manhunts*. Elma, WA: Fulco Publishing, 1955.

Goings, Aaron. "Red Harbor: Class, Violence, and Community in Grays Harbor, Washington." PhD dissertation, Simon Fraser University, 2011.

Goings, Aaron, Brian Barnes, and Roger Snider. *The Red Coast: Radicalism and Anti-Radicalism in Southwest Washington*. Corvallis: Oregon State University Press, 2019.

Goodrich, Richard J. "The Madman of Aberdeen." *Harborquest* 3 (August 1992): 8–9, 23.

Gordon, Greg. *When Money Grew on Trees: A. B. Hammond and the Age of the Timber Barons*. Norman: University of Oklahoma Press, 2014.

Graham, Hugh Davis, and Ted Robert Gurr. *Violence in America: Historical and Comparative Perspectives*, vol. 1. Washington, DC: US Government Printing Office, 1969.

Green, James. *Death in the Haymarket: The Story of Chicago, the First Labor Movement, and the Bombing that Divided Gilded Age America*. New York: Random House, 2006.

Greenwald, Maurine Weiner. "Working-Class Feminism and the Family Wage Ideal: The Seattle Debate on Married Women's Right to Work, 1914–1920." In *Women in Pacific Northwest History*, edited by Karen Blair, 94–134. Rev. ed. Seattle: University of Washington Press, 2001.

Hall, Greg. *Harvest Wobblies: The Industrial Workers of the World and Agricultural Laborers in the American West, 1905–1930.* Corvallis: Oregon State University Press, 2001.

Harper, Franklin, ed. *Who's Who on the Pacific Coast: A Biographical Compilation of Notable Living Contemporaries West of the Rocky Mountains.* Los Angeles: Harper Publishing, 1913.

Harrison, Charles Yale. *Generals Die in Bed: A Story from the Trenches.* New York: W. Morrow, 1930.

Hawley, Lowell Stillwell, and Ralph Bushnell Potts. *Counsel for the Damned: A Biography of George Francis Vanderveer.* Philadelphia: J. B. Lippincott, 1953.

Henderson, Charles Richmond. "Industrial Insurance. III. Benefit Features of the Trade-Unions." *American Journal of Sociology* 12, no. 6 (1907): 756–78.

Herringshaw, Thomas William. *American Blue-Book of Biography: Prominent Americans of 1912—an Accurate Biographical Record of Prominent Citizens of All Walks of Life.* Chicago: American Publishers' Association, 1913.

Higbie, Frank Tobias. *Indispensable Outcasts: Hobo Workers and Community in the American Midwest, 1880–1930.* Urbana: University of Illinois Press, 2004.

Holbrook, Stewart H. *Holy Old Mackinaw: The Natural History of the American Lumberjack.* New York: Ballantine Books, 1971.

———. *Little Annie Oakley and Other Rugged People.* New York: Macmillan, 1948.

———. *A Narrative of Schafer Bros. Logging Company's Half Century in the Timber.* Seattle: Dogwood Press, 1945.

Holden, Brad. *Seattle Prohibition: Bootleggers, Rumrunners, and Graft in the Queen City.* Charleston, SC: History Press, 2019.

Holden, Jan. "Billy Gohl: The Ghoul of Grays Harbor." *Old West* (Fall 1995): 26–30.

"How a Western City Grows: Hoquiam, Washington." *Coast: An Illustrated Magazine of the West* 5, no. 6 (June 1903): 206–19.

Huberman, Leo. *The Labor Spy Racket.* New York: Modern Age Books, 1937.

Hughes, John C., and Ryan Teague Beckwith, ed. *On the Harbor: From Black Friday to Nirvana.* Aberdeen, WA: Daily World, 2001.

Hunt, Herbert, and F. C. Kaylor. *Washington, West of the Cascades: Historical and Descriptive: The Explorers, the Indians, the Pioneers, the Modern.* Seattle: S. J. Clarke, 1917.

International Seamen's Union of America. *The Red Record: A Brief Resumé of Some of the Cruelties Perpetrated upon American Seamen at the Present Time.* San Francisco: Coast Seamen's Journal, 1895.

Jameson, Elizabeth. *All that Glitters: Class, Conflict, and Community in Cripple Creek.* Urbana: University of Illinois Press, 1998.

Jeffreys-Jones, Rhodri. *Violence and Reform in American History.* New York: New Viewpoints, 1978.

Jensen, Vernon. *Heritage of Conflict: Labor Relations in the Nonferrous Metals Industry up to 1930.* Ithaca, NY: Cornell University Press, 1950.

———. *Lumber and Labor.* New York: J. J. Little and Ives, 1945.

Kazin, Michael. *Barons of Labor: The San Francisco Building Trades and Union Power in the Progressive Era.* Urbana: University of Illinois Press, 1989.

Kenny, Kevin. *Making Sense of the Molly Maguires.* Oxford: Oxford University Press, 1998.

———. "The Molly Maguires in Popular Culture." *Journal of American Ethnic History* 14, no. 4 (Summer 1995): 27–46.

Kessler-Harris, Alice. *Out to Work: A History of Wage-Earning Women in the United States.* Oxford: Oxford University Press, 1982.

Kimeldorf, Howard. *Reds or Rackets? The Making of Radical and Conservative Unions on the Waterfront.* Berkeley: University of California Press, 1988.

Knight, Robert Edward Lee. *Industrial Relations in the San Francisco Bay Area, 1900–1918.* Berkeley: University of California Press, 1960.

Lamb, Frank H. *Fifty Years in Hoquiam: Memoirs of Frank H. Lamb.* N.p., 1948.

———. *Rotary: A Businessman's Interpretation.* Hoquiam, WA: Rotary Club of Hoquiam, 1927.

Leier, Mark. *Rebel Life: The Life and Times of Robert Gosden, Revolutionary, Mystic, Labour Spy.* 2nd ed. Vancouver: New Star Books, 2013.

———. *Red Flags and Red Tape: The Making of a Labor Bureaucracy.* Toronto: University of Toronto Press, 1995.

——. *Where the Fraser River Flows: The Industrial Workers of the World in British Columbia.* Vancouver: New Star Books, 1990.

Lens, Sidney. *Labor Wars: From the Molly Maguires to the Sit Downs.* Garden City, NY: Doubleday, 1973.

LeWarne, Charles Pierce. "The Aberdeen, Washington, Free Speech Fight of 1911–1912." *Pacific Northwest Quarterly* 66 (January 1975): 1–15.

Limerick, Patricia Nelson. *The Legacy of Conquest: The Unbroken Past of the American West.* New York: W. W. Norton, 1987.

Lind, Carol J. *Big Timber, Big Men.* Seattle: Hancock House, 1978.

——. "The Port of Missing Men." *Tacoma News-Tribune*, February 23, 1969.

Lockley, Fred. "Grays Harbor: The Largest Lumber-Shipping Port in the World." *Pacific Monthly*, June 1907, 720–29.

London, Jack. *The Sea-Wolf.* London: William Heinemann, 1917.

Loomis, Eric. *Empire of Timber: Labor Unions and the Pacific Northwest Forests.* Cambridge: Cambridge University Press, 2016.

Lukas, J. Anthony. *Big Trouble: A Murder in a Small Western Town Sets off a Struggle for the Soul of America.* New York: Simon and Schuster, 1997.

Magden, Ronald E. *A History of Seattle Waterfront Workers, 1884–1934.* Seattle: Trade Printery, 1991.

——. *The Working Longshoreman.* Tacoma, WA: R-4 Typographers, 1991.

March, C. J. *The Ghoul of Grays Harbor: Murder and Mayhem in the Pacific Northwest.* Minneapolis: Slingshot Books, 2019.

Martin, Robert. *Carnegie Denied: Communities Rejecting Carnegie Library Construction Grants, 1898–1925.* Westport, CT: Greenwood Press, 1993.

Marx, Karl. *Capital*, vol. 1. Translated by Ben Fowkes. London: Penguin Books, 1990.

Mayer, Heather. *Beyond the Rebel Girl: Women and the Industrial Workers of the World in the Pacific Northwest, 1905–1924.* Corvallis: Oregon State University Press, 2018.

Meyer, Stephen. *Manhood on the Line: Working-Class Masculinities in the American Heartland.* Urbana: University of Illinois Press, 2016.

Montgomery, David. *Workers' Control in America: Studies in the History of Work, Technology, and Labor Struggles.* Cambridge: Cambridge University Press, 1979.

Morgan, Murray. *The Last Wilderness*. Seattle: University of Washington Press, 1955.

Morn, Frank. *"The Eye that Never Sleeps": A History of the Pinkerton National Detective Agency*. Bloomington: Indiana University Press, 1982.

Murphy, Mary. *Mining Cultures: Men, Women, and Leisure in Butte, 1914–1941*. Urbana: University of Illinois Press, 1997.

Neiworth, Latrissa. "Gohl(y) Violence Colors Aberdeen's Past." *Ocean Breeze* (Aberdeen, WA, school newspaper), February 10, 1976.

Nelson, Bruce. *Workers on the Waterfront: Seamen, Longshoremen, and Unionism in the 1930s*. Urbana: University of Illinois Press, 1990.

Nixon, Rob. *Slow Violence and the Environmentalism of the Poor*. Cambridge: Harvard University Press, 2011.

Norwood, Stephen H. *Strikebreaking and Intimidation: Mercenaries and Masculinity in Twentieth-Century America*. Chapel Hill: University of North Carolina Press, 2001.

N. W. Ayer and Son's American Newspaper Annual and Directory: A Catalogue of American Newspapers. Philadelphia: N. W. Ayer & Son, 1917.

Oberdeck, K. J. "'Not Pink Teas': The Seattle Working-Class Women's Movement, 1905–1918." *Labor History* 32, no. 2 (Spring 1991): 193–230.

Page, Thomas Walker. "The San Francisco Labor Movement in 1901." *Political Science Quarterly* 17, no. 4 (December 1902): 664–88.

Peck, Gunther. *Reinventing Free Labor: Padrones and Immigrant Workers in the North American West, 1880–1930*. Cambridge: Cambridge University Press, 2000.

Pence, Dennis. *The Ghoul of Grays Harbor*. Aberdeen, WA: AuthorHouse, 2004.

Proceedings of the Annual Convention of the Pacific District of the International Longshoremen's Association, 1913.

Proceedings of the Annual Convention of the Washington State Federation of Labor, 1905–7.

Prouty, Andrew Mason. *"More Deadly Than War!" Pacific Coast Logging, 1827–1981*. Seattle: University of Washington Press, 1985.

Richards, Lawrence. *Union-Free America: Workers and Antiunion Culture*. Urbana: University of Illinois Press, 2008.

R. L. Polk and Company's Grays Harbor Cities and Chehalis County Directory, 1903–35.

R. L. Polk and Company's Seattle City Directory, 1900–1905.

Robbins, William G. *Colony and Empire: The Capitalist Transformation of the American West*. Lawrence: University Press of Kansas, 1994.

Roediger, David. *Working toward Whiteness: How America's Immigrants Became White, the Strange Journey from Ellis Island to the Suburbs*. New York: Basic Books, 2005.

Rosenow, Michael K. *Death and Dying in the Working Class, 1865–1920*. Urbana: University of Illinois Press, 2015.

Saxton, Alexander. *The Indispensable Enemy: Labor and the Anti-Chinese Movement in California*. Berkeley: University of California Press, 1971.

———. *The Rise and Fall of the White Republic*. London: Verso, 1990.

Schmid, David. *Natural Born Celebrities: Serial Killers in American Culture*. Chicago: University of Chicago Press, 2005.

Schwantes, Carlos A. *Hard Traveling: A Portrait of Work Life in the New Northwest*. Lincoln: University of Nebraska Press, 1994.

———. *Radical Heritage: Labor, Socialism, and Reform in Washington and British Columbia, 1885–1917*. Seattle: University of Washington Press, 1979.

Schwantes, Carlos A., and James P. Ronda, *The West the Railroads Made*. Seattle: University of Washington Press, 2008.

Schwartz, Harvey. *The March Inland: Origins of the ILWU Warehouse Division, 1934–1938*. Los Angeles: Institute of Labor Relations, University of California, 1978.

Schwartz, Stephen. *Brotherhood of the Sea: A History of the Sailors' Union of the Pacific, 1885–1985*. San Francisco: Sailors' Union of the Pacific, 1986.

Session Laws of the State of Washington, 1903. Tacoma, WA: Allen & Lamborn, 1903.

Smith, Robert M. *From Blackjacks to Briefcases: A History of Commercialized Strikebreaking and Unionbusting in the United States*. Athens: Ohio University Press, 2003.

South-western Washington, Its Topography, Climate, Resources, Productions . . . and Pen Sketches of their Representative Business Men. Olympia: Pacific Publishing, 1890.

State of California. *Eleventh Biennial Report of the Bureau of Labor Statistics for the State of California (1903–1904)*. Sacramento: W. W. Shannon, Superintendent State Printing, 1904.

State of Washington. *Sixth Biennial Report of the State Board of Control for the Term Beginning October 1, 1910, and Ending September 30, 1912*. Olympia: Public Printer, 1912.

State of Washington, Bureau of Labor. *Eighth Biennial Report of the Bureau of Labor Statistics and Factory Inspection, 1911–1912*. Olympia: E. L. Boardman, Public Printer, 1912.

———. *Fifth Biennial Report of the Bureau of Labor Statistics and Factory Inspection, 1905–1906*. Olympia: C. W. Gorham Public Printer, 1906.

———. *Fourth Biennial Report of the Bureau of Labor Statistics and Factory Inspection, 1903–1904*. Olympia: Blankenship Saterlee, 1904.

———. *Labor Laws of the State of Washington*. Olympia: Public Printer, 1907.

———. *Ninth Biennial Report of the Bureau of Labor Statistics, 1913–1914*. Olympia: Public Printer, 1914.

———. *Seventh Biennial Report of the Bureau of Labor Statistics and Factory Inspection, 1909–1910*. Olympia: C. W. Gorham, Public Printer, 1908.

———. *Sixth Biennial Report of the Bureau of Labor of the State of Washington, 1907–1908*. Olympia: Public Printer, 1908.

Stein, Garth. *A Sudden Light*. London: Simon and Schuster, 2014.

Taft, Philip. "Violence in American Labor Disputes." *Annals of the American Academy of Political and Social Science* 364 (March 1966): 127–40.

Taylor, Paul S. "The Sailors' Union of the Pacific." PhD dissertation, University of California, 1922.

Tentler, Leslie Woodcock. *Wage-Earning Women: Industrial Work and Family Life in the United States, 1900–1930*. Oxford: Oxford University Press, 1979.

Thompson, E. P. "The Crime of Anonymity." In *Albion's Fatal Tree: Crime and Society in Eighteenth-Century England*, edited by Douglas Hay and others, 255–344. New York: Pantheon Books, 1975.

Thompson, Gabriel. *Chasing the Harvest: Migrant Workers in California Agriculture*. London: Verso Books, 2017.

Todes, Charlotte. *Labor and Lumber.* New York: International Publishers, 1931.

Tripp, Joseph F. "An Instance of Labor and Business Cooperation: Workmen's Compensation in Washington State (1911)." *Labor History* 17 (Fall 1976): 530–50.

"A Typical Lumbering City: Aberdeen, Washington." *Coast* 6, no. 1 (July 1903): 6.

United States Commission on Industrial Relations. *Industrial Relations: Final Report and Testimony Submitted to Congress by the Commission on Industrial Relations Created by the Act of August 23, 1912.* Washington, DC: Government Printing Office, 1916.

United States Department of Labor, Bureau of Labor Statistics. *Union Scale of Wages and Hours of Labor.* Washington, DC: Government Printing Office, 1913.

Utter, Robert F., and Hugh D. Spitzer. *The Washington State Constitution.* 2nd ed. Oxford: Oxford University Press, 2013.

Van Syckle, Ed. *The River Pioneers: The Early Days on Grays Harbor.* Seattle: Pacific Search Press, 1982.

———. *They Tried to Cut It All: Grays Harbor, Turbulent Years of Greed and Greatness.* Seattle: Pacific Search Press, 1980.

Vickers, Marques. *Murder in Washington: The Topography of Evil: Notorious Washington State Murder Sites.* Larkspur, CA: Marquis Publishing, 2016.

Walker, Anna Sloan. "History of the Liquor Laws of the State of Washington." *Washington Historical Quarterly* 5 (April 1914): 116–20.

Weinstein, Robert. *Grays Harbor, 1885–1913.* New York: Penguin Books, 1978.

Weintraub, Hyman. *Andrew Furuseth: Emancipator of the Seamen.* Berkeley: University of California Press, 1959.

Weiss, Robert P. "Private Detective Agencies and Labour Discipline in the United States, 1855–1946." *Historical Journal* 29, no. 1 (1986): 87–107.

Wertheimer, Barbara. *We Were There: The Story of Working Women in America.* New York: Pantheon Books, 1977.

White, Richard. *"It's Your Misfortune and None of My Own": A New History of the American West.* Norman: University of Oklahoma Press, 1993.

Wilson, Emily M. *From Boats to Board Feet: The Wilson Family of the Pacific Coast.* Seattle: Wilson Brothers Family Foundation, 2007.

Woog, Adam. *Haunted Washington: Uncanny Tales and Spooky Spots from the Upper Left-Hand Corner of the United States.* Guilford, CT: Morris, 2013.

Wyman, Mark. *Hard Rock Epic: Western Miners and the Industrial Revolution.* Berkeley: University of California Press, 1989.

Yaffee, Steven Lewis. *The Wisdom of the Spotted Owl: Policy Lessons for a New Century.* Washington, DC: Island Press, 1994.

Zoretich, Frank J. "Plank Streets and Shady Dealings." *Pacific Slope*, February 1978, 12–13.

INDEX

ABOUT THE AUTHOR

Aaron Goings is associate professor of history at Saint Martin's University. He was previously senior researcher at the Institute of Advanced Social Research at the University of Tampere. His previous works include *The Red Coast: Radicalism and Anti-Radicalism in Southwest Washington* (Oregon State University Press, 2019), coauthored with Brian Barnes and Roger Snider; and *Community in Conflict: A Working-Class History of the 1913–14 Michigan Copper Strike and the Italian Hall Tragedy* (Michigan State University Press, 2013), coauthored with Gary Kaunonen.